Alfred the Great and the Viking Invasions

Beatrice Lees

MERKABA PRESS

Published 2017 by Merkaba Press

CONTENTS

EUROPE BEFORE ALFRED THE GREAT

"IN the year of our Lord's Incarnation 849 light rose out of darkness. Alfred, King of the English, was born in the royal 'vill' [villa regia] which is called Wanetinge [Wantage]." To later historians, as to the early chronicler who wrote these words, King Alfred has appeared as a phenomenon to be wondered at rather than to be understood, a lonely light shining in the midst of an impenetrable darkness.

The ninth century, the time of the break-up of the Empire of Charles the Great, and of the systematic plunder-raids of the Northmen, is by common consent included among the "Dark Ages" of mediæval history. Too near to the modern world for the dignity of the classic past, too far removed for the vivid interest of contemporary politics, it presents at first sight little but a dreary vista of civil wars and viking ravages in the realm of action, of childish credulity and gross superstition in the realm of thought. It falls between the heroic period of Charlemagne and the romantic era of the Crusades, before the great days of Empire and Papacy, of monasticism and feudalism, a barren waste of years, in which the figure of Alfred, the perfect king, stands out in brilliant relief against a shadowy background of barbaric ignorance and violence.

Yet when the shadows are faced they flee away, and the darkness grows luminous, a summer night full of vague promise and suggestion and the faint stirrings of life, haunted by memories of the day that is gone, and by dreams of the coming dawn.

The true significance of the Middle Ages lies, indeed, in the very fact of their "middleness." If they were the ancestors of a historic future, they were also the heirs of a "storied past," the inheritors of high traditions, Hellenic, Latin, and Hebraic. Behind them lay the philosophy and art of Greece, the law and imperial statecraft of Rome, the stern monotheism of the Jewish dispensation, with its fervour of militant faith, and its splendid oriental poetry and prophecy.

Mediæval Christendom was built up out of the ruins of older civilisations, and thinkers and writers borrowed their material from Græco-Latin and Judaic antiquity as naturally as architects and sculptors used the columns and stones of pagan Rome in constructing Christian basilicas. Western learning and Eastern fancy, legend and myth, superstition and mystic devotion, the fascination of the unknown and the dread of the infinite, all went to the making of the subtle atmosphere of thought that softened the harshness of the rude practical activities of mediæval life.

Nor were these classic and oriental forms the mere dry bones of a dead society. They came to the mediæval world filled with living force, moulded and transfigured by Christian idealism. They gained power and meaning from that hope of a future life and that sense of the mystery of the unseen which, however dimly apprehended, served to lift the men and women of the Middle Ages above their material surroundings, to quicken their imagination, and to kindle their awe and wonder. The history of the past became symbolic of a spiritual future. It was a Christian Empire of which St. Augustine wrote, which Charles the Great tried to revive in visible form. St. Augustine's "City of God" was at once "golden Rome, head and glory of the world" (Roma caput mundi, mundi decus, aurea Roma), and "Jerusalem the Golden" (Urbs Sion Aurea), "the New Jerusalem coming down from God out of heaven."

Only by realising the theocratic character of mediæval society, and the strength of religious and ecclesiastical influences, can mediæval history be understood. The Church was the true worldstate, the kingdom of God upon earth, a kingdom ruled by two powers, the "holy authority of the

Popes" and the subordinate, but divinely instituted, authority of Monarchy. The common aims and sympathies of the Christian faith held together jarring tribes and races in some kind of political unity, in the imperium christianum, Christendom, the community of all Christian people.

Though the phrase "the Ages of Faith" has been used to invest the Middle Ages with an unreal glamour, there can be no doubt that mediæval society was peculiarly alive to emotional and spiritual appeals, and the importance can hardly be overrated of that chain of events which brought the Western and Northern nations at a critical stage in their development under the sway of the complex religious system of Catholicism.

The marvellous organisation of the Catholic Church, with its two branches, Eastern and Western, had gathered up into itself the accumulated wisdom of three great civilisations. Jewish and oriental in origin, it absorbed much of what survived of Greek philosophy, of Roman law and political theory, welded this heterogeneous material into a more or less coherent body of Christian theology, and, through the writings of the Fathers, made that theology the common property of the educated world.

This meant that the heathen tribesmen who derived their Christianity from Rome learnt their classical lessons in an ecclesiastical school, with ecclesiastical reservations and expansions, while the sacred books of the Old and New Testament came to them overlaid with a mass of allegorical interpretation which recalls early nineteenth-century methods of Scriptural exposition. But it meant also that they caught a faint reflection of the beauty of Greek thought and the glow of Eastern passion, and that they, the barbarian conquerors of Rome, received those ideas of political unity, of authority and disciplined order, which were among the best fruits of Roman Imperialism. Above all, Latin Christianity, by its very precision and formalism, gave definition to vague yearnings, and laid down clear rules of faith and conduct, a "way of righteousness." It taught the pagan world the virtues of self-control, of mercy and pity, and sacrifice for a cause, and brightened the routine of everyday life by the ceremonies of a stately ritual.

At the same time, the influence of Christianity, great as it was, must not be exaggerated. Behind and beneath the imposing fabric of Catholicism, the older beliefs lingered, as, indeed, they linger still. Christian observances were in many cases the mere setting for pagan rites; primitive superstitions were absorbed into orthodox Catholic doctrine, or sank into the magic and witchcraft which the Church persistently but ineffectually condemned. The northern races, moreover, had their own fine traditions of loyalty and courage, their own delicate artistic feeling, and a rich store of imaginative legend, myth, and folk-song. Christianity assimilated this native culture without destroying it, but not without vitally affecting its development. Arrested in its natural growth, it entered into combination with Christian elements, to form in course of time a new civilisation in the West, which should be neither barbarian nor Roman, neither heathen nor altogether Christian, but truly Catholic in its reconciliation of opposing forces.

A long period of experiment lay between the Empire of the Cæsars and its mediæval successor, the "Roman Empire of the German Nation," and both the dulness and the interest of the ninth century spring from the fact that it falls within this time of transition. It is dull because the men of the ninth century, bound by the spell of the past, did not yet dare to be themselves, and copied where they might have created. Their theories, borrowed from more advanced civilisations, were somewhat forced and artificial. Their ideals had but little bearing on the realities of their daily experience. They were inarticulate, too, unable fitly to express the thoughts that "quivered on their lips," and the difficulty of entering into their inner life is enhanced by the scantiness and poverty of the records they have left.

Yet this immaturity has a charm of its own, for it means infinite possibilities of growth and development. The ninth century, with all its crudity, is interesting for its promise of a great future, for its youthful extravagance and hopefulness, for its strange inconsistencies and eager ambitions, for its curious blending of idealism with materialism. More especially it is interesting for the strength of the theocratic and ecclesiastical factors in the organisation of society, and for the part which they played in secular politics, both in the West and in the East.

The great historian Von Ranke saw the distinguishing characteristics of the ninth century in the contrast between the two monotheistic theocracies, Christendom and Islam, and in their gradual victory over the declining forces of ancient heathendom. In the East, as in the West, a worldstate embodying a creed had arisen, and mediæval Mohammedanism proved a formidable rival to mediæval Christianity.

The ceaseless struggle between East and West became, in the Middle Ages, a holy war against the enemies of Christ and his Church, and political quarrels were fought out over ecclesiastical questions. The separation of the Western from the Eastern Empire was intimately connected with the separation of the Latin and Greek churches. Even travel and exploration assumed the religious aspect of pilgrimages to the Holy Land, or to Rome, the "queen of the world," the visible seat and centre of the authority of the Church of the West.

The world itself, to ninth-century eyes, might seem to be divided into Christendom and "Hethenesse." Within the Christian pale were the Empires of the East and West, both claiming to be the orthodox descendants and representatives of the Empire of Constantine the Great. The Eastern or Byzantine Emperors ruled from Constantinople, the "New Rome," over restricted but still extensive territories in Southern Italy and Sicily, in the Balkan Peninsula and the Peloponnesus, and in Asia Minor. Under the supremacy of the newly revived Western Empire were gathered the future kingdoms of France and Burgundy, of Germany and Italy, while England and Ireland, politically isolated, were yet members of the Christian community. Outside that community lay the realm of heathendom, the conquests of Islam, and the still unconquered fastnesses of more primitive beliefs.

Islam, like Christendom, had fallen into two divisions, differing in creed and in politics. The Emirate of Cordova encroached on the boundary of the Western Empire south of the Pyrenees. The Caliphate of Bagdad threatened the Byzantine frontier in Asia Minor and held Jerusalem and the holy places of Syria. Between the two, the Mediterranean Sea swarmed with Saracen pirates, Moslem adventurers and freebooters, who lived by the plunder of Christians.

Beyond the Christian and Mohammedan Empires, again, stretched a fringe of dim, mysterious barbarism, full, to the mediæval imagination, of dreadful shapes and monstrous creations:

The Anthropophagi, and men whose heads Do grow beneath their shoulders. Fabulous India and "far Cathay," the wild Tartar savagery of the remote North-East, with the mist-enshrouded north-western lands of Slav and Scandinavian paganism, to ultima Thule, and the "sluggish waveless sea which men believe to be the girdle of the earth," contributed their marvels to the store of travellers' tales which gathered about the borders of the known world.

It was from the heathen North that, as the eighth century drew to a close, a new element entered into the political and social life of Western Europe with the beginning of the "Viking Age." When "the first ships of the Danish men" appeared off the coasts of England and Ireland, curiosity and astonishment mingled with the terror which they aroused. The West-Saxon "reeve" (gerefa) whose death at the hands of the Northern pirates the English Chronicle records "knew not what they were." A later version of the same story makes him take them for merchants. "Never," wrote Alcuin of the sacking of Lindisfarne by the Northmen in 793, "could such a voyage have been thought possible." The Irish called the invaders Gaill or strangers.

Some four generations later, when the "Viking Age" proper ended with the cession of Normandy to Rollo, the "pirate duke," the "strangers" had become a recognised and important branch of the western family of European nations. At the opening of the tenth century, kings and chiefs of Scandinavian race ruled over Russia and the greater part of England; Scandinavian colonists lined the shores of the Irish Sea and occupied the islands of the eastern Atlantic from the Hebrides to the Faroes; Scandinavian explorers had passed the Straits of Gibraltar in the South, and had attacked Iceland and discovered Greenland in the far North-West.

If from one point of view the viking expeditions recall the pirate raids of the Saracens in the Mediterranean, from another they seem to be a continuation or revival of the tribal migrations of an earlier age. As in the fourth and fifth centuries the dwellers by the North Sea, Angles and Saxons, Jutes and Frisians, went forth to conquer and settle on the coast of Gaul and in the distant province of Roman Britain, so, more than three hundred years later, the warships of Danes and Goths, Norwegians and Swedes, sailed out from the Baltic lands to plunder the kingdoms of the West.

What is really remarkable about the expansion of the Scandinavian peoples in the eighth and ninth centuries is not so much the novelty of the movement as its magnitude, its extent, and its persistence. These Northern adventurers passed down the English Channel, and through the Straits of Gibraltar to the Mediterranean, or struck across the ocean to Scotland and the Western Isles, and so by the Irish Sea to St. George's Channel, or rounded the North Cape and explored the White Sea and the haunts of Finn and Lapp, or followed the "East-way," to Russia or "Gardariki," and on to "Micklegarth," the "great city" of New Rome.

Scandinavia had, indeed, been the home of a seafaring race from the dawn of authentic history, "rich," as Tacitus noted, "in ships, in arms, and in men." The long line of broken, island-fringed coast, deeply indented with bays and fiords, the narrow straits and sounds, the dark pine-forests, vast lakes, and rugged mountains of the interior, had nourished a vigorous population of stalwart dalesmen and hunters, fishermen, sailors, and traders, a stout-hearted, independent people, full of vitality, practical sagacity, and shrewd homely mother-wit. This was the material out of which the perils and hazards of a life of piracy fashioned a type as characteristic as the Elizabethan "seadog," the "sea-king" who "ruled over men, but had no lands," who "never slept beneath sooty roof-beams, and never drank at the ingle-nook." These early buccaneers, like their sixteenth-century descendants, looked westward for their El Dorado, and from their exploits, and the daring ventures and stirring incidents of their roving life, sprang both the "fighting faith" of the "Walhalla" mythology, as distinct from the primitive beliefs of the Germanic races, and the later literature of Eddas and Sagas.

It is partly to the heroic and romantic nature of the viking movement that the difficulty of accounting for it is due. Not only are trustworthy records scanty, but the few that remain have been distorted by terror, or transformed by poetic imagination: the terror that added a clause to the Litany: "From the fury of the Northmen, good Lord, deliver us"; the imagination which produced the viking cradle-song: "My mother said they should buy me a boat and fair oars. . . . And so wend to the haven, and cut down man after man"; or the triumphant death-chant of Ragnar Lodbrok in the serpent-pit: "We hewed with the brand! I . . . have fought fifty pitched battles and one. . . . Laughing I will die." With the contemporary English and Frankish chroniclers, the feeling of horror was uppermost. They saw in the incursions of the heathen pirates a judgment of God, a punishment for sin, a fulfilment of prophecy. The vikings were "the evil that was to break forth out of the North," foxes that destroyed the chosen vine, wolves that devoured the fold, waters that flooded the land. Above all, they were "heathen men," "Gentiles," "a pagan folk."

To the Scandinavian poets or saga-tellers, writing after the event, perhaps in the Western Isles, or in the new colony of Iceland, the element of romance was predominant. They emphasised the personal note, and made the early raids, like the later invasions, the work of individual heroes, such half-mythical war-leaders as Ragnar Lodbrok and Ivar the Boneless.

Modern historians, again, have sought to trace the resumption of western migration to economic or political circumstances :--over-population, social unrest, the revolt of a spirited people against the growing restrictions of settled government.

Though there is truth in all these theories, and fate, desire, and necessity may each have had a share in bringing about the viking movement, its immediate cause, as Lappenberg suggested long ago, was probably the Saxon war of Charles the Great, which brought the Danes face to face with the Franks and revealed the riches of Christian civilisation to the Northern plunderers, while the break-up of the Western Empire under Charles the Great's unworthy successors gave them an opportunity of which they were not slow to take advantage. It is at least certain that the first clearly recorded viking raids on the coasts of England, Ireland, and Frisia coincide with that last quarter of the eighth century when the frontier of Christendom was being gradually pushed northwards, and the great King of the Franks was putting the crowning touches to the fabric of empire. In 810 the murder of Godfred, king of the Danes, the protector of the fugitive Saxon chief Widukind, alone prevented a serious war between Franks and Northmen. Charles the Great made peace with Godfred's successor, but the closing years of his life were darkened by fears for the future, and he gave anxious thought to the strengthening of the naval defences of the Empire.

The famous tale of the Emperor weeping for the troubles that were coming on his descendants, as he watched the viking pirate-ships in the Mediterranean, embodies a historic truth. Christian imperialism was about to meet pagan tribalism in a desperate and prolonged struggle. The ninth century was to be a time of storm and stress which has been compared to the "Doom of the Gods" of Northern prophecy, "an age of axes, an age of swords . . . an age of wolves." A new society would eventually emerge from this clash of conflicting forces, even as when the "Doom" had passed, a new earth rose out of the deep, but this was not to be till a century of war and piracy had made the "viking" or "wicing"--a word like "Saracen" of uncertain derivation, but of dread import--a name of terror throughout Western Christendom.

When, in 814, Charles, the "Great and Orthodox Emperor," was laid to rest in the cathedral at Aachen, the reign of Chaos seemed about to return. His son and successor, Louis the Pious, though accomplished and devout, was too weak a man for the heavy task imposed upon him. A pathetic figure, at odds with his own children and out of touch with the tendencies of the time, he drifted helplessly through a shifting scene of change and chance, of rebellion within and invasion from without. Northmen, Slavs, and Saracens beat against the boundaries of the Empire: discontented sons and ambitious vassals stirred up strife at home.

Yet the very dissensions and divisions of actual society served to emphasise the old ideals of peace and unity. It was one of the gravest charges against Louis the Pious that he had failed to carry on the work of his father, the Rex Pacificus, and had brought shame and distress upon the Empire. Great principles of conduct and government rose like giant shapes out of the general welter and confusion, only to fall back again into darkness. Men clung to the dream of political and religious unity, as they clung to the memory of the golden days of Charles the Great.

The life of Charles had been a concrete manifestation of typical Christian kingship, all the more attractive and comprehensible for its barbaric setting. Henceforth the sovereigns of Western Europe would model themselves, consciously or unconsciously, after this pattern, and in so doing they would carry on a still older tradition. Charles the Great might well stand for the mediæval conception of the "Happy Emperor" of his favourite book, St. Augustine's City of God, and that description of a Christian monarch, enforced by the authority of Roman jurists and of Fathers of the Church, and popularised by the legendary fame of "Charlemagne," became the ideal of all the best statesmen of the Middle Ages.

St. Augustine had taught that the happiness of the ruler lay in just rule, in the fear of God, and in the love of the heavenly kingdom. He had spiritualised the earthly Rome by linking it with the thought of the "City of God." Later political philosophers laid stress on the official character of the imperial and royal functions, on the duties and obligations that attended empire and kingship, and on the divine origin of those duties, and their intimate connection with the Church and the Catholic faith.

The continuity of ecclesiastical tradition explains the continuity of mediæval political theory. It explains also the growing power and influence of the Church, the representative of a consistent purpose and a definite moral standard in a world of capricious impulses and unrestrained license. Rome was still the symbol of law and order and civilisation for the nations of Western Christendom, but, by an insensible transition, republican and imperial Rome had given place to the city of St. Peter as the goal of their hopes and ambitions. The real strength of the Papacy lay in the spiritual nature of its claim to supremacy, which enabled it to rise superior to the accidents of fortune, even when Rome itself was convulsed by sedition. Leo III., the Pope from whom on Christmas Day, 800, Charles the Great had received the imperial crown, died in 816, discredited, and hated by the Romans, who had risen in rebellion against him. His four immediate successors had short and inglorious reigns, and not till Gregory IV. mounted the papal throne in 827 did the Church find its opportunity in the weakness and disruption of the Empire.

The first few years after the accession of Louis the Pious had not been without promise. Friendly negotiation, mission-work, and politic intervention in the dynastic complications of Denmark marked his relations with the Northern nations. The Slavs on the eastern frontier and the Saracens of Spain were held in check, in spite of frequent revolts, and the imperial authority was maintained in Italy.

The Emperor's first fatal mistake was made in 819, when he took as his second wife the beautiful and gifted Judith of Bavaria, of whom it was said that she governed the kingdom, and turned all men's hearts to her will. The birth, in 823, of Judith's son, the future Charles the Bald, was the opening scene of an often-repeated tragedy, the struggle between a scheming stepmother and the jealous children of the first marriage. Ambitious courtiers and prelates fanned the flame, until the smouldering intrigues in the Frankish court flared up into civil war.

16

Deprived of authority and again reinstated, in the year 833 Louis the Pious found himself opposed by the combined forces of his three elder sons, Lothair, Pepin, and Louis "the German." On the Alsatian "Field of Lies" (Campus mentitus), a place of lasting shame for the faith there broken, the Emperor was deserted by his army and adherents, and forced not only to resign his throne, but to do public penance at Soissons, and confess that he had unworthily administered the office committed to him. Though Pepin and Louis, supported by popular sympathy, restored their father to power in 834, he never recovered his former position, and in 839, after the death of Pepin, the Empire was divided between Lothair and Charles, leaving only Bavaria to Louis the German, and the imperial title and overlordship to the old Emperor.

In 840 Louis the Pious died, esteeming himself wretched to end his days in misfortune, yet grieving less for his own departure than for the uncertain future of his people. With his death the unity of the Empire vanished, and the heritage of Charles the Great was torn asunder by his grandsons. At the battle of Fontanet (Fontenoy-en- Puisaye), in 841, Lothair was defeated by his brothers with great slaughter, and two years later the treaty of Verdun set the seal to the dismemberment of the Empire and traced the first faint outlines of mediæval Italy, Germany, and France.

Lothair, as Emperor, ruled over Italy and a long, narrow strip of territory stretching from the mouth of the Rhine to the mouth of the Rhone, and including the two capitals of Rome and Aachen, a "middle kingdom," which took from him the name of Lotharingia. Louis received the eastern kingdom, the land of the East Franks, the later Germany. To Charles the Bald fell the kingdom of the West Franks, la douce France. A clearsighted contemporary poet, mourning the triple partition of the great united Empire, and the advent of lawless anarchy, noted as a sign of the times the division of the sovereign power among petty princes:

A kinglet in place of a king: for one realm, broken fragments of kingdoms.

(Pro rege est regulus, pro regno, fragmina regni.)

The centralised imperialism of Charles the Great had, in fact, broken up from its own weight, never to be revived in its integrity. The political system which was destined to replace it, a "feudal system" of administrative landlordism, was, perhaps, better suited to the needs of a period when local and territorial influences were strong, communication between different parts of the country was difficult, and the demand for military protection was urgent. Under the pressure of external invasion and internal necessity, the fragmina regni split into still smaller units, principalities, lordships, "fiefs," of all kinds and sizes, little states within a state. With this process of devolution and decentralisation went specialisation of function, and the consequent differentiation of organs in the body politic. A territorial, localised, military society would inevitably develop on aristocratic lines. The governing, fighting class rose, the dependent agricultural class sank, in the social scale. The "strong man armed" kept the city. The weak man "bowed his shoulder to bear, and became a servant unto tribute," sacrificing freedom for the sake of security. "In the time of Charles the Great," wrote the chronicler Nithard, who fought at Fontanet, "there was general peace and concord, now . . . dissensions and strife appear everywhere. Then there was universal abundance and joy, now there is universal poverty and sadness."

While the Empire was rent by internecine wars and private feuds, the monastic annalists were recording with increasing frequency the raids of Northmen and Saracens. Though in 826 Harold of Denmark had submitted to Christian baptism, he was driven from power in the following year, and from 834 onwards the Flemish and Frankish coasts were constantly harried by "pirate-ships," men and women were killed or carried into captivity, convents were sacked, and tribute was exacted. Louis the Pious made peace with the new Danish King, Horik, and took measures for the defence of the coast, but the troubles that followed his death incited the pirates to fresh efforts.

In 841 they sailed up the Seine and plundered Rouen, and in 843 they were in the Loire, ravaging Nantes. The battle of Fontanet had weakened the Franks, though the chroniclers doubtless exaggerate when they say that their whole strength was exhausted so that they could no longer defend their frontiers. As the eleventh-century Roman de Rou has it:

Là périt de France la fleur,

Et de Barons tout le meilleur;

ALFRED THE GREAT AND THE VIKING INVASIONS

Ainsi trouvèrent Païens terre

Vide de gens bonne à conquerre [conquérir].

Still, it is not without significance that when, two years after the treaty of Verdun, in 845, Paris was besieged by the Danes under the viking Ragnar, Charles the Bald could only save his capital by the payment of tribute, a Danegeld of "many a thousand-weight of gold and silver." Hamburg was destroyed in the same year, and the warships of the Northmen were soon a familiar sight in all the rivers of western Flanders, France, and Spain, from the Elbe to the Ebro. Nor was Italy in much better case. Before his death in 844, Pope Gregory IV. had seen the conquest of Sicily by the Saracens, and during the brief pontificate of his successor Sergius II. Saracen pirates pushed up the Tiber, sacked the Roman churches of St. Peter and St. Paul, and rifled the sacred tombs of the Apostles. Though the defeat of another Saracen fleet off Ostia in 849 gave Rome an immediate respite, Leo IV., who became Pope in 847, realised that the storm had only blown over, and set himself to restore the walls of the city, and to protect the Vatican quarter and St. Peter's by fortifications.

The second half of the ninth century, which almost exactly covers the life of King Alfred of England, opened with gloomy prospects, with wars and rumours of war, with famine and rebellion, "dissensions of princes and ravages of the heathen," and all the restless turmoil of a transitional period.

ENGLAND BEFORE ALFRED THE GREAT

BEYOND the Empire of Charlemagne, the island of Britain, a world within itself, lay in the open sea, with Ireland at its side. Remote and isolated in position, cold and sunless in climate, these northern isles were yet fertile enough to tempt the invader, and successive waves of population had swept across them from the days of the prehistoric tribesmen whose handiwork remains in barrow and dolmen, in stone circle and monolith, whose memory may, perhaps, linger in legends of dwarf and gnome and brownie.

The Celts,--Goidels, Brythons, or Belgæ,--who conquered the earlier races, were still a power in the land when Alfred was king, not only in distant Ireland and Scotland, in the hills of Cumbria and Wales, and the moors of the west, but in the heart of England itself, through intermarriage and survival, through the obscure persistence of peasant stocks, or through the subtle influence of custom and tradition. On the far-reaching and thorough Celtic settlement had supervened an incomplete and temporary Roman occupation, followed by a lasting but partial Germanic colonisation. A political line had been drawn in the first four centuries of the Christian era between the Roman province of Britain and the barbarous north behind the walls of Hadrian and Antoninus. In the fifth and sixth centuries a racial line had further separated "Welshman" from "Saxon." Later still, the bond of common Christianity had done something to obliterate these distinctions. Bede, writing at the beginning of the eighth century, could describe the five tongues of Britain as English, Welsh, Scottish, "Pictish," and "Book- Latin," the universal language of learning and the Church, of civilisation and of Rome.

While on the Continent the nations of mediæval Europe were slowly rising from the ruins of the Roman Empire, a number of tribal kingdoms were struggling into existence in that part of Britain which had been conquered by Germanic invaders. Whether the process of political development was one of aggregation or of devolution is matter of dispute. War bands may have grown into tribal kingdoms, and many small kingdoms may have coalesced into a few large states, or again, large but thinly populated states may have split up into small kingdoms, communities within a community. In any case, the result was the formation of a succession of loosely co-ordinated federations, under over-kings whose authority, dignified by Bede with the name of imperium, qualified them in the Anglo-Saxon vernacular for the title of Bretwalda, "ruler of Britain." The sixth and seventh centuries saw the kings of Sussex, Wessex, Kent, East Anglia and Northumbria reach such a position in turn. Oswy of Northumbria, who died in 671, was the seventh Bretwalda. The eighth, according to the Anglo-Saxon Chronicle, was the West-Saxon Egbert, King Alfred's grandfather, more than a hundred and thirty years later.

With Egbert's rise to power in the early ninth century, and the almost coincident appearance of the Danes off the British coasts, a new era began in English history. The ability and energy of the West-Saxon king gave Wessex the supremacy over all England. The Danish wars made that supremacy permanent. Consolidated by a common danger, stimulated by the enthusiasm of a holy war against the enemies of the Christian faith, and organised by the genius of a dynasty of great rulers, the West-Saxon kingdom stood forth as the leader among the petty English and Anglo-Danish states, until the very name of "Wessex," merged in the wider "England," survived only as an arcaism or a historical tradition.

Yet the political unity of England was no sudden growth. To the men of the ninth century local interests were far stronger than national patriotism. They were West-Saxons or Mercians first, and Englishmen only by contrast with Welsh or Scots, Danes or Franks. King Alfred himself was a Wessex man with Kentish antecedents, born in Berkshire, living nearly all his days south of Thames. Though when he died he could be styled "King of the Anglo-Saxons," or even "King over all Angle-kin," in 871, when he came to the throne, it was only the "kingdom of the West-Saxons," with Kent and its dependencies, over which he ruled. The sights and sounds of the South and West of England, the laws and customs, the legends and folk-lore of the southern peoples, must have set their mark deeply on his mind and heart, as they were destined, through him, to influence the whole course of the national development of England.

At the opening of the ninth century, the kingdom of the West-Saxons, even with the underkingdoms of Essex, Kent, Surrey, and Sussex, was but an insignificant principality, though rich and varied in natural resources. Bounded by the North Sea on the east, the Bristol Channel on the west, and the English Channel on the south, it stretched northward to the Thames valley, and included the modern counties of Essex, Kent Surrey, Sussex, and Hampshire, with the pleasant west country of Wiltshire, Dorsetshire, and Somersetshire, the half-subdued Devonshire, and the still British Cornwall. Whatever the dim beginnings of Wessex may have been, whether the original settlement of the Gewissæ, or West- Saxons, was made from Southampton Water, or, as some modern scholars hold, from the Thames valley, by the year 800 their power centred in the country about the ancient Belgic and Roman city of Winchester (Venta Belgarum), the seat of a bishop and already venerated as a burying-place of kings. Behind Winchester, Roman roads struck up to the Hampshire Downs and the vale of Thames, and then westward to Bath, or eastward to London and the Watling Street and the Continental route through Kent, by Rochester and Canterbury, to the port of Dover. South and west of the Kentish uplands and valleys lay the little kingdoms of Surrey and Sussex, crossed by the parallel ranges of the North Downs and South Downs, with the great forest of Andred, the Andredesweald, between them. Sussex and Surrey were probably colonised by tribes of Saxon stock, but Kent, the southern coast of Hampshire, and the Isle of Wight seem to have been conquered by men of Jutish blood, distinct in race, in speech, and in customs, a fact which was not without importance in later West-Saxon history.

The reputed founders of the royal house of Wessex, Cerdic, who bears a British name, and his son Cynric, are figures as unsubstantial as Hengest and Horsa, the traditional leaders of the Jutish invasion of Kent. The earliest extant version of the Anglo-Saxon Chronicle, a Winchester book, naturally enough dwells on the exploits of these West-Saxon pioneers, and works the legends and tales that grew up round their names into a series of hopelessly contradictory annals. A more historical king of the West-Saxons is Ceawlin, son of Cynric, the second Bretwalda, the victor in that sixth-century battle of Deorham which gave the West-Saxons the Romano-British towns of Gloucester, Bath, and Cirencester, and the surrounding districts, and carried their power to the Bristol Channel.

In the seventh century the political supremacy passed to Kent, to East Anglia, and to Northumbria, while Wessex, weakened by constant war, sank into a subordinate position. Not until 685 did the southern kingdom once more rise into prominence under Ceadwalla, a descendant of Ceawlin, a Christian king with a Welsh name, who fought his way to the throne, reigned for three stormy years, conquered the Isle of Wight, ravaged Sussex and Kent, and then, in a fit of devout contrition, resigned his crown and went on pilgrimage to Rome. He was succeeded by his kinsman Ine, one of the most noteworthy of the early West- Saxon kings. Before he, too, quitted the world to die in retirement at Rome, he had given Wessex that famous collection of "dooms" or customary laws, which were destined to be incorporated, after an interval of more than a century and a half, in the "code" of Alfred the Great. Ine's abdication in 726 was followed by a period of dissension and anarchy, and the West-Saxon kingdom, torn by internal strife, gradually became subject to Mercia, now rising to the height of its power under the strong rule of Ethelbald and his greater successor Offa.

By the second half of the eighth century Offa was practically supreme over all England south of Humber. Even when he died in 796, his son-in-law Beorhtric continued to govern Wessex as an under-kingdom of Mercia till his sudden death in 802. Then, if the Anglo-Saxon Chronicle may be trusted, Egbert "took" the West-Saxon kingdom, not to relax his hold upon it until his own death thirty-seven years later, when he had added to his original dominions the kingdoms of Kent, Surrey, Sussex, Essex, Mercia, and East Anglia, and the nominal suzerainty over Northumbria.

As the first ruler of a united England before the storm of Danish invasion tore asunder once more the ill-consolidated tribal kingdoms, as the grandfather of Alfred the Great, and the founder of the West-Saxon royal house, Egbert has won a fame which is hardly warranted by the sober testimony of fact. A few entries in the Winchester Chronicle, a few charters, some coins, a doubtful genealogy, the attribution of the mysterious title of Bretwalda, the records of victories which have left a faint echo in folk-song, these are all the traces that actually remain of a king of whom by the fifteenth century the story could be told that in the first year of his reign he held a Parliament at Winchester and with the consent of his people changed the name of his kingdom from Britain to England.

The fragmentary annals of the period reveal, indeed, a scene of confusion in the tribal states of England which might well be utilised by a young man of ability for his own aggrandisement, and if, in the uncertainty of our knowledge, Egbert can hardly be called an adventurer, he was at least a pretender, with pretensions, apparently, to the thrones of both Kent and Wessex. The ancient West-Saxon royal genealogy traces Egbert's paternal ancestry to Ingild, brother of Ine, through whom he is linked with the kin of Cerdic, the royal stock of Wessex. Egbert is said to have been the son of Ealhmund, the son of Eafa or Eaba, the son of Eoppa, the son of Ingild. If Ingild, Eafa, and Eoppa are only a shade less mythical than the demigods and heroes from whom the house of Cerdic derived its descent, there is some evidence for the existence of Ealhmund, Egbert's reputed father.

An Ealhmund is mentioned in a late Canterbury copy of the Chronicle as having been king of Kent about 784. A charter, the possible source of this entry, was granted by Ealhmund, rex Canciæ, to Reculver in 784, and it seems probable that he ruled Kent at this time as an under-kingdom of Mercia. Certain coins of an Egcberht rex, minted by Udd, and by Babba who also struck money for the Mercian kings Offa and Coenwulf (757-821) and for the Kentish usurper Eadberht Praen (796-798), suggest that Egbert, too, may have reigned for a short time as a vassal king of Kent. A series of fairly well-attested charters connected with Christchurch, Canterbury, further show Offa revoking Kentish land-grants made by rex Egcberhtus, and the Chronicle tells how Offa and his son-in-law Beorhtric of Wessex drove Egbert for three years from England into "Frank-land." Slight as are these indications, they seem to imply that Egbert was in some way connected with the determined effort of the men of Kent to preserve their ancient independence. He may have represented the old royal stock to which, apparently, Eadberht Praen, the apostate priest who led the final struggle against Mercia, claimed to belong. Whether he took part in that struggle, which broke out on Offa's death in 796 and lasted till 798, is, however, uncertain. The date of his exile cannot be precisely fixed, though it must have begun after 789, the year of Beorhtric's marriage to Offa's daughter, and before the death of Offa in 796. In any case, it fell within the reign of Charles the Great, and there is no reason to reject the interesting tradition, emphasised by William of Malmesbury, of the influence of the Carolingian civilisation on Egbert's later career.

Of that career little enough is known. The Chronicle briefly notes Egbert's accession to the throne of Wessex, but his kinship with the house of Cerdic can only be traced through Ine's brother, the shadowy Ingild. Even his hereditary possessions in Hampshire, which are often taken as evidence of his West-Saxon descent, were on either side of the river Meon, in that Jutish district which in race and history was more in sympathy with Kent than with Wessex. Nothing further is known of him till 814, when he harried the West- Welsh, or Celts of Western Devon and Cornwall. Eleven years later, in 825, his victory over the men of Devon at Gafulford left him free to turn against Mercia, now weakened by the civil war which had followed the death of Coenwulf, Offa's successor.

The battle of Ellandun, where Egbert defeated the Mercian King Beornwulf, though its site is disputed, was famous enough to be celebrated in an English song which may still be traced in the rhythmic Latin prose of Henry of Huntingdon. Egbert at once sent his son Ethelwulf, Alfred's father, into Kent, with the bishop of Sherborne, the ealdorman-of Hampshire, and a "great host." Baldred, the under-king, was driven over Thames, and Kent, Surrey, Sussex, and Essex submitted to the West-Saxon King, "because," says the Chronicle, "they had been formerly wrongfully forced from his kin," a statement which, if applied to Kent, goes-to strengthen the theory of Egbert's Kentish descent. Ethelwulf now became underking of Kent, while the East-Anglians in turn revolted from Mercia, and after slaying their overlord Beornwulf in battle, sought Egbert as "peace giver and protector."

Beornwulf's successor Ludeca fell in the following year, and in 829 Egbert deposed Wiglaf, the new Mercian ruler, and conquered the Mercian kingdom and "all that was south of Humber." It is here that the Winchester chronicler calls him "the eighth king who was Bretwalda.""The ninth," wrote Henry of Huntingdon in the twelfth century, expanding this passage, "was his grandson Alfred, who brought all parts of the kingdom under his sway." The North Welsh also "bowed" to Egbert, and he actually, as his coins show, called himself "King of the Mercians," though he allowed Wiglaf to return as under-king.

But too much must not be made of the unity achieved with such apparent ease. England was still merely a loose bundle of petty states, held together by one strong and successful warrior. Already, too, the cloud was gathering which was soon to burst over the country and sweep away all signs of a premature federation. The year 832--to be corrected to 835--is marked in the earliest extant manuscript of the Anglo-Saxon Chronicle by the ominous entry: "Here the heathen men harried Sheppey." In the following year a fierce naval battle against a fleet of thirtyfive Danish ships took place at Charmouth, and the vikings were victorious. In 838, an alliance between the Cornish men and the Danes threatened Wessex with a new and terrible danger, from which Egbert's great victory at Hengestesdune (Hingston Down), near Plymouth, delivered his kingdom. A year later, in 839, he died, and Ethelwulf, his eldest son, succeeded to the West-Saxon throne, while his younger son Athelstan became under-king of Kent, Essex, Surrey, and Sussex.

The death of Egbert, and the beginning of the struggle with the vikings which was destined so profoundly to affect English political and social history, are turning-points which invite a backward glance at that older England into which Alfred was born, but which his children were only to know under changed conditions.

Any attempt to reconstruct the English society of the ninth century must go back to earlier records, to archæological remains, to the history of Bede, the annals of the Anglo-Saxon Chronicle, the laws and charters, the letters and documents, the poems and lives of saints, which incidentally throw light on customs and traditions. Even so, the light is but dim and uncertain. It might be said of Alfred's age as an old biographer wrote of the life of Alfred himself: "The Pieces we have being mangled . . . they seem rather the Rubbish of a Broken Statue than the whole Parts of a Perfect Image." Yet, allowing for variations due to differences of race and locality, one thing at least is clear. Anglo-Saxon society was a country society, rooted in the soil, occupied chiefly with agriculture, living on and by the land. Perhaps this very fact may help us to get near to the true spirit of the past, for there is a quiet conservatism in Nature which is reflected in the continuity of economic custom. The rude forefathers of the hamlet live again in their remote descendants, whose toilsome days are still bound up with the unceasing course of summer and winter, seedtime and harvest.

There is very little about cities and city-life in the eighth- and ninth-century records. The English towns were ecclesiastical or military centres, royal residences, markets for the produce of the countryside, but they were comparatively few and unimportant. There was nothing in England to rival the splendour of Rome, or Aachen, or even Paris. Laws and charters reveal a rustic people, observant of natural features, marking their boundaries by river and hill, by the "broad oak," or the "withy-mere" which had caught their eye and fancy, tending their pigs in the forest, where the sound of the axe felling timber rang through the clearings, or following the heavy plough drawn by its team of patient oxen, across the wide expanses of hedgeless fields, cut up into strips by "balks," or banks of turf, overgrown with wild flowers and grasses.

The life of rural communities rises up before us as we read, of village and hamlet, of lonely homesteads, and monasteries set in solitary places, of the lord's hall and the peasant's hut; a simple life, limited in its demands and outlook, but wholesome and vigorous, and all the more intense for its very narrowness. These hard-working farmers and shepherds were also great fighters, mighty hunters, valiant trenchermen, feasting without restraint when occasion offered, drinking deep of ale and mead, and repenting with equal thoroughness when fines had to be paid for brawling in their cups, or when the fiery denunciations of the "mass-priest" woke their imagination with the terrors of the Day of Judgment.

Something of the West-Saxon village life may be gathered from the regulations in Ine's laws which show the ceorl and the gebur1 at work and at play, ploughing and hedging, stealing, quarrelling and carousing, incurring penalties and receiving compensation. Other figures also flit across the scene, the merchant, the "Welshman," the stranger, the fugitive, and the serf, while the landgrants mirror the face of the country and the manner of cultivation, the brooks and meres, fords and bridges, oaks and thorns, "gores" and "lynches."

The Latin prose of Bede's Ecclesiastical History, the English alliterative verse of the "Widsith" song, or the Beowulf epic, paint for us the hall of king or eorl, the great "mead-hall," with its raftered roof and its glowing central hearth, where the chieftain sat in council with his wise men, or feasted with his thegns about him, or rested unarmed on winter nights, while the gleeman touched the harp and chanted the deeds of heroes.

From early manuscripts, casual notices of dress or armour, and the mouldering relics in Anglo- Saxon graves, we can picture kings and warriors, bishops and monks, high-born ladies and rough peasants, in their habit as they lived, in tunic, super-tunic, and mantle, the men in breeches and stockings cross-gartered with bands of cloth or leather, with flowing hair and beard, the women veiled, in long tunics, often richly ornamented, the church dignitaries in vestments, the soldiers in mail shirts and round or peaked helmets, armed with shields, swords, spears, axes, and bows and arrows.

Language and literature suggest a brave and loyal folk, tinged with the fatalistic melancholy that is born of grey skies, and the relentless cold and darkness of northern winters, but responsive to the thrill of mystery and the charm of natural beauty. We see a world where men went in dread of demons and monsters, ghosts and witches, where their fancy played round the birdlike ship breasting the foam-flecked sea, the "whale's road," the "swan's road," and their eyes were quick to note the green of grassy headlands against brown furrows, the pale shining of water, or the fitful gleam of armour and weapons. We hear in their poetry, as they heard, the call of the cuckoo in spring woods, the croak of the raven, the bird of war, as it hovered over the battle-field, and the "dreadful evensong" of the wolf.

Yet the soul of the people remains unrevealed. Who shall tell us what these thegns and ladies who lie beneath their grassy barrows, with sword and shield, jewels and treasure, beside them, really thought and hoped when they walked in the sunshine? Was the ceorl, in the days when he was no cold constitutional abstraction, but a warmblooded human being, a mere savage, or an unlettered but not altogether uncivilised peasant, slow to understand, but tenacious of grip, and with some dim perception of the meaning of liberty and independence? There is no answer. This long-past age lies in an enchanted sleep, entangled in a maze of controversy, waiting for the magic touch that shall kindle it to life. Meanwhile, it is at least possible to piece together from scattered fragments the external framework of the social organisation.

Though the primitive democracy of the older school of constitutional historians must be rejected as based on insufficient evidence, it is probable that in the eighth and ninth centuries many of the village groups in England were independent lordless communities, learning through local politics the wider lessons of freedom and equality in a well-balanced state. Many other villages, however, were already under the rule of lords, lay or ecclesiastical. In both types, free and dependent, the same system of cultivation would obtain. The peasant proprietor, the lord's "man," and the lord himself all held strips of arable land in the open fields, with a proportionate share in meadow, wood, and waste. The arable was tilled, as a rule, by ploughs drawn by a yoke of four, six, or eight oxen, though a team of two oxen was not uncommon. The full eight-oxen team would be provided by combination among the villagers, where no one landholder was sufficiently wealthy to bear the whole expense. A rotation of crops and fallow in successive years was observed in cultivation, most frequently either in simple alternation, cornone year and fallow the next, or in a threefold course of "winter corn," wheat or rye, "springcorn," barley or oats, and fallow.

There is evidence in the "land-books" or charters that this kind of common cultivation and joint holding with individual rights in the separate strips was older than the ninth century. Agricultural co-operation was, in fact, the natural result of economic and climatic conditions which made the tillage of the soil costly and laborious. A heavy soil meant a heavy plough with a normal team of eight oxen, and this was as much beyond the means of the average ninth-century peasant as a steam-plough is beyond those of his twentiethcentury successor. The village generally formed a nucleus for the open fields, two, three, or four in number, which lay around it, while beyond stretched the meadow-land, the woods and copses, and the uncultivated wastes and commons. In hilly pastoral country, the village settlements seem to have been replaced by a more isolated way of life, in scattered homesteads and hamlets, but in the villages proper the houses clustered thickly together, so that the word "neighbour," the "near gebur" or "boor," acquired a new meaning of social obligation, and duty to a man's neighbour came to be ranked next to his duty to God.

Before the middle of the eighth century, as the writings of Bede and the laws of the later Kentish kings and of Ine of Wessex show, English society was marked by definite class divisions. The wooden huts of the straggling village street, the homes of "churl" (ceorl) and "boor" (gebur), must often enough have been dominated by the more pretentious "hall" of the thegn or ealdorman, with its belfry and its wide gates. All over the country, too, an ecclesiastical aristocracy was springing up. More and more the parish church became the centre and meeting-place of the village, while endowments were lavished by kings and nobles on the great monastic houses, grants of land and jurisdiction, and of immunity from secular service, which gave the clergy a privileged position, and at the same time involved them in worldly affairs. Ecclesiastical provisions, regulations as to the conduct of priests and monks, the observance of Sunday and the payment of tithes, fill a large space in the laws, the foundation of monasteries and the appointment of bishops are as prominent in the annals as the victories and succession of kings, and stories of miracles and wonder-working relics play an important part in popular literature. The high ecclesiastics were influential, also, in the work of government, but here they shared their power with the lay nobles and officials.

The actual administration of the Anglo-Saxon state is one of the most fiercely controverted subjects in this period of controversy. Every point, alike in central and in local government, has been made the occasion for disputes which need not be repeated here. There is too little direct evidence to warrant a positive conclusion, but the local village groups appear to have been linked, however slightly, to the central authority, by means of at least two intermediate administrative units, the hundred or its prototype, and the shire. The shires were under the rule of ealdormen, who, with the king's thegns and the higher clergy, regular and secular, formed the inner circle of witan, or wise men, whose signatures were appended to charters, and who acted as a deliberative and advisory royal council, with powers that varied with the varying strength of the monarchy.

Though the West-Saxons, in common with the other Germanic conquerors of England, recognised kingship as the normal form of government, in the eighth and ninth centuries their kings were, to some extent, held responsible to the people. Ine, Offa, and Egbert, if they were touched by the autocratic influence of Roman Imperialism, interpreted Roman theory by Germanic traditional practice. The king was chosen from the sacred stock which claimed kindred with the tribal gods and heroes, but there was acknowledgment, even in this limited right of selection, of the official character of kingship, a character on which the Christian Church laid stress, while the solemn coronation oath implied a mutual compact between king and people.

The political theory of the early Germanic states was a strand woven of the three threads of tribal tradition, Roman Imperialism, and Christianised Judaism. If the Mercian or West-Saxon king regarded himself as, like Saul, "the Lord's anointed," king "by the gift of God," if, like the Cæsars, he issued coins and used sounding titles, there was still much of the half-barbarous chieftain about him. In actual dignity and position he differed from his subjects rather in degree than in kind. He had royal demesnes, scattered over the country, and a right to take food-tribute on his progresses. A heavy fine was exacted for contempt of his authority, or for injury to his person, while he could grant to communities and individuals a special peace, protected by severe penalties. Yet, despotic though he might be in practice, in theory his power was limited, not only by the advice of his council, but by the almost sacred nature of the customary law, the inherited wisdom of the race, beyond and above any individual man, a thing to be reverenced and guarded, and not lightly tampered with.

It was these laws, "dooms," or customs which were "declared" and "interpreted" in the courts of justice, central and local, by king or ealdorman, by thegn or reeve, or, if needful, by the freemen who constituted the court. They formed an archaic body of law, in which a man's legal status was determined by a wergild, the price paid for his life to his kindred, where the kindred were the avengers of blood, and the individual was but a unit in a family group. In this system men were classed as twelfhynde, those with a wergild of twelve hundred shillings, sixhynde, with a six hundred shilling wergild, and twyhynde, with a wergild of two hundred shillings. The twelfhynde and twyhynde classification seems to have been used much as we use "gentle and simple," to cover the whole free population; it corresponded roughly to the old division into "beorl and ceorl," nobleman and commoner.

There was nobility of blood; a man could be born into the ranks of the eorls, and apparently also into the class of gesiths or thegns. There was an official nobility, too, dependent on service. The king's favour could raise a man to the rank of ealdorman, with all that it implied of high wergild and dignified position, and the "king's thegns" seem to have owed special services to their royal lord. Or, again, men could "thrive," or rise in the social scale by merit or good fortune. A ceorl could become a king's thegn, or even an eorl; amongst freemen there were no hard and fast class barriers; all were "lawful men," with wergild and kindred, legal rights and obligations duly proportioned to their respective grades in the social hierarchy, distinguished alike by privilege and responsibility from the servile class of theows or slaves, who were personally unfree, and required a definite act of manumission to raise them to the ranks of freemen.

The chief public obligations which the freemen of the early English state were called on to meet were, doubtless, the payment of tribute, the enforcement of justice, and the defence of the kingdom. The food-rents and services by which a tribal king or chief was in great measure maintained, go back to very early times. The primitive king travelled from one royal tun or "vill" to another, "eating up his rents" as he went, feasting in barbaric state in his simple hall, hunting in his forests, dispensing a rude justice to the neighbourhood, and then passing on, with wife and children, courtiers and servants, goods and chattels, to his next halting-place.

Justice was further administered by those local courts of which only dim and fleeting glimpses can be obtained. These seem to have been presided over by royal officials, bishop and ealdorman, sheriff and "reeve," and to have been regularly attended by the freemen who owed the service of "suit of court." Where the law to be administered represented the customs of the tribe no professional judges were needed. The official president of the court, supported by the "suitors," was competent to state the customary penalty. The trial was conducted by the ancient method of ordeal, by fire or water, or by compurgation, or "oath-helping," when the accused swore that he was innocent, and his "helpers" swore that his oath was "clean," or true. The oath-helpers varied in number with their dignity and the consequent value of their oaths, and with the gravity of the offence and the rank of the offender, but there was little or no idea of weighing evidence in the modern sense of the term. Decision of guilt was too hard a task for man, unless the criminal had been taken redhanded. In all other cases God must give the verdict through a ceremonial appeal.

If cattle-lifting, theft, and crimes of violence kept the courts of justice busy, the constant civil dissensions and tribal wars of growing states made the duty of military defence both imperative and burdensome. Fyrdung, service in the fyrd or national army, early became one of the most important and ordinary of the obligations laid upon freemen. It constituted, with the upkeep of fortifications and the repair of bridges (burh-bot and brycg-bot), the trinoda necessitas, or triple duty, which was a common incident of eighth- and ninthcentury land-tenure.

Ine's laws prescribed a definite scale of fines for neglect of the fyrd. The landowning sithcundman" or "born gentleman," who was also a landed proprietor, paid a hundred and twenty shillings and forfeited his land, the landless sithcundman paid sixty shillings, the "churlish man," thirty shillings. Fyrdung, then, was incumbent on all ranks of freemen, but the composition of the body thus formed and the exact nature of the services rendered are problems which have never yet been satisfactorily solved. It has generally been assumed that the fyrd was originally the nation in arms, serving under local officers, ealdormen or sheriffs, on the basis of one man for every hide, or family holding of a hundred and twenty acres:-- an ill-trained, ill-armed force of foot-soldiers, with a nucleus of better equipped mounted infantry, gesiths or thegns, king's followers and men of substance, who acted as a kind of royal bodyguard.

It has been thought, also, though the evidence is insufficient for proof, that by the eleventh century the fyrd had become a specialised force of mounted infantry, in which each soldier represented a land-unit of five hides, or six hundred acres, though in emergencies practically the whole free able-bodied population could be called into the field for defence against invasion. Another theory, however, would introduce the principle of specialisation much earlier, and make the fyrd of Alfred's day no citizen army, but a comparatively small body of mounted infantry, fighting on foot, but riding to the field of battle, in which the rank and file followed private lords rather than public officers, and the ceorls acted mainly as a sort of Army Service Corps, carrying provisions to the host, or perhaps, on occasion, working as sappers and miners, when roads or earthworks had to be made. Here, again, the evidence hardly admits of a certain conclusion, though, such as it is, it points to the retention of the current theory, with some modification.

Of the ninth centuryfyrd it may, perhaps, safely be asserted, that it did not invariably contain precisely the same elements, but that it was generally a large force, as compared with a werod, or troop of armed men, and that it was always a local force, or a combination of local forces. It seems probable that the fyrd which Egbert led to the north in 829, to receive the submission of Northumbria, was a more mobile and a less popular body than the army that he called out in 838 when news arrived of the landing of the great shiphere of the Danes, and of their alliance with the Welsh.

When he that heard and fared with the fyrd,

(Tha he thæt hierde and mid fierde ferde) as the Winchester chronicler wrote, the rude rhyme showing, perhaps, a touch of national pride in the West- Saxon soldiers who won the battle of Hengestesdune. At Ellandun, again, the battle against the Mercians was fought by the fyrd, but Egbert could detach a micel werod from the main body and send it under special commanders to subdue Kent.

Later on, in the Danish wars, the Chronicles mention the fyrd of the West-Saxons, the fyrd of the king of the Mercians, and the great fyrd that the Northumbrians gathered together to oppose the invaders. There is mention, too, of fights between the Danes and the men of Somerset or Dorset, of Kent or Surrey, under their ealdormen, and sometimes the local force is identified with the shire itself, as when in 860 "Osric ealdorman" with "Hamtunshire" and "Æhelwulf ealdorman" with "Berkshire" combined against the vikings who had attacked Winchester. As in former days "folk" and fyrd were interchangeable, so now fyrd and "shire" could be used indifferently.

There is nothing in all this, however, to show whether these local troops were normally mounted infantry or simple foot-soldiers. They are generally said to "fare," or to be "led" by the king, though ealdormen, king's thegns, and reeves are occasionally spoken of as "riding" on an expedition. The whole question will recur in connection with the wars of Alfred's reign, when notices of "riding" are found more frequently in the Chronicles. Of the earlier Anglo-Saxon fyrd, before the coming of the Danes, it can only be affirmed with any approach to certainty that it was a body of "territorials," connected with land, while the werod was based rather on a personal principle, and that all free laymen, from eorl to ceorl, owed some kind of fyrd service, either directly or by representatives.

The invasions of the Danes, which forced the English kingdoms to organise themselves permanently for defence, are accepted by all the western mediæval chroniclers as a scourge of God, by far the most terrible of the "five plagues" of Britain: Romans, Picts and Scots, Angles and Saxons, Danes, and Normans. The viking ships first appeared off the English coast at the close of the eighth century, though where these invaders came from, and to what race they belonged, are much disputed questions. The Franks called them all Northmen, the English knew them all as Danes, the Irish distinguished between the Dubh Gaill, or dark strangers, and the Finn Gaill, or fair strangers. To every nation of the West they were heathen pirates, shapes of dread and horror. The old chroniclers were right in drawing an analogy between their incursions and those of the Angles and Saxons, three hundred and fifty years earlier.

Like them they were at first mere raiders, bands of adventurers under warlike leaders, devastating the land like a pack of wolves, or a swarm of locusts, and then passing on. Like them, as time elapsed, their enterprise grew in scope and importance, until the buccaneers had been transformed into colonists, who settled and tilled the lands which they had first wasted, and then conquered.

The Anglo-Saxon Chronicle tells how, in the days of King Beorhtric of Wessex, that is, between 786 and 802, "three ships" of Danish men came to the English coast, and how the "reeve" (gerefa) rode down to see who the strangers were, and met his death at their hands. Ethelwerd, writing in the tenth century, makes the "reeve" into a king's reeve, an exactor regis, called Beaduheard, gives the place of landing as Dorchester, and says that the reeve took the pirates at first for merchants.

The very form of this story shows how early the coming of the vikings passed into legend and song, and how deep an impression their ravages had made on the popular mind. Even so Hengest and Horsa are said to have come to Britain with "three keels," or Ælle of Sussex and his sons with "three ships, or Cerdic and Cynric of Wessex with "five ships," according to one annal, "three ships" according to another. Even so, too, but with a happier issue, in the Beowulf epic, did the thegn who watched the coast for Hrothgar, King of the Danes, ride down to the shore to challenge Beowulf and his comrades, when they landed from their "lofty keel." The West-

Saxon reeve Beaduheard was, as Henry of Huntingdon, in repeating the tale, sadly notes, with pardonable exaggeration, only the first of "many millions" of Englishmen to be slain by the Danes.

In 793 the earliest authentic record of a viking raid on England occurs in connection with the famous sack of the church and monastery of Lindisfarne, which moved Alcuin to write letters of sympathy and exhortation to his countrymen from his retreat at the Carolingian court. Dreadful portents, tempests, and lightning, and "fiery dragons flying in the air," heralded, it is said, "the devastation of God's church at Lindisfarne by the harrying of heathen men."

The next year the pirates came again, to attack Jarrow, but they were scattered by a storm, sent, so the monks believed, by St. Cuthbert, for the discomfiture of his enemies. In the twelfth century Simeon of Durham could sketch, with vivid touches, the still unforgotten scene of terror:--the wolf-like invaders and their helpless victims, the plundering of churches, and the slaughter of priests, monks, and nuns.

The opening of the ninth century saw the diversion of the viking activity to the coasts of Ireland and western Scotland, of Frisia, and of France. For nearly forty years England had peace, while Ireland was ravaged from Donegal to Kerry, and St. Columba's rich island sanctuary of Iona was despoiled three times. It was not till the last years of King Egbert's life that Kent and Wessex were seriously troubled by raids of "heathen men." The Isle of Sheppey was harried in 834, and a descent was made on Charmouth in Dorsetshire in 836. These expeditions, which began in the year after the battle of the "Field of Lies," seem to be connected with the revival of viking incursions on the Frisian and Flemish coasts, and were probably carried out by detachments from the great Danish host which at this time took advantage of the civil war between Louis the Pious and his sons to sack the wealthy trading towns of the Rhine and Scheldt, Dorstadt, Utrecht, and Antwerp.

More formidable, and somewhat different in character, was the invasion of south-western England in 838 by the allied forces of the Danes and the Cornishmen. It has even been suggested, though the evidence is very slight, that this attack came from Ireland, where the vikings, probably in this case Norwegians, under their able leader Turgesius, Thorgest, or Thorgils, were beginning to settle in the land they had won. The casual raids were now developing into organised campaigns, planned with knowledge and purpose. England's forty years of peace were to be followed by forty years of constant anxiety, and of fierce struggle with no despicable foe.

That the Northmen were trained soldiers and skilled in seamanship is evident both from the testimony of the contemporary chronicles and from the remains of viking ships, armour, and weapons which have been unearthed in Norway and Denmark, and, to a much smaller extent, in France and England. The most perfect specimen of a viking ship was discovered at Gokstad in southern Norway, and has been attributed to the eighth or early ninth century. It is long, narrow, and shallow, some seventy-nine and a half feet from stern to bows, sixty-six feet in the keel, about five feet deep, and more than sixteen feet broad in its widest part, built of oak planks, nailed, and bolted together with iron, and caulked with plaited cowhair. It was undecked, though there may have been lockers at stern and bows, and the bottom was covered with loose boards, with storage room beneath them. Rowed by sixteen oars a side, with shuttered rowlocks cut through the oak planking, it had also a mast forty feet high, a yard, and a square sail. It was steered by means of a short broad oar on the starboard side, worked by a movable tiller. Remains were found of a tent-like deck awning, white, with red stripes, which must have been secured by ropes to the sides of the vessel, of an iron anchor, a cauldron for cooking, plates, cups, and other iron utensils, and a wooden draught board, with lines scored on the back for the old game of "nine men's morris." Three smaller boats, twenty-two and a quarter feet and about fourteen feet long in the keel, lay with the Gokstad ship.

Such must have been the "long ships" which struck terror into English hearts when their square sails, white or striped, were descried far out at sea, bearing down on the coast with a favouring northeast wind behind them or creeping up the wide estuary of the Thames, between low marshy banks, to carry desolation to the very heart of the fertile and tranquil country. Their descendants, long and narrow and of light draught, with pointed stern and bows, still ply on the lakes and rivers of Norway, Denmark, and Finland, and still put out to sea with square sails set to catch the breeze.

An average-sized viking ship of the ninth century would probably carry from forty to fifty men, with weapons and food, but a large vessel might well hold from eighty to a hundred warriors, and though many expeditions were undertaken by very small squadrons, or even by three or four "keels" (ceolas), a great fleet might number hundreds of ships. The command was often divided, and the large fleets, in spite of their admirable organisation, appear to have been rather aggregations of groups than united wholes.

Under such chosen sea-kings as Turgesius, who led the "great royal fleet" to Ireland, or Rorik, the kinsman of King Harold of Denmark, whom a chronicler calls "the gall of Christendom" (fel Christianitatis), these "noble sea-levies" must have looked stately enough in their full battlearray, the round shields hung in a close row above the oars, with metal bosses glittering in the sunlight, the "golden war-banner" shining in the bows, the huge carved prows shaped like the heads of dragons or monsters. "Ships came from the west," runs a Northern lay, "ready for war, with grinning heads and carven beaks."

The vikings, too, who sailed in these fleets were splendid men, whose appearance won unwilling admiration from the Western chroniclers:-- "men of great stature and fair of face, and most expert in arms." Disciplined and well-equipped warriors, they were as much at home on land as at sea, and could beach their boats, commandeer horses, and ride on a foray, with the same reckless courage with which they faced the gales of the North Sea, or ventured across the Atlantic Ocean, in their small open ships.

Egbert's victory at Hengestesdune in 838 gave Wessex a brief respite from viking invasion, but with his death in 839 and the accession of his son Ethelwulf, the raids began again, and grew more and more serious and determined as time went on. A comparison has often been drawn between Ethelwulf and his contemporary, Louis the Pious. The likeness is, indeed, too striking to be overlooked:--the strong father, working for peace and unity; the weaker son, clinging to his inheritance in the face of internal discontent and external danger; the rebellious children at home, the hostile Northmen abroad. Yet the whole action of the island drama is on a smaller scale. There is less of pity and terror in the catastrophe; the Danes were resisted more successfully; the brothers, Ethelbert, Ethelred, and Alfred, united against the common foe instead of weakening their forces by civil war; above all, where the West Franks had to make the best of a Charles the

Bald, the West-Saxons found an Alfred the Great.

It is partly, perhaps, due to the fame of Alfred that legend has busied itself
with his father's history until the true Ethelwulf is lost in a cloud of
mythical ancestors, saintly advisers, and ecclesiastical eulogists. The habit of
regarding him as an English Louis the Pious is further responsible for many
of the current theories of his weakness and incapacity. The king who went
in person to Rome with gifts in his hand and devoted the tenth part of his
land to God's service, was himself turned into a churchman by admiring
biographers. William of Malmesbury says that though he was ordained sub-
deacon, he was permitted by the Pope to resume the secular life on the
death of Egbert without other heirs. Henry of Huntingdon makes him
bishop of Winchester. St. Swithun becomes his tutor, and St. Neot his
kinsman, and his descent is traced through Germanic heroes and gods to
Jewish patriarchs and the Christian Deity, the Father of all.

Apart from these legendary accretions, a good deal is known about
Ethelwulf's life. His name figures in Continental annals and in English
records. He had close and interesting relations with the West Franks and
the Papacy, and he seems to have been a man of cultivated taste and sincere
piety, whose lack of capacity has been somewhat hastily inferred from the
absence of evidence for his direct military activity in the Danish wars, and
from the vicarious energy of his ealdormen and bishops in the defence and
government of the country. After the battle of Ellandun he was sent with
Wulfheard, ealdorman of Hampshire, and Ealhstan, Bishop of Sherborne,
to receive the submission of Kent. He then became under-king of Kent and
its dependencies, Essex, Surrey, and Sussex, and he grants or signs charters
connected with Kentish affairs as "king," "king of the Kentishmen," "king
of Kent" (rex, rex Cantuariorum, rex Canciæ), from 828 to 838. In 839
Egbert's death gave him the West-Saxon throne, and he appears to have
been succeeded in the Kentish under-kingdom by Athelstan, who is
variously described as his eldest son and his younger brother. The question
is obscure, but it is probable that Athelstan, who signs charters as "king"
and "king of Kent," from 842 to 850, was the son of Egbert, and that he
governed East Anglia as under-king before his translation to Kent.

The year after Ethelwulf's accession, that fateful year 840 which saw the
death of Louis the Pious, saw also the renewal of viking attacks upon

England. One of the last acts of the ealdorman Wulfheard before he "fared forth" was the repulse of thirty-three shiploads of pirates at Southampton, a victory speedily followed by the defeat of the men of Dorset at Portland, and the death of their ealdorman Æthelhelm. In the following year Herebryht, the Mercian ealdorman, was slain by "heathen men," and there was harrying on the eastern coast, in Lindsey, in East Anglia, and in Kent.

The civil war in the Empire had given the Northmen an opportunity, and in 841 a great fleet under the viking Oscar appeared in the Seine, plundered Rouen, and threatened the Abbey of Jumièges. It seems to have been the same fleet which, in 842, attacked both the flourishing port of Cwantawic (St. Josse-sur-mer, or Étaples), and the English towns of London and Rochester. In 843, also, unless the chroniclers have confused the events of this year with those of 836, Ethelwulf, like his father, seven years earlier, was defeated by "thirtyfive shiploads" of Danes at Charmouth, while in 844 the vikings slew Redwulf, king of Northumbria.

The main body of the Northmen had now entered into alliance with the rebellious Bretons. They sacked Nantes, and in 843 wintered for the first time on the island of Noirmoutiers, at the mouth of the Loire. The next year they joined the discontented party in Aquitaine, devastated southern France, and then advanced on the Christian kingdom of the Asturias, and even sailed down the coast of Portugal and Spain to Cadiz, and penetrated as far inland as Seville. Driven back by the disciplined troops of the Spanish Moors, they turned northwards once more, and in the March of 845, a viking fleet of a hundred and twenty ships plundered Paris, and only retired on the payment of a heavy tribute by Charles the Bald. Ragnar, the leader of this expedition, has often been identified with the Ragnar Lodbrok of legendary fame, whose story is closely interwoven with English traditions, and the retreat from Paris was early attributed to miraculous causes, a magic fog preventing the advance of the ships, the intervention of St. Germanus, or the divine judgment, visiting the sacrilegious invaders with pestilence and death.

It was in this same year, 845, that Hamburg, the new archbishopric of the north, was ravaged by King Horik's Danish fleet of six hundred sail. In 846 a Flemish monastic chronicler declared that the Danish pirates had subdued almost the whole province of Frisia. Hard winters, bitter winds, and torrential rain aggravated the misery of the people by destroying the growing crops and vines. The land was desolated by war and famine. In Aquitaine packs of wolves three hundred strong roamed unchecked through the country, devouring the men and women whom those human wolves, the vikings, had spared. The Northmen besieged Bordeaux in 847 and seized Dorstadt, which they had burnt in the previous year.

On every hand fire and sword, bloodshed and rapine, struck terror to men's hearts and paralysed their energies. Ireland, like Frisia and France, lay helpless at the feet of the heathen conquerors. Only in England some power of resistance seemed left, when the men of Somerset and Dorset under their ealdormen, with Ealhstan, the warlike Bishop of Sherborne, defeated a Danish host at the mouth of the river Parret, on the Somersetshire coast.

But in England, too, the future looked dark enough when, not long after the Somersetshire victory, Alfred, the youngest child of King Ethelwulf, was born. The long ships of the vikings still hovered like birds of ill omen just across the Channel, waiting to swoop down on their destined prey. Though as yet their attacks had been casual and intermittent, the work of detached bodies of Danes or Norsemen, under leaders whose names have passed from memory, all through Alfred's childhood they were growing more regular and formidable, until, with his dawning manhood, the full "fury of the Northmen" fell at last upon England. Henceforth the "Great Army" of the vikings, the Micel Here or Here of the Winchester Chronicle, became the central fact in the life of every Englishman, the constant preoccupation of the statesman and the soldier, the main theme of the chronicler and the moralist, a nightmare terror to trembling women and children, the dreadful yet half-welcome rod of God's wrath to monks and nuns eager for martyrdom.

Nearly three hundred years later, the chronicler Henry of Huntingdon felt something of that old horror and despair, when he wrote of the viking invasions, the "fourth plague" of Britain:

There was no profit to the victors when they conquered, for a fresh fleet and a greater army ever appeared. . . . God Almighty sent forth these fierce and cruel people, like swarms of bees:--Danes and Goths, Norwegians and Swedes, Vandals and Frisians: --who spared neither age nor sex.

THE CHILDHOOD AND BOYHOOD OF ALFRED

848-866

WHERE the northern slope of the Berkshire Downs falls gently to the basin of the Thames, on the edge of the Vale of White Horse, amidst cornfields and green water-meadows, lies the little town of Wantage. Here, as a modern statue in the wide old market square records, "Alfred the Great, the West-Saxon King," was born, "A.D. 849." The only contemporary evidence for this accepted tradition is the opening of Asser's Life of Alfred, which has been copied by later chroniclers:

In the year of our Lord's Incarnation 849, Alfred, King of the Anglo-Saxons, was born in the royal "vill" [villa regia] called Wanating, in the district named Berrocscire [Berkshire], which district is so called from the Berroc wood, where the box-tree grows most abundantly.

Isolated as is this mention of Alfred's birthplace, there is no reason to doubt its truth. Its very unexpectedness, indeed, makes for its credibility. Wantage, though a royal "vill," was too small and inconspicuous to have been deliberately chosen by an unscrupulous biographer for the scene of his hero's entrance into the world. On the other hand, it was quite a possible place for the birth of a son of the house of Egbert, which held large estates in the neighbourhood, originating, possibly, in the grant of land "about Ashdown" made in the middle of the seventh century by Cenwalh, King of the West-Saxons, to his kinsman Cuthred, grandson of Cynegils, a former King. The ham at Waneting was bequeathed by Alfred to his wife, and remained crown-land till the twelfth century. Asser may even have derived his information from the King himself. The local touches, the etymology of "Berkshire," the box-trees in the Berroc wood, suggest a special personal knowledge, for it was unusual in the ninth century to preserve details of birth, save in those ecclesiastical biographies where signs and portents heralded the advent of a future saint or martyr.

Death, the achieved fame, the completed earthly career, the "faring forth" into the unseen, alone seemed worthy to be remembered. The kings and nobles whose obits were carefully registered, that prayers might be offered for their souls, whose virtues were commemorated by annalist and bard, had, as a rule, crept almost unheeded into life. The Anglo-Saxon Chronicle, with its frequent entries of death and burial, succession and descent, passes over in silence the births of famous men. Wantage, then, may still boast of being "the cradle of the most illustrious King Alfred," and Berkshire may retain the name of Alfred the Great on her roll of worthies.

The actual year of Alfred's birth is more open. to dispute, though there can be little question that it was either 848 or 849, and the evidence is rather in favour of the earlier date. There are two contemporary authorities: Asser's Life of Alfred, and the West-Saxon royal genealogy and regnal table which is prefixed to the Parker or Winchester manuscript of the Anglo-Saxon Chronicle. Unfortunately, they do not agree. The regnal table is carried down to Alfred's accession, when "there were gone of his age three and twenty winters," when, that is, he was twenty-three years old. As he came to the throne in 871, "after Easter," this would throw back his birth to 848. Asser, on the contrary, says that Alfred was born in 849, and became King "in the twenty-third year from his birth."

Neither Asser nor the regnal table can claim to be infallible in matters of chronology, but of the two, the regnal table is somewhat the more trustworthy, since it is very ancient, and is intimately connected with King Alfred. It occurs both at the beginning of the Anglo-Saxon Chronicle and at the end of the English version of Bede, as well as in a still earlier fragmentary form, and in each case it breaks off at Alfred's accession. It seems likely, therefore, that it was put together from older materials and brought up to date under the king's supervision before the completion of the Alfredian Chronicle in 891. Asser, who probably wrote his book a little later, about 893, borrows his chronology from the Anglo-Saxon Chronicle, reckoning from the Incarnation, but he also dates each year by the birth of Alfred. Since the Chronicle has no entries between 845 and 851, he may possibly have taken the date of Alfred's birth from the regnal table. If so, he apparently understood the phrase "there were gone of his age three and twenty winters" to mean, not "aged twenty-three," but "in the twenty-third year of his age."

The point, after all, is not of vital importance. It is likely enough that Alfred himself would not have been able to give the day of his birth, though he would have known that he was but a youth of some twenty-three winters when he took upon his shoulders the full burden of government. The fashion of "keeping birthdays" does not, indeed, appear to have been observed in ninth-century England, partly, perhaps, on account of the superior claims to reverence of the day of the patron saint after whom a child was named, but chiefly because, as was still the custom in Iceland in the nineteenth century, the midwinter Nativity of Christ, the Christmas Day with which the year may have begun, was celebrated as the one great birthday festival.

If the Anglo-Saxon records are vague and unsatisfactory in their chronology, they preserve the genealogies of royal houses with reverent care. It mattered little when or where a ruler was born, but it mattered very much who his father was, and if he came of the true royal stock, the "right kingly kin" (cynecynn). The kings of Wessex were specially concerned to prove that their kin went back to Cerdic, the first of the royal line, and through him to the traditional forefathers of the race of Gewissœ, or West-Saxons, "Gewis," Wig, and Freawine, and behind them again to the mythical Woden and his son Beldaeg.

It is significant that no genealogy of Egbert, Alfred's grandfather, is found until the death of his son Ethelwulf, when the family had firmly established its somewhat doubtful claim to the West-Saxon throne. The Anglo-Saxon Chronicle inserts, under the year 855, a notice of Ethelwulf's death, which took place two or three years later, with a long and distinguished pedigree of his house, which has been thought to mark the close of an early collection of English annals. This pedigree gives the descent of Ethelwulf son of Egbert from Ingild, brother of Ine of Wessex, and links it on to the older West-Saxon genealogies in the Chronicle, which trace Ine's ancestry to Cerdic, and from Cerdic to Woden. Then, borrowing apparently from the genealogy of the Bernician dynasty, it adds Woden's descent from the fabulous demigod "Geat," and finally, drawing here from no known source, mounts up through some nine generations of dim, mysterious beings,

44

whose names, varying in the different manuscripts of the Chronicle, recall old heroic poems, and legends of heathen kings, to connect them at last by the device of a son born to Noah "in the ark" with the patriarchs of the Old Testament, and so with Adam the first man, and with Christ, the spiritual second Adam.

In the West-Saxon regnal table, too, the notice of Ethelwulf's reign is followed by a genealogy, showing his descent from Cerdic, and including not only Ine's brother Ingild, but his two sisters, Cwenburh, and Cuthburh the foundress and first abbess of Wimborne Minster, where one of Ethelwulf's sons was afterwards buried.

The pedigree of Ethelwulf, the first to introduce a Christian element into the pagan genealogy of the royal house of Wessex, is also the last of its kind in the Anglo-Saxon Chronicle. Yet the West- Saxon kings continued to pride themselves on their divine ancestry, and Asser is careful to trace Alfred's descent from Cerdic through both his parents. He incorporates Ethelwulf's full pedigree in his text, and supplements it by the genealogy of Alfred's mother Osburh, the daughter of Oslac, the royal butler or cupbearer, a Jute of the stock of Stuf and Wihtgar, kinsmen of Cerdic and Cynric, from whom they are said to have received a grant of the Isle of Wight. Stuf and Wihtgar are legendary figures, whose story comes from the suspicious fifth-century annals of the Anglo- Saxon Chronicle, but the tradition of Osburh's origin may well be genuine, and if Ethelwulf also numbered Jutes among his father's Kentish ancestors, there must have been a strong Jutish strain in Alfred's blood.

Of Oslac, the father of Osburh, nothing is known beyond Asser's statement, nor is it easy to say in what the duties of the king's butler (pincerna) consisted at this early period, though Oslac was, doubtless, a great nobleman, and a high official in the primitive court and household of his royal son-in-law. Osburh herself was, in Asser's words, "a most pious woman, noble in mind and noble in race," a worthy mother of kings. Her four sons, Ethelbald, Ethelbert, Ethelred, and Alfred, ruled over Wessex in succession. Her only daughter, Ethelswith, became the wife of the king of Mercia.

Ethelbald signs charters with his father Ethelwulf, as filius regis or dux filius regis, from 847 to 850, and in 851 he was present at the battle of Ockley

(Aclea), when the Danes were defeated by the West-Saxon fyrd. If, as is probable, he was then at least fifteen years old, he would be born about 836, some twelve years before Alfred, and three years before his father's accession to the throne of Wessex. As Ethelswith was married in 853, it seems likely that she was next to Ethelbald in age. If she were fifteen at the time of her marriage, she would be two years the junior of her eldest brother, and Ethelbert and Ethelred would then come between her and the youngest child, Alfred.

Athelstan, the under-king of Kent, who signs charters from 841 to 850, and who gained a great naval victory over the Danes in 851, has been thought to be the son of Ethelwulf by an earlier marriage, but though this is possible, the evidence on the whole supports the theory that he was Ethelwulf's brother, a younger son of Egbert, and that Egbert on his death, like Ethelwulf after him, divided his dominions, and granted the underkingdom of Kent, with Surrey, Sussex, and Essex, to his second son, though his elder son retained the overlordship of the whole, with the direct government of Wessex.

There is little to show what motive governed the choice of the names given to the children of Ethelwulf and Osburh. The Os stem in the names of Osburh and her father Oslac connects with the Œsir, Anses, or high gods of northern mythology, and was common in the royal houses of Northumbria. All Osburh's children, however, except Alfred, received names compounded with their father's Ethel prefix, which is found throughout England, and signifies "noble." Ethelbald and Ethelred were the namesakes of famous Mercian kings; Ethelbert may have been called after the first Christian king of Kent. Alfred alone bore a name somewhat unusual in England in his time, with that Ælf or Alf root which, like the Os stem, goes back to the old belief in Œsir and Alfar, Anses and Elves, the creative and sustaining forces of nature, the spirits of the earth and air.

The prefix Ælf or Alf was used in the royal families of Northumbria and East Anglia, and the name Ælfred or Alfred occurs, though somewhat rarely, in English documents before the birth of the child who was to make it illustrious and popular. In the first half of the ninth century it appears in lists of witnesses to charters in Hampshire, in Worcestershire, and in Berkshire, while in 831, an Ælfred held the unexplained office of pedisecus at the court of Wiglaf of Mercia.

If, in accordance with their traditional custom, the elves from whom King Alfred derived his name presided over his birth, they brought rich gifts to his cradle, and endowed him with all the grace and virtue of a fairy prince of romance. Asser describes him as his parents' favourite, beloved by all, surpassing his brothers both in beauty of form and face, and in charm of speech and manner--"there from his Infancy appearing in him not only a sweetness of Favour and Countenancetenance

tenance above the rest, but also an Excellence of Spirit, of Wit and Disposition," in the stately seventeenth-century English of Sir John Spelman. Something must be allowed here for the natural partiality of a biographer for his hero, but the stories of Alfred's childhood that have been preserved show him as a thoughtful, sensitive boy, with an eager curiosity, and an insatiable thirst for knowledge. Though Asser deplores the neglect of his early education, the West-Saxon court, in which he spent the greater part of his boyhood, was no bad training-school for a life of public duty and responsibility. A shifting scene, full of interest and variety, it was well suited to call out an intelligent child's powers of observation and reflection.

The royal "vills," "hams," and "tuns" of Wessex and its dependencies were scattered up and down the country, and the King and Queen moved their gipsy-like caravan of children, retainers, and household goods from one botl (dwelling) or setl (seat) to another, as occasion demanded. Christmas they often spent at the Dorset Dorchester, Easter at the Wiltshire Wilton, but they also wandered through the Home Counties and the shires of southern and western England. The itinerary of Ethelwulf and Osburh cannot be fully traced from the scanty indications in charters and chronicles, but Alfred's childish eyes must at least have often rested on the rolling chalk downs of Berkshire, Kent, and Surrey, the green valley of the Thames, the ancient cities of Winchester and Canterbury, and the white stretches of Watling Street, that great Roman road which seemed to the Saxons like the star-strewn path of the Milky Way. The love of the "fair countryside, the fairest of God's creations," which breathes through his writings, must have grown with his growth among the woods and fields, the streams and grassy hills of his native land.

From those early years in the wide open spaces and calm silences of nature, he probably drew much of the quiet strength and patience of his manhood. Nor was the human element wanting in his upbringing. About him, as the court travelled through the long leisurely day, or kept its modest state in the royal hall, would be a constant stir of life, the coming and going of officials and ministers, priests and soldiers, bishops like the saintly Swithun of Winchester, or the warlike Ealhstan of Sherborne, ealdormen like Eanwulf of Somerset or Osric of Dorset, fresh from fighting the Danes.

The times were threatening, and there was grave talk among the West-Saxon nobles, and strenuous preparation, for the Northmen were busy on the Frisian coast and about the mouth of the Rhine, where in 850 the pirate Rorik, "gall of Christendom," secured a permanent base at Dorstadt, and became the Emperor's vassal. Alfred's first dream-like memories must have been of the viking invasions of his babyhood. The "heathen men" were to the English children of the early ninth century much what "Boney" and the French became to their descendants more than nine hundred years later, phantom shapes, all the more fearful because vague and undefined.

It was probably detachments of Rorik's followers who fell upon England in 851, when Alfred was about three years old. Wessex and Kent were ready for them, and they met a gallant resistance. The men of Devon, under their ealdorman Ceorl, beat the invaders back from the south-west "with great slaughter"; the Kentish under-king Athelstan, with his ealdorman Ealhere, repulsed a naval attack on Sandwich, fighting, according to some manuscripts of the Chronicle, "on shipboard." Nine Danish boats were taken and the rest saved themselves by flight.

Another great fleet of three hundred and fifty ships, which made for the estuary of the Thames, was more successful. Canterbury and London were stormed, Beorhtwulf, King of the Mercians, and his fyrd were routed, and the vikings crossed the Thames and marched into Surrey. It would have gone hard with southern England had not Ethelwulf and his son Ethelbald at the head of the West-Saxon fyrd checked the advance of the Danes and defeated them in the bloody battle of Aclea (Ockley, or Oakley). "There was the greatest slaughter in the heathen army that we have ever heard tell of to this present day," wrote the contemporary chronicler.

An ancient tradition, still lingering in local song and legend in the nineteenth century, has placed this victory near the picturesque little Surrey village of Ockley, at the foot of a spur of the North Downs. Great Oakley in Essex has also made, with less reason, a similar claim. A third possible site, which on both philological and military grounds has something to be said in its favour, is Church Oakley, near Basingstoke in Hampshire. This place is called Aclei in Domesday Book, where Ockley is written Hoclei. It is in the heart of Wessex, near the Roman road from Silchester to Winchester, which was probably the objective of the Danish march. But Ockley, too, is on a Roman road, the Stone Street or Stan Street, which ran from London to Chichester, and cut through the parallel ranges of the Downs and the great Andredsweald forest which lay between them.

As the Chronicle expressly says that the Danes crossed the Thames into Surrey, while Ethelwerd adds that the battle was fought "near the wood which is called Aclea," the philological objection is hardly strong enough to necessitate the rejection of the Ockley site. The vikings may have been trying to reach the south coast in order to meet their fleet coming from the Thames, with a view to an attack on Winchester from the sea.

In any case, the strategy of this campaign suggests a power of organisation which should go far to exonerate Ethelwulf from charges of cowardice or indolence.

He, with his eldest son, Ethelbald, and with Athelstan of Kent, had taken counsel with the West-Saxon witan at Wilton in 850. The following year saw a well-planned defensive scheme bravely carried out--the local leaders with their followers watching the coasts, the King with the main army intercepting the enemy before a junction could be effected between their fleet and their land forces, and thus warding off the threatened danger from his chief city.

This crowning victory of the "fortunate year" 851 made a deep impression on men's minds. It was used as a date to reckon from, and Henry of Huntingdon, in the twelfth century, dwells upon it with evident pride, describing the fallen warriors lying like corn beneath the sickle, the rivers of blood, and all the horrors of the ghastly field. "God," he concludes, "gave the fortune of war to those who believed in Him, and brought unspeakable destruction on those who despised Him." The ninth-century chronicler Prudentius of Troyes had the same thought when he wrote of Rorik's host, "part of them, attacking the island of Britain and the English, were defeated by them with the help of our Lord Jesus Christ."

This idea of the struggle with the Danes as a holy war would be familiar to Alfred from his nursery days. The world as he first knew it must have seemed a place of conflict between the Christian forces of light and the heathen powers of darkness. The saints and demons of his Catholic teaching would materialise as English and Danes when he listened to the stories of Hengestesdune and "Parret-mouth," Sandwich and Aclea, while the lust of battle was sanctified to him, as to the crusaders of a later age, by the sense of a just and righteous cause. The little sons of Ethelwulf may often have "played at vikings" before the days when play turned to grim reality. Alfred's one mention of childish games is of boys "riding their sticks" and imitating their elders.

If faith and patriotism thus combined to train and discipline the character of Alfred, there was also much in his surroundings to appeal to his imagination. From the green ridges above his birthplace looked down the mysterious "White Horse," work of a vanished race, destined to be associated with the victories of his own later years. Near by was "Wayland's Smithy," the ancient sepulchral monument early said to be haunted by the magic smith of Northern mythology, "the famous and wise goldsmith Weland," as Alfred calls him in the Boethius. From the barrows on the downs, so legend told, the mighty dead came forth at night to sit before their doors. In marsh and fen might lurk monsters as fell as Beowulf's foe, the fire-breathing Grendel. Across the sea might still come floating an oarless ship, in which a royal child lay asleep among weapons, with a sheaf of corn at his head, like Alfred's fabled ancestor Sceaf, "the Sheaf." The fancies of an outworn creed mingled with the wonders of Christian martyrology and saint-lore to people the earth with unseen presences and to lend enchantment to common things.

Asser bears witness to Alfred's love for those old poems of his race, with which his retentive memory was stored. "By day and by night he would listen to them, hearing them constantly repeated." By day, perchance, as he rode from hall to hall in golden summer afternoons, by night, as he sat before the blazing wood-fire on frosty winter evenings, and saw visions in the flames while the gleeman sang to the sound of the harp.

The only story of Alfred's childhood which has been preserved in detail prettily illustrates this early taste.

One day [writes Asser] his mother showed a certain book of Saxon poems which she had in her hand to him and his brothers, and said, "I will give this manuscript to that one of you who can learn it first." Moved by these words, or rather by divine inspiration, and attracted by the beauty of the initial letter of the book, Alfred thus answered his mother, anticipating his brothers, who were his seniors in years, but not in grace: "Will you," he said, "really give this book to that one of us who can first understand it and repeat it to you?" With a glad smile, she assented. "I will give it," she said, "to that one." Then he, straightway taking the book from her hand, went to a master and read it. Having read it, he brought it back to his mother and repeated it.

This seeming simple tale has been obscured by a cloud of controversy, raised chiefly by its inconsistency with Asser's previous statement that Alfred remained "illiterate" till the twelfth year of his age, or after, and by the improbability of a young child learning to read in a short space of time. Both difficulties are avoided by the supposition that Alfred merely learnt to repeat the poems by heart, a view very generally adopted, but opposed by Mr. Plummer, who sees no way of escaping from the conclusion that Alfred actually read the book, since Asser distinctly says that "he went to a master and read it" (legit), while, though he afterwards "recited" it (recitavit) to his mother, the Latin recitare means simply "to read aloud," and is used by Asser himself in this sense in several passages.

It may readily be granted that a clever boy of five or six years old could easily be taught to read a "set book" of poetry, but it is also probable that the constant repetition involved in the reading would impress the poems on his memory, and it may be pointed out that the classical recitare often implies the declamation of poems in public, and that in Alfred's translation of Orosius, it is rendered by the Anglo-Saxon singan and giddian, to sing and chant. Indeed, with the few and wellloved books of childhood, "reading over and over again" passes almost insensibly into "knowing by heart." Alfred's mother, moreover, promised the book to the son who should "learn" it (discere) first, and the whole point of the anecdote as Asser tells it is to show Alfred's precocious quickness and powers of memory, even before his regular education had begun. The attempts to settle the question by putting the incident later in Alfred's life, after his father's second marriage, may be dismissed as pure guesswork, unsupported by any contemporary evidence. The discussion has been unfortunate, in that it has diverted attention from certain points of deeper interest in the story.

In spite of Asser's complaints, Alfred seems to have been surrounded, at least in his very early childhood, by the influences of a cultivated home, where he learnt to know and prize books, to take pleasure in artistic skill, and to value the national treasure of folk-song. The taste and love of beauty which he afterwards displayed, the appreciation of English poetry which led him carefully to preserve the Anglo-Saxon songs, and to have them taught to his children, may have been inherited from the grandfather who owed his education to the courts of Offa of Mercia and of Charles the Great, and from the father who kept in touch with Frankish learning and refinement, and whose costly gifts of embroidery and English metal-work in gold and silver roused admiration even in luxurious Rome.

The winning of the poetry book should probably be placed about the year 854, between Alfred's two visits to Rome. His sister, who is not mentioned in connection with it, had then already left the West-Saxon court for a home of her own. The brothers who competed with Alfred were presumably the young Ethelbert and Ethelred, for Ethelbald had long been engaged in public cares.

After the struggle of 851, the vikings, if a somewhat doubtful entry in the Anglo-Saxon Chronicle may be believed, spent the winter in the Isle of Thanet. They were certainly there in 853, when Ealhere and Huda, the ealdormen of Kent and Surrey, attacked them with their local forces, and were defeated after a bloody battle in which the two ealdormen fell. In 853, too, Burhred, the successor of Beorhtwulf on the Mercian throne, with his witan or council, sought the help of the West-Saxons against the North Welsh, and Ethelwulf not only came to his assistance in person, but cemented the alliance by giving him the hand of his only daughter, Ethelswith.

The marriage took place after Easter, according to Asser, in the "royal vill" (villa regia) of Chippenham, in Wiltshire. Alfred may already have started for the Continent, for it was in this year that his father first sent him to Rome with a great company of attendants, noble and non-noble. The embassy seems to have been intended to prepare the way for Ethelwulf's own journey, two years later.

He had long cherished the idea of a pilgrimage to the shrines of the Apostles. As early as 839, he had sent ambassadors to the Emperor to ask permission to pass through the Frankish dominions on his way to worship at Rome, alleging as the cause of this pious resolve a vision seen by an English priest, who, rapt out of the body, learnt what great plagues and invasions of heathen men were in store for those Christians who would not repent of their sins. Why the little Alfred accompanied the embassy of 853, "we may," with Sir John Spelman, "diversly conjecture, but not determine."

Later legends put St. Swithun in charge of the expedition and made it the result of a dream in which Ethelwulf was directed by an angel to send his youngest son to the Pope, that he might receive the royal unction, and become the first of a long line of anointed kings of England. Legendary, also, in all probability, is the story reported by William of Malmesbury that Alfred was said to have first met his future literary adviser, Grimbald, on this journey, and never to have forgotten his kindly hospitality. All that is certainly known is that the embassy reached Rome in safety and that the child Alfred was warmly welcomed by the Pope, Leo IV.

The building and fortification of the "Leonine City" had just been completed, and the English travellers must have wondered at the new gate of St. Peregrinus, with its proud inscription in honour of "Golden Rome," "Rome the head of the world," and the great walls with their forty-four strong towers. They must have heard tales, too, of the splendid dedication ceremony of June, 852, of the coronation of Louis II., the son of the Emperor Lothair, in 850, and of the naval victory over the Saracens off Ostia in 849. All around them were evidences of the destruction wrought by fire and sword, and evidences also of the wealth and piety which had hastened to repair those ravages. The ancient city of the Cæsars was already almost transformed into the city of the Popes. Christian churches and monasteries, often built from the materials of older temples, clustered about the mighty ruins of imperial Rome--the forgotten monuments and deserted palaces, the silent Forum, the vast Coliseum, of which Anglo-Saxon pilgrims of the seventh century repeated the prophecy: "When falls the Coliseum, Rome shall fall, and when Rome falls, the world."

These things were of the past: of the present were the shrines of St. Peter and St. Paul, newly decorated after the Saracen raid by the lavish generosity of the Pope, the wonder-working relics of saints and martyrs, the endless stream of pilgrims, many of them English, pouring into the holy city at the call of penitence, of curiosity, or of devotion.

By the middle pof the ninth century, the Catholic Church had fallen from primitive simplicity into complexities of doctrine and a material conception of the spiritual life. The purgatorial system with its realistic presentation of the world beyond the grave, of the joys of heaven and the pains of hell, had long been elaborated with a Dante-like vividness of detail. A Christian mythology, beautiful and terrible, was rapidly replacing the ancient polytheism of Rome or of the North. The symbolic expression, half original, half adapted from older forms of belief, fostered a spirit of mysticism in the educated, a crude superstition in the ignorant. Visions and miracles, signs and tokens, strange deliverances and marvellous judgments, mingle with protests against magic and witchcraft in the literature of the time. While theologians disputed over abstract questions of doctrine, transubstantiation, Trinitarianism, predestination, image-worship, the concrete relics of the saints were sought after with a passionate credulity, bought, stolen, translated from one church to another, magnificently enshrined, fervently worshipped, by learned and unlearned, clergy and laity alike.

Though Alfred only once, in his later writings, speaks of having seen Romeburh, no imaginative child, trained in the Christian faith, could fail to be deeply moved when he trod "the threshold of the Apostles," and knelt in awe before the shrines where so many English kings and pilgrims had knelt before him.

An extant letter from Pope Leo IV. to Ethelwulf mentions his gracious reception of the young "Erfred," whom he has invested "as a spiritual son," with the belt and robes of the consular office. The entry in the Parker manuscript of the Anglo-Saxon Chronicle1 for the year 853 apparently describes the same ceremony: "And in that year king Ethelwulf sent Alfred his son to Rome. Then was the lord Leo Pope in Rome, and he hallowed him to king and took him as bishop's son," or godson.

The "taking as bishop's son," or "bishoping," probably means that the

Pope, in accordance with early Catholic custom, was Alfred's sponsor in the rite of confirmation. This answers to the spiritual sonship of the papal letter, and was so understood by Asser, who writes that the Pope "anointed Alfred as king, and confirmed him, receiving him as the son of his adoption." Confirmation would involve unction, and it has been suggested that the investiture as consul to which the Pope refers, with the anointing which formed part of the confirmation ceremony, were interpreted in the light of after events as regal unction, a "hallowing to king," which was worked up by later monkish historians into a formal coronation at Rome.

The Chronicle and Asser, however, keep the "hallowing to king" distinct from the "bishoping," and their statements are so explicit that it seems impossible to doubt that the writers believed that some sort of royal anointing had taken place, an opinion presumably shared by Alfred himself. Both passages were almost certainly composed after Alfred's accession in 871, by men acquainted with the Latin annals and biographies of the Frankish Empire. The entry in the Chronicle, which is distinguished in the Parker manuscript by two marginal crosses, and is closely followed by Asser, shows Latin influence in the use of the word domne, for dominus, lord, a Latinism, which is also found in the English version of Bede. The clerk who wrote it may well have had in mind such parallels as the papal unction of the two young sons of Charles the Great in 781, as kings of Italy and Aquitaine, or the anointing of Louis II. as Emperor in his father's lifetime, or he may, perhaps, have recalled how David, the youngest son, was anointed by the prophet as king in the midst of his brethren.

When fate had swept away Alfred's three elder brothers in swift succession, and the memory of the visit to Rome had grown dim, it would be easy to attribute something of prophetic insight to the Pope, and to mistake the half-forgotten ceremony of consular investiture for regal unction, even without confusing it with the ritual of confirmation. The letter of Leo IV. makes it clear that the honour actually conferred on Alfred was the titular dignity of consul, which was granted somewhat freely by the Popes of the ninth century, when it had ceased to carry with it any real authority. The Byzantine splendour of the consular insignia may have caused them to be regarded by the English as royal robes. A consul, as Leo's letter implies, was girt like a king with a sword. He may also, at this late period, have been crowned with a golden diadem and invested with the purple and white cloak or trabea which was originally only worn by consuls in triumphs.

That the difficulties involved in the story of Alfred's regal unction were early felt, may be indicated by the fact that the Peterborough manuscript of the Chronicle (E) omits the incident altogether, while the late bilingual Canterbury manuscript (F) puts it after the death of Ethelwulf, and a spurious Winchester charter makes Ethelwulf speak of it in connection with his own pilgrimage in 855. Since, however, the anointing was performed by Leo IV., who died in July, 855, it must have occurred during Alfred's first visit to Rome, in 853.

He was in England again in 855, when Ælfred filius regis witnesses a Rochester charter, which is dated by Ethelwulf, "when I set out to go beyond the sea to Rome." This charter is also witnessed by Æthelberht rex, and it appears likely that Ethelwulf, on the eve of his departure, divided his dominions in the approved West-Saxon fashion, leaving his eldest son Ethelbald as regent of Wessex, and Ethelbert, his second son, as under-king of Kent.

That he further made an attempt to conciliate both the clergy and the laity by promises and rewards is probably the thread of truth in the tissue of fiction which veils the famous "Donation of Ethelwulf." The Parker manuscript of the Chronicle, under the year 855, has an entry:

Here the heathen men first sat over winter in Sheppey.

And that same year "booked" Ethelwulf king the

tenth part of his land over all his kingdom to the

praise of God and his own eternal health.

In Asser's text this becomes:

Ethelwulf, the aforesaid venerable king, freed the

tenth part of his realm from all royal services and

tribute, and offered it to God, the Three in One, in

everlasting alms or inheritance, in the cross of Christ,

for the redemption of his soul and the souls of his

forefathers.

Asser, then, apparently took the "booking," or granting by charter, of the Chronicle, to mean that Ethelwulf had given a tenth part of the kingdom to be held by the Church "in free and perpetual alms," quit of all public service save prayer and intercession. Such grants, on a smaller scale, were common enough, and the later confusion of Ethelwulf's gift with the grant of tithes has no basis beyond the recognition of the sacred character of the tenth part. The monks afterwards supported Asser's view by spurious charters, framed in the interests of their own privileges and exemptions. Two genuine charters of 855 set the matter in a different light. One, the Rochester charter already cited, books lands to a thegn (minister) with full power of bequest, "for the tithing (decimatio) of fields which, God permitting, I have ordered to be made to my other thegns (ministri)." These lands, as the endorsement shows, were ultimately granted to a monastery. In the other charter, also a Rochester "book," witnessed by Ethelbearth rex and Elfred filius regis, in a meeting of the witan, Ethelwulf grants land to a thegn, quit of all royal services, "for the expiation of my sins and the absolution of my crimes."

Mr. Stevenson has pointed out that in land grants to laymen, which contain exemptions from worldly services, and expressions of penitence and pious hope, there was generally "an understood reversion" to religious uses, and that in many cases there is proof that such reversion had actually taken place. He concludes that Ethelwulf "booked" a tenth part of his own lands to his thegns in the first instance, with reversion to the Church after the deaths of the grantees. If this be so, it may imply a desire on Ethelwulf's part to promote the internal peace and harmony of his kingdom during his absence at a critical juncture.

The outlook for Wessex was, indeed, dark in 855, with the vikings settled on the coast of Kent, and the whole of the North Sea and English Channel, from Frisia to Aquitaine, swept by their fleets. They harried the country about the Scheldt, sailed plundering up the Seine, and sacked and burnt the cities on the Loire, Nantes and Angers, Tours and Blois. Their leaders are now often mentioned by name in the Frankish chronicles, Rorik and Guthrum and Godfred, pirates of royal birth, Sihtric and Bjöm, the raiders of the valley of the Seine.

In England the Danes had settled in the Isle of Sheppey in the east, and were threatening Mercia from the west. A charter of Burhred, the Mercian King, is dated in 855, "when the pagans were in the country of the Wrekin (in Wreocensetnu)." In this same year also, "Horm, chief of Black Gentiles," was killed by the Welsh King Roderick ap Merfyn.

Yet Ethelwulf hardly deserves the reproaches which have been heaped upon him for going on pilgrimage instead of remaining at home to defend his kingdom. He had waited long before carrying out the scheme which he had planned at the beginning of his reign. He was growing old, as men counted age when public life began almost in childhood, and disease and death often came prematurely. Judged by contemporary standards, his action probably appeared altogether admirable, the crown of a virtuous life.

The Frankish annals duly record how " Edilvulf, King of the Anglo-Saxons," was honourably received on his way to Rome by Charles the Bald, King of the West Franks, and how he was conducted to the frontier with all royal observances. Asser alone notes that Alfred accompanied his father, who "loved him more than his other sons." It may be that the child was already motherless, for Ethelwulf married his second wife only a year later. Sorrow for Osburh's death may even have been one of the compelling causes of his journey, but here all the contemporary authorities are silent.

The English pilgrims may have reached the Holy City before the death of the old Pope Leo IV., in the middle of July, 855. They must certainly have witnessed the disorderly scenes which followed the election of his successor, Benedict III., who was opposed by a strong party in Rome. The papal biographer gives a list of the splendid gifts which the West-Saxon King offered to Pope Benedict, among them a crown of pure gold, a sword ornamented with gold, and a gold-embroidered tunic, royal insignia, it would seem. Rich stuffs, golden vases and images, and four silver-gilt gabatæ or hanging lamps, "of Saxon workmanship," are also mentioned, with largesse of gold to the Roman clergy and nobles, and of silver to the common people.

A later story, which comes from William of Malmesbury, makes Ethelwulf restore the "Saxon School" in Rome, which had been destroyed by fire, and establish a tribute of "Peter's Pence" or Romescot, to maintain it. It was to commemorate this tradition that Raphael introduced the figure of Ethelwulf into his Vatican fresco, L'incendia del Borgo, with the inscription "Astulphus, king of England, came here as a pilgrim and gave tribute."

The Borgo or Burgus, so-called from the Anglo- Saxon burh, was the name given to the English settlement on the Vatican Hill, which was also called the Schola Saxonum in the ninth century, though the schola seems originally to have meant the whole body of "Saxon" settlers, the "English colony," organised on military lines for purposes of defence. The Vicus Saxonum, a district which stretched from the palace of Nero to the banks of the Tiber, included the scholæ or schools of the other Germanic races, Frisians, Franks, and Lombards. The "Saxon School" was burnt down early in the ninth century, and again at the beginning of the pontificate of Leo IV., who was said to have checked the flames by making the sign of the cross. Leo himself rebuilt the church of S. Maria, now represented by the church and hospital of Santo Spirito in Sassia, Saxia, or "Saxony," on the site of the ancient burh, and the Germanic scholæ formed part of the new walled "Leonine City."

Ethelwulf's share in the work of restoration, though not unlikely in itself, is not mentioned by early writers, and the idea that he began the payment of "Peter's Pence," an older and rather obscure tribute to the Papacy, was probably due to some confusion between his personal gifts in 855 and the bequests to Rome in his will. A spurious charter of post-Conquest date even makes Ethelwulf establish the English School to serve God day and night for the benefit of his people. Another story relates how he obtained exemption from working in chains for the English criminals in Rome.

These trivial tales serve at least to show the impression made by Ethelwulf's visit to Rome, and by his pious munificence and devotion. It was with a true instinct that Raphael in his fresco placed him side by side with a later papal tributary, Godfrey de Bouillon, one of the leaders of the first Crusade. The pilgrim kings of the eighth and ninth centuries were, in truth, the forerunners of the crusading kings of the eleventh and twelfth centuries, and, like them, they won a posthumous and legendary fame, in which romance and reality are strangely intermingled.

After a year's sojourn in Rome, Ethelwulf turned his steps homewards. He must have been at the West Frankish court by the summer of 856, when he was betrothed to Judith, the young daughter of Charles the Bald, the granddaughter of that earlier Judith whose charm and ambition had brought such disaster on the Empire.

The marriage was celebrated on the first of October, in the royal palace at Verberie near Senlis. There is no warrant in ninth-century sources for the modern view that the union was the result of deep-laid political schemes, the seal of an alliance between West-Saxons and West Franks against their common foes the Northmen. What seems to have chiefly struck the chroniclers who do more than merely mention the marriage is the fact that Hincmar, archbishop of Rheims, blessed the bride, crowned her with a diadem, and gave her the name of queen, contrary to West- Saxon custom, and that she was afterwards permitted to sit by her husband's side on the royal throne.

If Asser may be believed, the reason for the inferior position accorded to the West-Saxon queen was to be sought in the horror felt for the crimes of Eadburh, daughter of Offa of Mercia, and wife of Beorhtric of Wessex. When her husband died of the poison prepared by her for her enemies, she fled, so runs the story, to the court of Charles the Great. Charles asked her, with a grim jocularity, whether she would prefer to marry him or his son. She chose the son for his youth, whereupon the great King said, with a smile: "Had you chosen me, you should have had my son; since you have chosen my son, you shall have neither him nor me." Eadburh was then appointed abbess of a nunnery, but in a few years she was deprived of her post, on account of the wickedness of her life, and she eventually died in great poverty and misery at Pavia, where she was frequently seen, accompanied by one servant, begging her daily bread. "I often heard this," says Asser, "from my lord Alfred, the truth-telling King of the Anglo-Saxons, as he had heard it from a number of truthful witnesses, many of whom could remember the events."

The anecdote is worth preserving, both as an illustration of the taste of the time, and as an early link between England and that legendary history of Charlemagne which was already growing up on the Continent. The literary relations between Wessex and "Frankland" had, indeed, long been close and friendly. Ethelwulf had a Frankish secretary, and corresponded with Lupus

Servatus, the learned abbot of Ferrières. At a slightly later date Asser's writing shows marked traces of Frankish influence, while the Frankish annalists are generally well-informed on English affairs.

The actual form of service used by Hincmar of Rheims at the marriage of Ethelwulf and Judith is still extant, and the chronicler Prudentius of Troyes speaks of the pomp and state of the young Queen's journey to her island kingdom. Though she was a mere child, of twelve or thirteen years old, while her husband was a man of about fifty, with grown-up sons, there is no indication that the marriage roused dissatisfaction in Wessex. Asser, however, states that on Ethelwulf's return from Rome, though the people received him gladly, he was met by a serious revolt on the part of his eldest son Ethelbald, who conspired with Ealhstan, Bishop of Sherborne, and Eanwulf, ealdorman of Somerset, to exclude his father from the throne.

The rebels gathered west of the forest of Selwood, in the Dorset and Somersetshire district; the West- Saxon nobles were divided against themselves, and the country was on the verge of civil war, when Ethelwulf, with "excessive clemency," refused his people's offers of help, and consented to divide his kingdom with his son, leaving Ethelbald to rule in Wessex, while he himself retired to the "eastern provinces" of Kent and its dependencies, though he probably retained the suzerainty or overlordship throughout his dominions. The whole account reads much like a page of Carolingian history: the undutiful son, the trusted councillors betraying their master, the division of the realm, even the marriage of the old King to a young wife, of whom his elder children might well be jealous--all have their parallels in the Frankish annals.

Since the Parker manuscript of the Anglo- Saxon Chronicle altogether ignores the rising, and merely says that Ethelwulf came to his people, and they were fain (glad) thereof, Asser's narrative has been regarded with suspicion. The same Chronicle, however, also passes over in silence the undoubted marriage of Ethelbald with his father's widow, and Asser's story is borne out by the reckoning of five years to Ethelbald's reign in the Parker Chronicle, and in the West-Saxon regnal tables, while the Annals of St. Neots put Ethelwulf's death in 857 and make Ethelbald reign two and a half years jointly with his father, and two and a half years alone. As Ethelbald died in 860, this would fix his accession in 855, the year when Ethelwulf went to Rome. The papal records, too, state that Ethelwulf "left his possessions and lost his own kingdom" for the sake of his Roman pilgrimage. The Anglo-Saxon and Frankish authorities agree in placing his death about two years after his return, in 858.

He was buried at Winchester, or, according to a curious entry in the Annals of St. Neots, at the little royal ham of Steyning in Sussex. His will, known only from the description in Asser and from the mention in the will of Alfred of "the writing concerning the heritage of King Athulf," appears to have divided the kingdom between Ethelbald and Ethelbert, and to have left his family lands to his children and kinsmen, and his personal property to his sons and his nobles, with considerable bequests for religious and charitable purposes.

He decreed, if Asser may be trusted, that for the good of his soul one poor man should be fed and clothed for ever from every ten hides of his hereditary lands which were cultivated and inhabited. He also gave a sum of three hundred mancuses, or some forty pounds, a year, to Rome, two-thirds of it to keep up the lights in the churches of St. Peter and St. Paul, and one-third as an offering to the Pope. These clauses have often been connected with the grant of tithes and the tribute of Peter's Pence, and Ethelwulf's will has been confused with his earlier "Donation." There is some justification for this in the fact that, except for the continued payment of Peter's Pence, there is no evidence that the provisions of the will were carried out, nor, indeed, could the King legally lay a permanent charge on his family lands, in which he had only a life interest, though he could, doubtless, express a pious wish, and trust for its fulfilment to the charity of his successors.

Ethelbald's short reign as sole King was uneventful for Wessex. He shocked public sentiment by marrying his father's child-widow Judith, won a certain meed of praise by his benefactions to the monks of Abingdon, died prematurely, and was buried at Sherborne, in the diocese of his friend, Ealhstan, that "Selwood-shire" which had been the scene of his revolt against his father. No panegyric follows the brief notice of his death and burial in the Chronicle, nor need Henry of Huntingdon's rhetorical phrases be taken seriously when he writes: "All England wept for the youth of King Ethelbald, and there was great lamentation over him. . . . England felt afterwards how much she had lost in him."

Judith, widowed a second time while still in her teens, sold her lands in England and retired to Senlis, where she lived in queenly state under the guardianship of the bishop and of her father Charles the Bald, until she incurred the ban of the Church by eloping with the Count of Flanders, Baldwin of the Iron Arm. That she cherished kindly memories of her English sojourn would seem to be indicated by the later marriage of her son Baldwin II. to Alfred's daughter Æfthryth, the ancestress of Matilda of Flanders, wife of William the Conqueror.

On Ethelbald's death, Ethelwulf's second son, already under-king of Kent, Surrey, Sussex, and Essex, became King of Wessex also. Contrary to the custom of his house, he delegated no portion of his authority to his younger brothers, possibly because Ethelred and Alfred were too inexperienced to be placed in responsible positions in dangerous times.

While England enjoyed immunity from viking ravages, every year in the Frankish annals has its tale of raids and sacrilege, of wasted villages and burning towns. In each great river, Somme or Seine, Loire or Rhone, rode a pirate fleet, generally with an island base for winter quarters. Favoured by the perennial dissensions in the Carolingian house, the Northmen sacked Paris in the Christmas season of 856, a deed of horror and audacity which seemed to those who chronicled it like the profanation of Jerusalem by the Babylonians. Orleans, Blois, Chartres, suffered in turn, the valley of the Rhone was devastated, and in 860 the vikings even coasted along the Mediterranean shore, and burnt Pisa and other cities.

It was in 860, too, shortly after Ethelbert's accession, that the Danes of the Somme, led, apparently, by one Weland or Völund, attacked Wessex. Charles the Bald had tried to bribe them to drive their brother pirates from the Seine, but in spite of heavy taxation he failed to raise the requisite sum, and while waiting for payment the fleet slipped across the Channel, sailed up Southampton Water, and plundered Winchester before the fyrd could intercept and repulse them. "There came up a great host of ships, a sciphere," says the chronicler, "and 'broke' Winchester, and against that host fought Osric ealdorman with Hamptonshire and Ethelwulf ealdorman with Berkshire, and put the host to flight, and held the place of slaughter."

The defeated raiders recrossed the Channel, and for five years England was again at peace, lying in a breathless calm, on the edge of the storm which still swept the Continent.

In 861, Charles the Bald, exasperated by a second sack of Paris, succeeded in persuading Weland to besiege the island settlement of the vikings of the Seine, but the device of setting a thief to catch a thief was no more successful than in later days in England. The besieged bought off their besiegers, and took up winter quarters with them. Charles now resorted to the wiser policy of systematically fortifying and guarding the banks of the river, and by a fortunate victory he forced the Danes to come to terms. Weland did homage, and ultimately accepted Christianity.

Meantime, the vigilance and energy of Robert the Brave, Count of Anjou, kept the pirates of the Loire in check, but the struggle was fierce and continuous, and the inhabitants of the western kingdoms lived in daily terror of death and outrage at the hands of the Northmen, while across the eastern frontier of the Empire poured a new and even more terrible enemy, the savage Ungri or Huns, whose coming Hincmar of Rheims reluctantly chronicles.

It was in 865 that the vikings, who had been ravaging the banks of the Rhine in the previous year, appeared once more off the Kentish coast, and settled in the Isle of Thanet. The men of Kent adopted an expedient which had already been tried by the West Franks: they bought off the invaders, only to find that "during the peace and the promise of money, the army (here) stole away by night and harried all Kent eastwards." It is noteworthy that neither king nor ealdorman is mentioned in connection with this raid and the previous negotiations. The "men of Kent" seem to have acted quite independently. It may be that the sands of Ethelbert's life were already running low. The Chronicle assigns him a reign of five years, puts his accession in 860, and makes Ethelred succeed him in 866. Hence he probably died either late in 865, or early in the following year.

The Northmen timed their attacks wisely, when the kingdoms they invaded were weak, or divided against themselves. On all sides danger threatened when Ethelbert was laid beside his brother Ethelbald at Sherborne. Asser and the Chronicle alike praise the peace and honour of his reign, repeating, perhaps, Alfred's own idealised recollections of those few quiet years in the midst of strife, a Golden Age, when men could sleep in security, with no fear of the pirate fleet. It is to this time that the famous passage in Asser's

Life of Alfred must apply, where he describes the talented boy, conscious of intellectual power, thirsting for knowledge, eagerly learning Anglo- Saxon poetry by heart, but remaining "unlettered" (illiteratus) till the twelfth year of his age, or later, owing to the carelessness of his parents and guardians.

Whether "unlettered" be taken to mean merely ignorant of Latin, as has been suggested, or altogether untaught, it is likely enough that from Alfred's return from his second journey to Rome, when he was about eight years old, to the accession of Ethelbert, when he was in his twelfth or thirteenth year, his formal education was neglected by his father and elder brother. Absorbed in the cares of state and the pleasures of the court, they would give small thought to the unusual aptitude for learning shown by the child Alfred. Asser tells how in later days the great King was wont to lament that when he had youth and leisure he could find no master to teach him, and Alfred's preface to the Pastoral Care of Gregory the Great notes the lack of scholars in Wessex when he came to the throne in 871. Yet ten years earlier, after Ethelbert's accession, he apparently learnt to read without difficulty, and, perhaps, began the compilation of the little book of Hours, psalms, and prayers, which Asser saw long afterwards.

The decay of learning in Wessex was, doubtless, gradual, and the Danish wars hastened the slow literary decline which probably set in with the death of Ethelwulf. St. Swithun, one of the last representatives of the old tradition, only died in 861, shortly after the sack of his cathedral city by the Northmen, and his influence must have lingered for a while among those who had known him. Alfred himself could remember how, before the viking ravages, the churches throughout all England were filled with treasures and books.

When, in his maturity, the King found the longdesired opportunity to carry out his educational schemes, memories of his boyhood may have suggested the lines of study he laid down for his children and for the pupils in his court school-- psalms, and Anglo-Saxon books and songs, with reading and writing in both Anglo-Saxon and Latin, a training in "liberal arts" which should precede the strenuous physical discipline of hunting and other bodily exercises.

In Ethelbert's peaceful days Alfred himself may first have learnt the hunter's craft for which he was renowned, notwithstanding the delicacy which hung about him from his infancy. His signature as filius regis appended to his brother's charters implies that he continued to follow the court in its wanderings through the country. From these scattered indications, then, it is possible to gain some idea of the external conditions under which he passed the years of childhood and early youth, those years of growing curiosity in the world of men and affairs, of dawning ambition and uneasy self-realisation.

Of his inner life and the workings of his mind and conscience less has been revealed, though Asser has left it on record that "from his cradle he desired wisdom before all things." Temperament and experience would combine to make him thoughtful beyond his age, and to rouse his sense of responsibility. To the child, nurtured in the doctrines of the Catholic Church, who had seen Rome and the West Frankish court, and had heard of the ancient splendour of the Empire, learning and godliness must have seemed the highest good. The vision of his manhood may have flashed upon his boyish eyes, that high ideal of an ordered Christian State, of a contented and God-fearing people, ruled by a king and an aristocracy using the knowledge that is power for the well-being of the community.

Touches of human feeling redeem Asser's confused and wordy account of his hero's precocious piety, his zeal in almsgiving, his prayers as he lay prostrate before the shrines of saints, the illness called ficus which God sent in answer to his petition for an infirmity which should chasten without disfiguring or incapacitating him. His ecstasies and prayers were but the natural expression of spiritual crises in a boy for whom religion had opened the gates of emotion.

Such psychological phenomena are not confined to any one age, or form of faith. The disciple of Wesley, bemoaning his sins at night in the dark garden, the youthful Francis of Assisi, publicly beggaring himself for love of his fellows, were of the same stuff as the stripling Alfred, rising at cockcrow to pour out his passionate heart before God and the saints. Devout, imaginative, studious, he must have shrunk from the rough contact of the actual world, the scandals and quarrels in the Imperial house, the arrogance and corruption of the Papacy, the ruthless cruelty of the heathen Northmen. Where he looked for civilisation he found deepening barbarism, where he sought a contemplative seclusion, he was forced into violent action.

Of all his biographers, Sir John Spelman, who had seen something of the Civil War in England, and knew how it fared with scholarly spirits fallen upon unquiet days, has best appreciated the suffering of the young Alfred, who thirsted more after literature than either possessions or sovereignty.

But [as he finely concludes] He that had a Work for him to do, of which he little ever thought, had provided him a School, which, though nothing acceptable in Appearance, was far more proper to enable him for the service that he was to do than were the Schools of Letters. And that was the School of Travel [travail] and Adversity.

ÆLREDUS SECUNDARIUS

866-871

WITH Ethelred's accession Alfred was drawn into the full current of public life. Though he was not entrusted with the independent government of an under-kingdom, and continued to sign charters merely as filius regis, he enjoyed the first place in his brother's counsels, and Asser speaks of him as secundarius, a term implying, apparently, some kind of authorised viceroyalty, connected, it may be, with his position as next in the line of succession to the West-Saxon throne.

Ethelred has been described as Alfred's favourite brother, and it is possible that nearness of age, early associations, and the premature deaths of Ethelbald and Ethelbert would create a specially close relation between the survivors. Together they had watched their parents and their royal brothers successively pass away. Together they were now called upon to face the greatest danger which had threatened England within the memory of man.

In 866, the year in which Ethelred "took" the West-Saxon kingdom, "a great army (micel here), came to the land of the English and wintered in East Anglia, and were 'horsed' there, and the East-Angles made peace with them." Thus runs the entry in the Anglo-Saxon Chronicle, significant in its brevity: the first ominous note of the warstorm that was about to burst on the devoted country. This was no simple coasting raid, no casual river expedition, or harrying from an island base. It was the beginning of a deliberate systematic policy of conquest and settlement on the mainland. The flat rolling pastures of East Anglia, with their herds of grazing horses, seem to have offered an easy prey. The vikings left their ships and transformed themselves into mounted infantry, fighting still on foot, but riding on their foraging inroads, and sweeping the countryside, as an old author notes, after the fashion of the "dragooners," or mounted foot-soldiers of the German wars of the seventeenth century. The East-Anglian folk, like the men of Kent before them, bowed to the inevitable, and made a precarious peace with their unwelcome visitors.

The vikings now turned to fresh fields of plunder and conquest. They crossed the Humber into Deira and seized York, the ancient Roman city of Eboracum. Northumbria was rent at the moment by civil war. Ælle, a usurper, was disputing the crown with the rightful ruler Osbert, and the pressure of a common danger united the rivals too late. They led a mycel fyrd against York, where the invaders had taken up a defensive position behind the crumbling walls. The Northumbrians broke into the city on March 21, 867, only to be defeated with fearful slaughter in a savage hand-to-hand struggle. Ælle and Osbert fell, and the exhausted remnant of the army made peace with the Danes.

The legends which have gathered round this Northumbrian campaign and round the East- Anglian raids which preceded and followed it bear witness to the general recognition in the popular mind of the importance of the crisis. No impersonal political cause seemed sufficient for such great disasters. Love, hate, and revenge, the primitive passions, were evoked to account for the misfortunes which had befallen England, and the invasion of Northumbria was woven into the saga of the mysterious Ragnar Lodbrok and his sons. By the twelfth century the Viking Age had become matter for romance, and tales were current in England of the betrayal of a beautiful Northumbrian woman by one of the rival kings--Osbert in one version, Ælle in another,--of the rebellion of her kinsmen, and the calling in of the Danes by her outraged husband. Another tradition makes Ælle cast the famous viking Ragnar Lodbrok into a pit full of serpents, and the Northumbrian expedition is undertaken by Ragnar's sons, Ingvar and Ubba, to avenge their father's murder. They take Ælle prisoner and put him to death with horrible tortures. A third story connects Ragnar Lodbrok with East Anglia. He is cast ashore on the coast, received hospitably by King Edmund, and murdered by a jealous huntsman, who is then sent adrift in Lodbrok's boat, and, landing in Denmark, accuses Edmund of the murder of the Scandinavian chief. Ragnar's sons, Hingvar and Hubba, invade East Anglia and martyr Edmund, "Christ's most blessed Confessor."

In all these romances the leader of the vikings is Ingvar, Hingvar, or Ivar, the "Ivar the Boneless" of the sagas, the crafty son of Ragnar, whose quickness of wit more than compensates for his weakness of body. He is the brain of the English expeditions, a man of foxlike cunning, wily and astute, a typical Norman statesman, while his brother, Ubba or Hubba, is the typical Norman soldier, brave, strong, and persistent.

Fact and fiction are inextricably mingled in the history of the three brothers, "Hingwar, Hubba, and Healfdene," whom English mediæval tradition has associated with the Danish wars of the ninth century. They were, almost certainly, of Danish origin, yet Hubba is described as dux Frisiorum, leader of the Frisians, while Hingwar has been, with much probability, identified with Ivar the comrade of Olaf the White, the Norse King of Dublin, who raided western Scotland in 870, and brought a great spoil of English, British, and Pictish captives to Ireland. The Irish annals call Ivar "King of the Northmen of all Ireland and Britain," and make him the brother and successor of Olaf the White. The later English and Continental chroniclers know only "the tyrant Ingvar," most cruel of all the pirate kings. In the strictly contemporary accounts, the Anglo-Saxon Chronicle and Asser, he is merely mentioned incidentally as the brother of Healfdene. The sagas replace Ubba and Healfdene by the half-mythical "Snake Eye," "White Shirt," and Björn Ironside. The Irish sources give him, in addition to Olaf, a younger brother, Oisla or Avisle, whom, in conjunction with Olaf, he murders "with guile and parricide."

From this confusion of detail it may perhaps be inferred that the great adventure of the conquest of Britain attracted rovers from far and near, vultures hovering over the doomed quarry. Ivar may have come from Ireland, Ubba from the Danish settlements in Frisia, Healfdene from Denmark itself, or from the Continent. A fourth "son of Ragnar," Björn, is found among the vikings of the Seine, and possibly also in the perilous voyages to Spain and northern Italy. The clans would rally to the sound of battle, and kinsmen would gather together in the land of promise, as, in the eleventh century, the sons of the Norman house of Hauteville, descendants of the vikings, overspread the fertile provinces of southern Italy and Sicily. To Alfred and his fellows, at least, these shadowy pirate chiefs must have been substantial enough, and the question of the hour was how to meet the imminent peril of their further incursions into the heart of England.

In 868 the host of Ivar and Ubba marched from York southwards into Mercia. They left behind a puppet king, one Egbert, to rule the country north of Tyne, but they seem to have kept Deira in their own hands, using York as a base of operations.

The southern kingdoms were not unprepared for their coming. The bonds between Mercia and Wessex were drawn closer by the marriage of Alfred to the daughter of a Mercian ealdorman, and when news arrived of the approach of the pagan army, Burhred, the Mercian King, and his witan, at once appealed for help to Ethelred of Wessex and his brother Alfred, to whom Asser now gives the title of secundarius. The mention of Alfred in conjunction with his brother, marked by a marginal cross in the Parker manuscript of the Chronicle, bears out the theory that he held a recognised position of authority.

The united fyrds of Mercia and Wessex met the invaders at Nottingham on the Trent, one of the "Five Boroughs" of the later Danelaw, where they had apparently either thrown up an earthwork, a geweorc, as winter quarters, or occupied an already existing camp. Here Alfred had his first sight of the vikings, but there was little fighting, since, though the fort withstood the attacks of the English, the pagans consented to make terms. Burhred allowed them to remain at Nottingham till the spring, when they returned to York, and "sat there," says the Chronicle, "one year," preparing, perhaps, for a more daring enterprise. In 870, the here, a compact and disciplined body of horsemen, rode through Mercia into East Anglia, burning and plundering the rich monasteries of the fenland on their way to winter quarters at Thetford in Norfolk.

A stream of ecclesiastical legend here combines with the secular traditions of the heroic struggle to obscure the actual sequence of events. Yet the main incidents of the story, as told by the English historians of the twelfth century, and by the picturesque mediæval forger "Ingulf of Croyland," may be accepted as true in the spirit, if not in the letter. These chroniclers describe the ruthless march of the heathen army, the gallant but hopeless stand of the men of Lindsey under their local leaders, the stately abbeys and religious houses going up in flames, Bardney and Croyland, Medeshamstede or Peterborough, "once full rich, but now brought to naught," and the water-girt Ely. They dwell on the slaughter of monks and nuns, the scattering of the relics of the saints, the destruction of manuscripts, the loss of church treasures, the torture and suffering, softened by a touch of nature when the viking chief saves the life of a beautiful child in the sack of Croyland.

The men who lived through such experiences as these had neither time nor heart to write about them, but many vivid details would be preserved in the memory of the people, a store of material for those who came after. Such may have been the origin of the history of St. Edmund which was told by his armour-bearer to St. Dunstan, and transmitted to his tenth-century biographer, Abbo of Fleury.

In the winter months the Danes took up a strong position at Thetford, where the river Thet joins the Little Ouse. The East-Anglians gave them battle, but were defeated, and the ruin of the country seemed complete when its King, Edmund, fell into the hands of the enemy and was mercilessly put to death. The Chronicle and Asser only say that "the Danes gained the victory, slew the King, and won the land." The legend which made Edmund an English St. Sebastian is of later growth. It tells how he was bound to a tree, scourged, shot at by the Danish bowmen until he was as thickly covered with arrows as a hedgehog with spines, and finally beheaded and cast into a wood, whence his body was miraculously recovered by his people.

Over the remains of the martyr-king rose one of the most splendid abbeys of mediæval England, and the royal manor of Bedricsworth, his burialplace, grew into the populous town of St. Edmund's Bury or Burg. Coins inscribed with his name were struck in his honour in East Anglia before the ninth century was at an end. The conqueror of his conquerors, he became the favourite saint of Guthrum-Athelstan, the royal Danish convert of the time of Alfred, and of Canute the Great, the first Danish King of all England, a hundred and fifty years later. His fame spread rapidly and widely, and he stands out as the central figure of the Christian cycle of Danish legends, as Ragnar Lodbrok is the centre of the corresponding heathen cycle.

But these things were still far away in 870, when the Danish leaders were regarded merely as savage marauders, with no romance or glamour about them, and King Edmund was but one among their many unfortunate victims. The events of 870 were grim realities for Ethelred and Alfred of Wessex, and they must have waited with heavy hearts, knowing that the invasion of their own kingdom could not be long delayed.

For the present, however, there was peace south of Thames, and Alfred might enjoy a brief interval of quiet home life before the full burden of public responsibility was laid upon him. He had been married in 868 to Ealhswith, a Mercian maiden of royal blood, of whom singularly little is known. Asser does not even mention her name, though he states that she was the daughter of Ethelred "Mucill," comes or ealdorman of the "Gaini," and of Eadburh, of the Mercian royal house. He adds that he had often seen Eadburh before her death, a much respected woman, who in her long widowhood was a pattern of virtuous life, but for Alfred's wife he has no word either of praise or blame.

The name of Ealhswith occurs in the different manuscripts of the Anglo-Saxon Chronicle, where her death is variously entered under the years 902 and 905; in Alfred's will, where he bequeaths the "hams" at Lambourn, Wantage, and Ethandun, with a sum of money, to "Ealhswith"; and in a charter of 901, which she signs as the mother of Edward the Elder, Ealhswith, mater regis. She is also the reputed foundress, or co-foundress with her husband, of St. Mary's Abbey at Winchester, the "Nunnaminster" or nuns' minster, where she is said to have died in retirement.

Her father's second name, " Mucill" or "Mucel," a word erroneously understood by early writers to mean "big" or "great," is found among the duces or ealdormen who witness Mercian charters from 814 to about 868. As another Mucel dux witnesses several of the same charters between 836 and 848, Mr. Stevenson has concluded that there were two ealdormen of the name, father and son, and that the son was Alfred's father-in-law. Ealhswith further appears to have had a brother, Athulf or Ethelwulf, who was an ealdorman, and died, according to the Chronicle, in 903. All research has failed in identifying the district of the "Gaini," over which Ethelred "Mucill" is said by Asser to have ruled.

It was during Alfred's protracted wedding festivities, if Asser may be believed, in the midst of revels which were carried far into the night, that the young bridegroom was suddenly struck down by a strange and painful illness, hitherto unknown to the physicians, which still continued to torment him after twenty-five years, when Asser was writing his book. It was attributed by the spectators to "fascination," or the evil eye, or to the envy of the devil; others, again, thought that it was a peculiar kind of fever, or the ficus from which he had suffered "from infancy." Regardless of consistency, Asser goes on to explain that this ficus had been sent as a discipline in answer to Alfred's prayers "in the flower of his youth"; that he afterwards prayed for a lighter affliction, which should not, like leprosy and blindness, render him useless or despicable, and that he was healed of the ficus, only to find a new infirmity substituted for it at his marriage.

Alfred came of a short-lived stock, and he may well have inherited a constitutional delicacy which showed itself in various ways at different periods of his life, but it is impossible to determine the precise nature of his illness from Asser's vague and contradictory narrative. It has often been supposed that Alfred was an epileptic, but this is hard to credit of one who worked so hard and continuously, and who was remarkable for the sanity of his mental outlook. Nor would epilepsy have been unfamiliar to the English physicians of the time, or likely to be mistaken for the ficus. A more probable theory, based on the Anglo-Saxon medical use of the term ficus, would make the childish ailment hæmorrhoids, and the later trouble some form of stone. This would explain many of the symptoms, as described by Asser;-- the sudden attacks and equally sudden cessation of agonising pain, the constant irksome discomfort, the depression and lassitude of hours of comparative health, are all well-known symptoms of this complaint. It is even possible that Alfred's nervous dread of leprosy and blindness was induced by the subtle working of a disease which specially affects the circulation and eyesight. Yet whatever his physical weakness may have been, he seems to have resisted it manfully. No bodily suffering could break his spirit, and he found the best corrective for morbid fancies in the pressing need for action, when at last the fatal hour struck for Wessex.

St. Edmund won the crown of martyrdom on November 20th, 870. With the new year, the vikings advanced south-westward to the West-Saxon frontier, and encamped close to the royal "vill" of Reading, on the tongue of land between the south bank of the Thames and its tributary the Kennet. The Parker manuscript of the Chronicle only states that "the army (here) came to Reading." The Peterborough manuscript says more explicitly that they "rode," perhaps along the ancient warpath of the Icknield Way. They poured into Wessex, writes Henry of Huntingdon, "like a stream, carrying all before it." The leader of the host was no longer Ivar, who may now have gone to harry the west coast of Scotland with Olaf the White, but his brother Healfdene, with another King called Bagsecg, and a number of "jarls," or lesser chiefs.

On December 31st, three days after their arrival at Reading, they sent out a foraging party under two of the jarls, while the remaining troops secured the camp by throwing a rampart across the neck of the little peninsula, from river to river. Asser, the sole authority for this entrenchment, calls it a vallum. It was probably a dyke, or earthwork, of the nature of the geweorc at Nottingham, or of Alfred's own later geweorc at Athelney.

As the jarls and their horsemen rode westwards, through woods and fields, Ethelwulf, ealdorman of Berkshire, with an advance guard, recruited chiefly from his personal followers, met them at Englefield, between Pangbourne and Theale, completely defeated them, and slew one of their leaders.

The Danes fell back on their camp, and four days later, Ethelred and Alfred, at the head of the main West-Saxon army, effected a junction with Ethelwulf and appeared before Reading with a micel fyrd. They drove the bands of stragglers whom they found outside the camp up to the rampart, with great slaughter, but the Danes within the entrenchment rushed "like wolves" from "all the gates," and in their turn attacked the Christians, and put them to flight. Ethelwulf, the lion-like hero, was left dead on the field. His body, in the words of Ethelwerd, "was secretly carried off, and taken into the province of the Mercians, to the place which is called Northworthige [Northweorthig] but in the Danish tongue, Deoraby [Derby]." Perhaps, as Professor Stenton suggests, he was a Mercian by birth and early allegiance, and his people buried him in his own country.

Gaimar, the Anglo-Norman poet-chronicler of the twelfth century, says that the English fled eastwards to Wistley Green, and escaped across the Loddon by the ford at Twyford; a curiously circumstantial account, but unsupported by any other evidence. It is more likely that the retreat would be to the west, where the royal demesne lands, from the "ham" at Wantage to the "ham" at Lambourn across the Downs, would furnish shelter and supplies, or to the south, to cover Winchester, which lies in a direct southerly line from Reading.

The Danes seem now to have evolved a definite scheme of action, and to have organised their campaigns with a skill and method which demanded equal activity on the part of their antagonists. At Nottingham and at Thetford, while they kept in touch with the waterways, they seized central points, and either threw up earthworks, or used older fortifications, whence they could harry the surrounding country. At Reading, where they were stationed on a river frontier, they worked rather from circumference to centre. They threatened both Winchester to the south and London to the east, held the line of Thames, and kept the way open for reinforcements from Scandinavia or the Continent to come to them.

From Reading it would be easy to climb the Downs and march westwards into the heart of Wessex, along the Ridgeway, the old track which still crowns the heights, or to drop down by the ruined Silchester to the Roman road leading due south to Winchester. The victorious Danish army appears to have chosen the western route. Four days after the fight at Reading they were on Æscesdun, the modern Ashdown, the long range of chalk hills which runs east and west between the valleys of the Ock and the Kennet. At some point on this ridge took place the third and greatest of the many struggles of what has been called "Alfred's year of battles."

Few sites have been more disputed than that of the battle of Ashdown. It has been located in Ashdown Forest in Sussex, at Ashdown in Essex, at Ashendon in Buckinghamshire, at Assedone, an eleventh-century manor near Ashampstead, between Pangbourne and Streatley, at Aston, near Lowbury Hill, at the eastern end of the Berkshire Downs, and at Ashdown Park, in the Manor of Ashbury, at their western end.

The claims of Sussex, Essex, and Buckinghamshire are easily dismissed. The whole campaign centred in the Berkshire and Wiltshire hills, and it would require more than the recurrence of a not unusual place-name to justify its transference to the extreme south or east of England, or to Mercia. The identification of Assedone with Æscesdun seems to rest on a mistaken etymology. Aston, again, is the "East town," not the "Ash dune," and Ashdown Park only derives its name from its situation on the Ashdown ridge. The whole range of downs, in fact, seems to have been called "Ashdown," not, probably, from the ash-trees which grew on the slopes, but from Æsc, some forgotten chieftain of bygone Saxon days. "Ashdown," wrote Dr. Wise, the editor of Asser, in 1738, "seems to be a district or country rather than a Town," and he adds that the Downs were still called Ashdown by the shepherds. This is borne out by the entry in the Peterborough manuscript of the Anglo-Saxon Chronicle for 1006, which speaks of going "along Ashdown" to Cuckhamsley Hill, and by a passage in the Abingdon Chronicle which mentions Alfred's victory "on" (super) Ashdown. Dr. Wise himself thought that the battle-field was near Ashdown Park, below the earthwork of Uffington Castle, and under the White Horse, the figure cut in the chalk of the northern face of the Downs, which he took to be a memorial of the victory. In this theory, Uffington Castle serves the Danes for a camp, while Ethelred, like an eighteenth-century general, lies the night before the engagement at Hardwell Camp, about half a mile to the west. Wayland's Smithy becomes the burial-place of the Danish King Bagsecg, and the jarls rest beneath the Seven Barrows.

Though skeletons and Anglo-Saxon weapons have been dug up in the neighbourhood, there is really nothing except conjecture to fix the battle at this spot. Equally conjectural, if plausible enough, is the alternative theory which makes the Danes encamp on Lowbury Hill at the eastern end of the ridge, and the West-Saxons march up from Streatley to fight them on the Compton Downs. It seems, indeed, vain to hope to identify the actual battle-field. The very fact that there is no genuine ancient tradition for its site suggests that it was soon forgotten. Camden, the sixteenthcentury antiquary, who used Asser's book, and knew the Vale of White Horse, mentions Alfred's battles at Ockley and Ethandun in his descriptions of Surrey and Wiltshire, but says nothing of Ashdown, and other early scholars have followed his example. After all, it matters little. The whole district is memory-haunted. The green highway of the Downs has seen the passing of many peoples since prehistoric times, and the upland fight of Alfred and the Danes has become one with the undying legends of the hills.

If the scene of the drama must thus be left indeterminate, the action, at least, is fairly clear, from the accounts given by Asser and the Anglo-Saxon Chronicle. Asser, in particular, who had gone over the field of battle and had talked to trustworthy eye-witnesses, has preserved many intimate details.

The Danes mounted the Downs from their base at Reading, whether merely for plunder, or in pursuance of a scheme of invasion, is uncertain. Their host was in two bodies or "folks," one under the kings Healfdene and Bagsecg, the other led by the "jarls" or lesser chieftains. The English made a similar disposition of their forces. Ethelred commanded against the kings, and Alfred was at the head of the division which was opposed to the jarls. The advantage in position was with the heathen army, which occupied higher ground than the Christian forces.

In the early morning of January 8th, the Danes began to descend the hill in close formation. Alfred was ready for action, but Ethelred was at prayer and refused to move, "saying that he would not leave that place alive until the priest had finished the mass, nor desert divine for human service." Asser is of opinion that the subsequent victory showed that this piety availed much with the Lord, but Alfred may be excused for chafing at the delay. He was young and impetuous. The enemy was coming on fast. He, then, the secundarius, took on himself the responsibility of the whole command. He gathered the troops in close array around the standards of Wessex, and led both divisions to the assault, charging uphill "like a wild boar." Ethelred, "girt about with arms and prayers," followed and the battle became general.

There was in that place [writes Asser] a solitary stunted thorn-tree, which I have seen with my own eyes. About it the hostile forces joined with a great shouting, their men fighting for an evil cause, ours for life and loved ones and fatherland.

All through the short winter day the battle raged, but as evening closed in, the broken Danish army fled in headlong rout towards their camp at Reading, pursued until nightfall by the triumphant West-Saxons. The level ridge of Ashdown was thickly strewn with the bodies of the dead. King Bagsecg fell on the field, slain, tradition said, by Ethelred's own hand, and with him fell the five great jarls, Sidroc the Old and Sidroc the Young, Osbearn and Fræna and Harold, amidst heaps of unnamed warriors. The stream of fugitives was still pouring into Reading on the following day. Never, it was said, since the coming of the Saxons to Britain had there been so great a slaughter.

Later chroniclers, writing under strong royal and ecclesiastical influences, magnified the part played by Ethelred, and the effects of his piety. William of Malmesbury even says that the victory, imperilled by Alfred's rashness, was saved by the King's timely arrival. Alfred certainly acted with a courage and independence which throw an interesting light on the development of his character at this time. The quiet student and devout penitent was now transformed into a hot-headed young soldier, impatient and self-confident, but full of generous ardour, courting danger and despising caution. The blood of his warlike forefathers must have stirred within him as he led that wild rush up the grassy slope in the pale light of the January morning, with all his future kingdom lying at his feet, the prize of victory.

One of the legends of the White Horse connects it with St. George, who is said to have killed the Dragon at Dragon Hill, on the Ashdown range. In Alfred Wessex was to find her true dragonslayer and champion in the long war with the many-headed Danish hydra, and it was on Ashdown that he must first have realised something of the meaning of that strenuous task.

Great as the victory of Ashdown had been, it was not followed up by Ethelred and his brother. Healfdene was allowed to remain at Reading, recruiting his shattered strength, while the West-Saxon army apparently rested on its laurels. An Abingdon tradition may possibly give a clue to this seeming inaction. The Chronicle of the Abbey compares Alfred to Judas Iscariot, because he forcibly deprived the monastery of the "vill" of Abingdon, with all its appurtenances, a poor return to God for the victory over the Danes on Ashdown. It is possible that Alfred may now have been occupied in securing the upper reaches of the Thames by fortifications at Abingdon, which would hold the Danish camp at Reading in check, and would also be easy of access from the royal "hams" at Wantage and Lambourn, on either flank of the Berkshire Downs. The monastery had undoubtedly been plundered by the Danes in 871. Only the walls were left standing, and the monks had fled with their relics and documents.

If a policy of western defence were thus Alfred's aim, he must have been disappointed when, a fortnight after the battle of Ashdown, the Reading Danes, abandoning the western line of attack, made a bold dash southwards into Hampshire. The West-Saxon army can hardly have been disbanded, for, led by Ethelred and Alfred in person, it caught up the enemy at Basing, on the Loddon, about twelve miles from Reading, on the direct road to Winchester. The battle which followed was claimed by the Danes as a victory, but practically they owned themselves beaten, for they gave up their advance into Southern Wessex, and retreated empty-handed to their camp. The West-Saxons seem now to have fallen back on a new line of defence, the lofty downs south of the Kennet valley, which guarded Winchester, Salisbury, and Wilton.

It is probable that the next few weeks saw some of the many "uncounted raids" of ealdormen and of king's thegns and of "Alfred the King's brother," of which the Chronicle speaks, implying that, for Alfred at least, these skirmishing expeditions preceded his accession to the throne. In any case, with the coming of spring, the heathen army took the field in force, and another of the great battles of this eventful year was fought at Meretun, a place which has been identified with Merton, in Surrey, Merton near Reading, and Marden near Devizes, but which is, almost certainly, Marton near Bedwyn in Wiltshire, an important strategical post, on the Roman road from Winchester to Marlborough, commanding the approaches to Winchester and Salisbury, and not far from the point of junction of the three counties, Berkshire, Hampshire, and Wiltshire.

Asser, oddly enough, omits this battle altogether, but the Chronicle briefly describes the division of the heathen host into two "folks," the flight, a feigned flight, possibly, of both bodies of the Danes, their rally and final victory, and the death of Heahmund, Bishop of Sherborne, with "many other good men." He was buried at Keynsham near Bristol, and the fact that he was afterwards honoured as a saint incidentally serves to fix the day of the battle in which he was killed as that of his festival, March 22nd.

About a month later, "after Easter," which fell this year on April 15th, King Ethelred also passed away, worn out by incessant labour and anxiety, or perhaps, as some of the later chroniclers say, wounded to death in the battle of Marton. The sumor lida or "summer army" of Danish marauders of the Chronicle has even been turned into a fabulous Danish king "Somerled," who gives Ethelred the fatal stroke. He was laid to rest in Wimborne Minster, where a seventeenthcentury inscription on a brass of earlier date preserves the memory of "St. Ethelred the Martyr, King of the West-Saxons, who fell by the hands of the heathen Danes."

After ruling the kingdom for five years [writes Asser] with diligence, honour, and good repute, through much tribulation, he went the way of all flesh, and, buried in Wimborne Minster, he awaits the coming of the Lord and the first resurrection of the just.

Alfred now came to the throne, "with the full consent of all the inhabitants of the kingdom," according to Asser, elected by the witan and acclaimed by the whole people, if later writers may be trusted. There is no contemporary record of a formal election, for Asser's vague generalities have little weight, and the Chronicle simply says, after the notice of Ethelred's death: "Then Alfred son of Ethelwulf (Æthelwulfing) his brother took (feng to) the West-Saxon kingdom."

In all probability Alfred's accession was a foregone conclusion. Though Ethelred left at least two sons, they must have been disqualified by their youth. It is even possible that the position of Alfred as secundarius carried with it some association in the sovereign power and the recognition of a right to succeed to the crown. To the believers in Alfred's papal coronation and "anointing to king" his accession, of course, presents no difficulties. It is also often assumed that Ethelwulf had regulated the royal succession by his will, leaving the West-Saxon crown to Ethelbald, Ethelred, and Alfred, in turn, and giving Kent to Ethelbert and his descendants. This arrangement is supposed to have been subsequently set aside, as far as Ethelbert was concerned, while Ethelred and Alfred inherited the kingdom in accordance with its provisions. This theory rests on Asser's account of Ethelwulf's will, with the references to it in the Latin version of Alfred's will. It is probably due to a misconception of the meaning of the clauses cited by Alfred, which seem in the original Anglo-Saxon text to apply only to Ethelwulf's private lands.

Asser merely states that Ethelwulf by his will divided the kingdom "between his two elder sons," thereby, apparently, confirming the earlier settlement which had made Ethelbert under-king of Kent. The private estates were inherited, by a family agreement, by Ethelwulf's four sons in order, and it is possible that the same rule of descent was observed in the kingdom, but there is very little on which to base such a conclusion.

In Alfred's case the question of title has been needlessly complicated. He was the obvious person to succeed on his elder brother's death, the one mature survivor of the royal house of Wessex. It is probable that, in conformity with the custom of the time, he was solemnly crowned, though only a late and untrustworthy tradition places his "second" coronation at

Winchester, and connects it with the "first" coronation and unction at Rome. He brought the regalia used in the papal ceremony back to England with him, it was said, and bequeathed them to his successors.

Among the ancient regalia which were melted down in the Civil War of the seventeenth century was "the principal crown with which the kings Alfred, Edward, etc., were crowned." Sir John Spelman describes it as "of a very ancient Work, with Flowers adorned with Stones of somewhat a plain Setting," and conjectures that Alfred, in his days of prosperity, "fell upon the Composing of an Imperial Crown . . . of a more August and Imperial Form than has been formerly in Use in this Kingdom." This seems to have been "the crown of Edward the Confessor," ascribed to Alfred in the fourteenth century, when the monks of Westminster were attempting to prove that even if the "first king of all England" had not been crowned in the Abbey, they were in possession of the very crown which the Pope had placed upon his childish head in Rome.

Less mythical, if not altogether above suspicion, is "KingAlfred's oath on the day of his coronation," preserved in the cartulary of his monastic foundation at Athelney. It agrees with the form of oath taken by the English kings of the eleventh century, the ancient threefold pledge to keep the Christian Church and people in peace, to put down wrong and robbery, and to do justice and mercy. In after years Alfred fulfilled that pledge in all sincerity, but in 871 the burden rather than the glory of kingship must have been present to him, and the care of Church and State must have lain heavily on his young shoulders, with the country ravaged and exhausted by war, and the Danes pouring into Wessex in overwhelming force.

Shortly after the battle of Marton, "a great summer army," a sumor lida, of pirates--migratory adventurers, as opposed to the more permanent winter settlers--sailed up the Thames, to reinforce the Reading army and share its triumphs. There may have been some fighting of which no distinct record has survived, but the main body of the Danes probably continued to hold North Wiltshire and the line of heights south of the Kennet. It was from here, presumably, that, about a month after Ethelred's death, they advanced on the royal "vill" of Wilton, in the very heart of Wessex, much as, seven years later, they came down on that other Wiltshire "vill" of Chippenham. Now, as then, they seem to have taken Alfred unawares, with only a small band of followers, a lytel werod, about him. He made, however, a gallant stand on the hill above Wilton, south of the river Wiley. After fighting all day, the Danes took to flight; but when the Saxons pursued rashly, they rallied, turned upon them, and drove them from the field.

The Chronicle, in summing up the history of this eventful year, speaks of "nine folk-fights," or pitched battles, without reckoning skirmishes and raids. Three unknown engagements must then be added to the six great fights of Englefield, Reading, Ashdown, Basing, Marton, and Wilton, and though the English might console themselves with the thought of the "thousands" of Danish dead, and of King Bagsecg and the nine "jarls" who slept among them, only two clear victories, Englefield and Ashdown, could be counted to them, while their own losses had been heavy, and they had been forced back almost to Winchester.

It was no wonder, as Asser says, that the strength of the West-Saxons was reduced, or that Alfred was at last driven to make terms with the invaders, covenanting, apparently, that they should leave Wessex, but paying, doubtless, a heavy price for the inestimable boon of peace. Alfred must surely have had the "folk-fights" and "raids" of 871 in mind when he wrote in his translation of Orosius, departing widely from his original, how Philip of Macedon bethought him that he could not continue to wage war against the Athenians "with folk-fights," and how he constantly "harried" them with raiding bands or hlothas, until they were all scattered and divided, and he was able to make an unexpected dash for Athens with his fyrd.

The military operations of 871 may be compared with the somewhat similar campaign of 1006, in the same district, during the later Danish wars, when the here came after Martinmas to the Isle of Wight, and went up at midwinter through Hampshire and Berkshire to the Thames at Reading, whence their predecessors had started in 871, and so to Wallingford and Cholsey, and along Ashdown to Cuckhamsley, while the fyrd gathered on the Kennet, only to be put to flight; the men of Winchester trembled at the passing of the plundering host, and the king and witan reluctantly bought peace with tribute. But in 1006 England had half-hearted defenders, under a "redeless" king, a leader without judgment or stability. In 871, their hope was in a king, young indeed, as yet, and untried, but destined to prove, in the words of his kinsman, the chronicler Ethelwerd, "the immovable pillar of the West-Saxons."

ÆLFRED CYNING

871-878

AFTER the peace which followed the battle of Wilton, the Danes withdrew to Mercia, and for four years Wessex has no history, and the name of Alfred passes from the pages of the Chronicle, as the centre of interest shifts to the Midlands and the north. Only an occasional reference in later records, and a few charters of doubtful authenticity, bridge the gap between 871 and 875. Even Asser becomes a mere echo of the Chronicle, while the Frankish annalists are too busy with the affairs of Empire and their own struggle with the vikings to spare a thought for the distant West-Saxon kingdom.

There is evidence, however, in Alfred's writings, that the people at his accession were all "broken" by the heathen folk, and that learning and civilisation were at a low ebb. When Asser says that Alfred took the reins of government "somewhat reluctantly," he may well have been repeating what he had heard from the King himself. Alfred's preface to the Pastoral Care, by its insistence on the cares which beset him and the troubles which came upon his kingdom, suggests a not unnatural depression and sense of lonely responsibility in the young ruler, the last of the sons of Ethelwulf, left to face unaided a dark and stormy future.

His first foes seem to have been those of his household. Difficulties which had arisen about the interpretation of his father's will were submitted to the decision of the West-Saxon witan at Langandene, possibly Long Dean in Wiltshire, in a meeting which may probably be assigned to the beginning of the reign. It came about, writes Alfred in the preamble to his own will,

that king Ethelred died. . . . Then, when we heard of many complaints concerning the inheritance, I brought the will of king Athulf (Ethelwulf) to our meeting (gemot) at Langandene, and it was read aloud before all the

West-Saxon witan. When it had been read, I prayed them all, by the love they bore me, not to hesitate for love or fear of me to declare the folk-law, and I gave them my pledge, that I would never bear any of them a grudge for speaking according to law, lest any man should say that I had wronged my kin, whether old or young.

It appears that Ethelwulf had left a joint life-interest in certain lands to his three sons, Ethelbald, Ethelred, and Alfred, and that after Ethelbald's death the two younger brothers made this over to Ethelbert. When Ethelbert died, Ethelred took the whole, with the witness of the witan, but he engaged that on his death these lands, with those which he had acquired independently, should revert to Alfred. In 871, then, Alfred found himself the sole legatee. "All my kinsmen had passed into the sleep of death," runs the Latin version of his will, "and so the inheritance of Ethelwulf my father devolved upon me."

But another agreement had also been drawn up by Ethelred and Alfred in the days of the Danish invasion, arranging that if either of them should be suddenly cut off, the survivor should provide for his brother's children from the family estates, other than those which Ethelwulf had thus specially bequeathed to his sons. It was, perhaps, in connection with this later settlement, that Alfred found himself called upon to face the discontent of his nephews or their guardians.

Ethelred certainly left two sons, who are mentioned in Alfred's will--Æthelwald, who afterwards put forward a claim to the crown, and Æthelhelm. A possible third son, Oswald, signs charters as filius regis up to 875. Of the other members of the royal house nothing is known. The witan, too, the advisers who gathered round the young King, are but indistinct and nameless figures. The older generation of notable prelates and ealdormen, Swithun and Ealhstan, Eanwulf and Osric, had passed away. Ethelwulf of Berkshire and Bishop Heahmund of Sherborne had fallen in the recent war. It is significant that neither Asser nor the Chronicle mentions any bishop or ealdorman by name from the accession of Alfred in 871 to 886, eight years after the close of his first great struggle with the Danes.

The signatures to charters in these years are mainly those of unremembered men. Ethelred, Archbishop of Canterbury, is an exception, but Kent at this time seems to have stood aloof in an isolation the more striking when compared with the leading part it had played in the former viking invasions. The personal details in the contemporary authorities for the first half of Alfred's reign are singularly royal in character, records of the deeds of kings, Danish and English.

It is likely enough that Alfred, in the early years of his rule, had to rely chiefly on his own judgment and administrative capacity in the work of government. But he was a born organiser, and after the first effort he probably found much that was congenial to him in a life of public action. The leader of the charge at Ashdown, the rider of raids in the Berkshire valleys, was not one to shrink from danger or exertion. Nor had the country as yet suffered vitally from the Danish war. If Berkshire and Wiltshire were scarred by the passage of the marauding host, Winchester was unharmed, and the great monastic houses of the west, Malmesbury and Glastonbury, Sherborne and Wimborne, seem to have escaped desecration. There was plenty of reserve strength in the kingdom, but the treaty with the Danes had shown its immediate weakness and the exhaustion of the army, and there can be little doubt that Alfred set himself at once to discipline his weary troops, and to inspire them with fresh courage.

The army which had defended Wessex in the "Year of battles" was no mere slow-moving levy of ill-equipped peasant proprietors. Local contingents may indeed have been present at Ashdown, in the micel fyrd which Ethelred and Alfred took a week to bring into action at Reading. The Berkshire ceorls at least would probably turn out to protect their homesteads when the enemy was at the gates. But the brunt of the fighting seems clearly to have been borne by the trained, wellarmed horsemen who formed the military following of the great lords. Even while the fyrd was gathering at the opening of the campaign, ealdorman Ethelwulf had met the Danish foragers at Englefield with his "comrades," his "gesiths" (sodales) says Asser, a small force, apparently, with which he afterwards joined the main body.

The "raids" which the Chronicle contrasts with "folk-fights" were ridden by aristocratic leaders, ealdormen and king's thegns, and Alfred the King's brother himself, each, it seems, with his own band of "gesiths" or companions. The lytel werod with which Alfred took the field at Wilton may possibly have been largely composed of soldiers of this kind, men of the thegn class, with horses and swords, the ministri of the charters, the "men who follow me" of Alfred's will.

At Basing, again, the rapid southward movement of Healfdene's troops was, perhaps, checked by Ethelred's mounted infantry, but at Marton the shire-levies of the three adjacent counties, Berkshire, Hampshire, and Wiltshire, may have taken part in the battle. This, however, is all guesswork, for the Chronicle, in its long entry for 871, only once expressly mentions the fyrd in connection with the fighting at Reading. In every case it simply notes that "KingEthelred and his brother Alfred fought against the army (here)," or, "against all the army."

If the exact distribution of troops in any particular action cannot be determined, it appears at least certain that the West-Saxon fyrd, no less than the Danish here, included a considerable body of mounted infantry at the beginning of Alfred's reign. But the here, a confederacy of companies of volunteer adventurers, organised for attack and conquest, was literally a "people in arms," while the fyrd, mobilised for national defence, was a more loosely compacted force, fluctuating in composition, a shifting group of local militiamen, the farmers and villagers of the open countryside, with a permanent nucleus of "professional" soldiers, horsemen drawn from court and hall, from walled town or fortified camp.

At the close of 871 the vikings, true to their compact with Alfred, left Reading, and went down the Thames to take up winter quarters in London, on Mercian territory. The vow to send alms to Rome and India, which in some manuscripts of the Chronicle Alfred is said to have made when he "sat" or encamped against the here in London, has been connected with this "wintering," but the passage is suspicious, and there is no other evidence to prove that the West-Saxons remained under arms through the winter following the "year of battles."

A silver coin which bears the name of Ulfdene XRX (rex), and the monogram of London (Londonia), has also been attributed to this period. It shows Healfdene, the "barbarian" King, in a more favourable light than the monastic records of plunder and destruction, but to Mercia and Northumbria he must have come as a very scourge of God. Burhred, King of the Mercians, had apparently been occupied with a Welsh inroad on his western frontier during the West-Saxon troubles.

He now bought off the Danish army with so heavy a "Danegeld" that Werferth, Bishop of Worcester, was forced to lease church lands "on account of the immense tribute to the barbarians in the year when the heathen sat in London."

In thus paying blackmail to the invaders, both Alfred and Burhred seem to have imitated the weaker policy of the West Frankish kings towards the vikings, while they neglected their wise precaution of guarding the river-ways by systematic fortification. Still, if the details given by the later mediæval writer "Ingulf" embody a genuine Croyland tradition, Burhred did what he could to save his kingdom, by granting out the devastated church lands of the fen country to military tenants, and thus interposing a barrier between the heart of Mercia and the Danes in East Anglia. If so, he only succeeded in postponing the death-struggle.

In 872 the "Great Army" moved its winter quarters from London to Torksey on the Trent, a strong position in Lindsey, which now formed part of Northumbria. Thence, in spite of a second treaty of peace with Mercia, they worked up the Trent to Repton, the burying-place, according to "Ingulf," of the Mercian kings. Here they spent the winter of 873-874, harrying the land far and wide. Though there is no record of an organised resistance, it is hardly likely that the Mercians surrendered without striking a blow for freedom.

Henry of Huntingdon is, perhaps, in the right, when he says that the three kings Guthrum, Oscytel, and Anwynd now joined their fellows, and "they were made invincible." Burhred was driven from the country, and in his place the vikings set up a tributary king, one Ceolwulf, "an Englishman by race, but a barbarian in wickedness," who has had hard measure dealt out to him by later historians. The Chronicle calls him an "unwise king's thegn"; to William of Malmesbury he is a "halfman" (semivir), to Sir John Spelman, "an Infamous Renegado of the Saxons." He seems to have been a mere tool of his Danish masters, and to have held the kingdom entirely at their will and pleasure, by a formal agreement, confirmed by oaths and the giving of hostages. He issued charters, however, and coined money in royal fashion, and "Ingulf" has a curious account of his oppressive methods of raising tribute, which may well be founded on fact when he describes the crushing tax laid upon Croyland Abbey, the penury and dispersion of the brethren, the melting down or sale of the sacred vessels, the silver and jewels of the monastery.

The hand of the Dane was heavy on the English Church, and the pressure of taxation must have completed the ruin which the earlier raids had begun. The East-Anglian bishopric of Dunwich became extinct; at Elmham and Lindsey, and apparently also at Lichfield, the episcopal succession was interrupted; the Mercian see of Leicester was removed to Dorchester in Oxfordshire, to be near the West-Saxon border; only Worcester and Hereford remained unchanged. Burhred, the last independent King of Mercia, went over sea, to die not long afterwards at Rome in the odour of sanctity, and to be buried "in St. Mary's church, in the Englishmen's school." His wife, Ethelswith, Alfred's sister, survived till 888, when she, too, died in Italy, at Pavia, on her way to the Holy City.

The army of invasion now turned seriously to the work of conquest and settlement. In the year 875 it broke into two divisions; Healfdene led one detachment into Northumbria, while the other, a mycel here, under the three kings Guthrum, Oscytel, and Anwynd or Amund, took up winter quarters at "Grantebridge," or Cambridge, the "vill" on the river Granta which afterwards became a famous Danish centre. Healfdene marched through Deira to the Tyne, and encamped at the mouth of the river Team, near Newcastle. Egbert, the under-king whom the Danes had set over Bernicia in 867, had been deposed to make way for a certain Ricsig, who may have been the leader of an anti-Danish movement, for his kingdom was recklessly harried by Healfdene's troops.

Churches and monasteries were burnt, monks and nuns were molested and slain, in a very frenzy of cruelty. The land was given up to fire and slaughter from the eastern to the western sea. The monks of Lindisfarne fled from their island abbey. The abbot himself, with a band of faithful brethren, wandered homeless for years, bearing with him the "holy and uncorrupted body" of St. Cuthbert, the relics of St. Aidan and St. Oswald, and the precious volume of the Lindisfarne gospels, till at last they found a resting place at Chesterle-Street, the forerunner of the magnificent shrine at Durham. The Danes even carried their ravages into Strathclyde and the country of the Picts. The Ulster annals mention a great slaughter of the Picts by the Dubhgaill, the "Black Strangers" or Danes, in 874. Ricsig died, of a broken heart, it was said, and was succeeded by another ephemeral king, Egbert II., who reigned for only two years.

In 876, after the Pictish expedition, Healfdene seems to have fallen back from Bernicia to Deira, where he effected a permanent settlement. "He dealt out the land of the Northumbrians," says the Chronicle, "and they continued ploughing and tilling it." Simeon of Durham sums up the Northumbrian population in 878 as, "the army, and such of the natives as survived." The swords were beaten into ploughshares, the savage raiders were transformed into peaceful colonists, and the first great kingdom of the later Danelaw was established, with its centre at York, while the English maintained some shadowy authority, under Danish overlordship, in the Bernician country to the north of the Tees.

While Healfdene thus drops out of history, fading into obscurity amidst dim Christian traditions of violent death and divine vengeance, Wessex, the scene of his former defeats and triumphs, becomes once more the theatre of war. The second great invasion, the attack of the army of the three kings on south-western England, began in 876. Unfortunately, the Chronicle, the only contemporary English authority, is here so abrupt as to be almost incomprehensible. King Alfred, unmentioned since 871, suddenly reappears in the summer of 875, faring out to sea with a fleet, a ship here, fighting against "seven shiploads" of vikings, taking one of their ships, and putting the rest to flight.

As this account immediately follows the notice of the settlement of Guthrum's army at Cambridge, where it remained for a year, it might be supposed that the sea-fight took place off the east coast. Yet in the next entry both West-Saxons and Danes are found at Wareham, on the Dorset coast, a hundred and seventy miles or more distant. "Here," runs the opening of the annal for 876, "the army (here) stole away from the West-Saxon fyrd, into Wareham."

The tenth-century chronicler Ethelwerd adds that it was the Cambridge army which thus moved south-westward, and joined forces with the "western army," which it had not done before. Unless this is a mere misunderstanding of the "West-Saxon fyrd" of the Chronicle, it implies concerted action of a novel kind, between the Cambridge army and the "Black Strangers," or Danes of the Irish Sea. This is not unlikely, since they may, possibly, have also co-operated in the campaign of 878, and the Irish Danes were now directing their attacks against Wales and western England, leaving Ireland to enjoy a long interval of comparative peace.

During the English wars of 870 and 871, the Irish and Frankish annals show a lessening of activity among the "Northmen" of the Continent and the "Strangers" of Ireland, while in 873 there was renewed harrying in the Loire country, and in Frisia, followed by treaties of peace similar to those which the West-Saxons and Mercians had made with Healfdene. The Cambridge army may have attracted the roving hordes of pirates who thus found their Frankish and Frisian hunting grounds to some extent closed to them, and Wareham would be no bad point of convergence for all the different bands of adventurers.

But it is a far cry from Cambridge to Wareham: so far, that many historians have supposed that Guthrum's host took ship from the east coast, and sailed round to Dorset by sea. This is, however, to ignore the fact that they are said to have "stolen away" from the West-Saxon fyrd, for if they embarked in Mercia, there would be no need to evade a West-Saxon army of defence. Nor is there any real difficulty in assuming that a lightly armed force, probably mounted, living on the country through which it passed, could cover the distance from Cambridge to Wareham, less than two hundred miles, quickly and easily.

When once the Danes had "stolen away" from the West-Saxon fyrd, there would be no further obstacle to their advance on Wareham. "They rode (chevacherent)," writes Gaimar, "straight to Wareham and besieged it. In a single day they took the town (burc)." The passage in the Chronicle, then, may be understood to mean that the Cambridge army entered Wessex from Mercia,-- by a night march, according to Asser,--slipped past the watching fyrd, and got clear away on the road to Wareham and the south, as Healfdene's men would have done in 871, had not the West- Saxons intercepted them at Basing. This interpretation agrees with the use in the Chronicle of the phrase, "the army (here) stole away from the fyrd," to describe the night-ride of the Danes from Wareham to Exeter, where the same manœuvre seems to have been repeated. The viking fleet apparently joined the army at Wareham with additional troops and supplies, while the main body took the land-route.

At Wareham the Danes would find a naturally strong position, further strengthened by art. Asser, who must have known the place well, as it lay in his diocese of Sherborne, calls it a castellum, a fortified town, or burh; to Gaimar, also, it was a burc. The great square of earthworks, which still remains, is famous as one of the finest examples of a genuine "Saxon camp." It lies between the rivers Frome and Trent, which join below it, and fall into Poole harbour. Surrounded by water on all sides except the west, it was, as Asser says, "the safest of sites." Here Guthrum and the army of the three kings established themselves, and, if Ethelwerd may be believed, proceeded to ravage the surrounding country. The nunnery within the enclosure, of which Asser speaks, probably fell a prey to the marauders, though there is no record of its fate.

Alfred seems to have followed the invaders with the West-Saxon fyrd, and to have come up with them at Wareham, for he now opened negotiations, and again made peace, "giving money," says Ethelwerd, and there is no reason to doubt his accuracy. The Danes swore solemnly to leave the West-Saxon kingdom, the usual condition of such a treaty, but enforced with unusual ceremony. Asser speaks of the giving of hostages, and of the swearing on Christian relics, "in which the King chiefly trusted, after God," while the Chronicle makes the vikings take their own "ring-oath," on the "holy ring" or armlet, sacred to the gods, the great oath which Odin himself is said to have taken--and broken--"which they had never sworn before to any people." These words find curious confirmation in the account of the treaty between Louis the German and the Northmen in 873, when the vikings swore, not by the holy ring, but by their weapons, "in accordance with the rites of that people."

The "ring-oath," then, created a peculiarly binding obligation, but all obligations sat lightly on the Danes. They left Dorset, only to take up winter quarters in south-western Wessex. "As was their wont, heeding neither hostages nor oath, nor the keeping of their pledged faith, the horsed here stole away from the fyrd by night into Exeter."

A scribal error in the text of Asser's Life of Alfred, whereby occidit, "killed," has been substituted for occidentem, "west," is responsible for the well-known story of the slaughter of Alfred's cavalry by the vikings, before their ride to Exeter.

Apparently the Danish raedehere, or mounted infantry, once more found the West-Saxons off their guard, and made a bolt by night for Exeter, an ancient Roman city, where they fortified themselves. Alfred, whose trust in his relics had probably led him to relax his vigilance, tried to retrieve his error by riding after them with the fyrd, another indication that he had a considerable mounted force, but he failed to overtake them, and had to content himself with investing Exeter.

Meanwhile the Danish fleet, or ship here, put out to sea, and coasted slowly along the Dorset shore, laden probably, as before, with supplies and reinforcements for the beleaguered garrison. The whole movement was much like the campaign of the previous season, on a smaller scale. It is now that some of the later chroniclers describe how Alfred built "long ships," manned them with "pirates," and blockaded Exeter by sea, while his army invested it on the landward side, and how the viking fleet of a hundred and fifty ships, full of armed soldiers, fought the King's vessels, and, weakened by a month of stormy weather at sea, was defeated, and foundered off Swanage from injuries received in the battle. This account appears first in the thirteenth-century historical compilations of the monks of St. Alban's Abbey. It is not improbable in itself, but its source is unknown, and in every way the simple entry in the Chronicle is to be preferred: "The fleet (sciphere) sailed west about, and they met a great storm at sea, and a hundred and twenty ships perished at Swanage."

It was doubtless in consequence of this naval disaster that the Danes at Exeter not only gave Alfred as many hostages as he wanted, and swore mighty oaths, but kept "good peace," and retired into Mercia at harvest-tide. This would be the late summer of 877, so the Exeter raid may be placed in the winter of 876, and the Swanage shipwreck, perhaps, at the beginning of the following year.

It is surely more than a mere coincidence that in September, 876, the Northmen reappeared in the Seine, just across the Channel from Wareham, with a fleet of about a hundred great ships called "barks" (bargas). Though Alfred had shaken off his burden for the moment, he must have anxiously watched the enemy closing in on Wessex from every side. Over him, as over the king Damocles of whom he wrote in his Boethius, a naked sword hung by a fine thread.

ALFRED THE GREAT AND THE VIKING INVASIONS

Though the concentration of the viking forces on England since 867 had meant a respite for the Continental kingdoms, the Empire was still torn by civil war, and devastated by the ceaseless internecine feuds of the Carolingian house. Save for the mention of a raid in the Loire valley in 868, the Frankish annalists are silent concerning the doings of the Northmen between 866 and 873, but they only describe at greater length the rebellions of the imperial princes against their fathers, and the undignified quarrels of Charles the Bald and his brother Louis the German over the inheritance of their nephews, Lothair II., King of Italy, and the Emperor Louis II., the sons of Lothair I.

Lothair of Italy died in 869. The year 870 saw the partition of Lotharingia, the "middle kingdom," by the treaty of Mersen, and in 875, on the death of Louis II. without sons, Charles the Bald went down into Italy by the invitation of the Pope, John VIII., and received the imperial crown from his hands. In the weakness of the Empire, the Papacy had steadily gained strength. Nicholas I., who succeeded Benedict III. in 858, did much to raise the prestige of the Holy See.

Since Gregory the Great, it was said, no such Pope had been seen in Rome. "He ruled kings and tyrants, and dominated them by his authority, as if he had been the lord of the world." A statesman, with a lofty theory of the spiritual supremacy of the Papacy, he enforced the extreme claims of the Church with consistent boldness, during the nine years of his reign. His successor, Hadrian II., carried on his work till 872, when John VIII., an able and practical man of affairs, mounted the papal throne.

But neither statesmanship nor courage could avail to stem the tide of lawlessness in Italy, where the Roman nobles, the petty princes of the southern provinces, and the predatory Saracens of the Mediterranean combined to waste the land. John VIII. sent urgent and picturesque letters to the new Emperor, begging for help against his many foes. At first he pleaded to deaf ears. Louis the German had died in 876, and Charles the Bald was busy trying to wrest eastern Lotharingia from his brother's sons. It was not till the defeat of Andernach had dashed his hopes in this direction that he began again to think of his Italian responsibilities and ambitions. Meantime the vikings were in the Seine, negotiations with them had failed, and the troops which had been called out had done nothing. Charles "began to think about a ransom," and a winter's plundering, with the Pope's pressing appeals, served to translate the thought into action.

At the beginning of May, 877, a tax of five thousand pounds of silver was raised to pay off the vikings, an "exaction to be paid to the Northmen in the Seine, to induce them to leave the kingdom." It was a singular policy, to give tribute to the vikings, to set the Emperor free to help the Pope against the Saracens. While, moreover, it enabled Charles the Bald to go to Italy for the second time, it turned the fury of the Northmen upon England, for the vikings were true vagrants, and, like the modern slum population, were only driven from one refuge to betake themselves promptly to another.

The great Seine fleet of about a hundred sail, which probably represented a force of from four thousand to six thousand men, may possibly have gone to join the English pirates, and to replace the ships that lay sunk below the cliffs of Swanage. It was, apparently, a recollection of this Seine expedition which misled the early writers who antedate by twenty years the first invasion of Normandy by Rollo, its future duke, and place it in 876.

The troubled year 877 closed with the sudden death of Charles the Bald, "in a miserable hovel," on his way back from Italy; an inglorious ending to his fifty-four years of ignoble struggle for wealth and position. "All the days of his life," writes a contemporary chronicler, "wherever it was necessary to resist his enemies, he would either openly turn his back or secretly run away with his soldiers." He died at the beginning of October, some three months before the final desperate attempt of the vikings to win the kingdom of Wessex. The dark hour of the Empire coincided with the crisis of Alfred's fate.

By the autumn of 877 the army of the three kings seems to have settled in Mercia, with its headquarters at Gloucester, and to have followed the example of Healfdene in Northumbria, by "dealing out" the land. Ceolwulf would now, doubtless, be required to fulfil the agreement he had made in 874, to resign his kingdom to his Danish masters whenever they should demand it. Though his power was restricted, however, he still remained under-king of western Mercia. "The army (here)," says the Chronicle, "departed at harvest-tide into Mercia, and some of it they dealt out, and some they gave to Ceolwulf."

This "deal" or partition of 877 may be the origin of the later distinction between Danish and English Mercia. The exact line of division is uncertain, but it probably corresponded more or less closely to the boundary fixed by Alfred in his treaty with Guthrum in 878. The land east of Watling Street, the valleys of the Trent, the Welland, the Nen, and the Bedfordshire Ouse, would thus fall to the Danes, while Ceolwulf would retain the valleys of the Severn and the Warwickshire Avon, the Cotswold country, and the modern Shropshire, Staffordshire, and Cheshire.

The Danes set up no new kingdom in central England, as they had done north of Humber. They appear to have formed a sort of confederacy, grouped round the "Five Boroughs," Lincoln and Stamford, Nottingham, Derby and Leicester, and other military centres, but of the first beginnings and gradual development of their settlements nothing is known; they only come into the light of history in the reign of Alfred's son, Edward the Elder.

A considerable section of the Danish host, at least, found no permanent home in Mercia. Of the three kings who commanded the Cambridge army, Oscytel and Anwynd are not mentioned again by the contemporary authorities, but Guthrum now stands out as the leader of a formidable combined attack on Wessex from the north and west. The viking fleet which in 878 was defeated in Devonshire was, perhaps, acting in connection with the force which, earlier in the year, seized Chippenham and overran Wessex. From 878 to his death, as a Christian king, in 890, Guthrum's fortunes were closely interwoven with those of King Alfred, his great opponent.

THE TESTING OF ALFRED: THE WAR IN THE WEST AND THE WINNING OF LONDON

878-886

THREE times in the course of seven years the Danes of the "Great Army" struck at the throne of Wessex. Once, in 871, from the east, an overland attack, from the Thames valley, with Reading as a base-camp; again, in 876 and 877, from the south, a combined land and sea campaign, starting from the fortified ports of Dorset and Devonshire; lastly, in 878, from the west, the land forces resting on Chippenham and the Bristol Avon as a base, and possibly co-operating with the fleet in the Irish Sea.

This war in the west country, with its sudden vicissitudes of fortune, when the whole future of the West-Saxon kingdom hung in the balance, took hold of the popular imagination. Folk-tale and ecclesiastical legend grew up about it, and the dry narrative of the Chronicle has touches of eloquence in recording it. In reality, very little is known about those critical weeks in which the fate of Wessex was decided. Almost every detail is questioned, the site of every battle is disputed, and the romantic additions are discredited. Yet still the story of Alfred in Athelney keeps its ancient charm, and still, as in the days of William of Malmesbury, the people point out the scenes of the great King's misfortunes.

The royal "vill" or "ham" of Chippenham, the first point to be attacked by the Danes in 878, lies in Wiltshire, on the Bristol Avon, about halfway between its sharp southward bend at Malmesbury, and its equally abrupt turn to the west at Bradford. It must have been a place of some importance, as Alfred's sister was married there to Burhred of Mercia in 853, but it was apparently unfortified, as it does not occur in the early list of burhs which includes Wareham, Exeter, and Malmesbury.

It has been suggested that Alfred may have gone to Chippenham for the Christmas season, and that the Danes surprised him in his winter home. This is possible, but there is nothing to show that he was in North Wiltshire at the time of the inroad, and the Dorset Dorchester, which was a more usual place for the Christmas sojourn of the West-Saxon court, would also be more accessible from Devonshire after the siege of Exeter. For the same reason, though Asser seems to make the Danes go straight from Exeter to Chippenham, ignoring the settlement of Mercia, it is more probable that they made their dash into Wiltshire from the neighbouring Gloucestershire, as the Chronicle and Ethelwerd imply.

It was at midwinter, in the January of 878, "after twelfth-night," that Guthrum's army, the here, stole into Chippenham. This attack during the Christmas festival is sometimes spoken of as an act of peculiar treachery, or at least of cunning, on the part of the Danes, but as a matter of fact, their raids appear to have been often made in the winter, sometimes with a view to taking up winter quarters. Thus Healfdene's march from East Anglia to the Thames was in December; the battle of Ashdown was fought early in January, almost exactly seven years before the capture of Chippenham; and Exeter was also, in all probability, taken in the winter months.

The special excellence of Guthrum's army lay in its power of swift and silent movement, rather than in any subtle strategy. Twice already it had "stolen away" from the West-Saxon fyrd, before it stole into Chippenham. But on both the previous occasions there had been a fyrd in the field for the Danish here to elude. Now, the men of Wessex, like the Mercians and Northumbrians before them, seem to have been struck with panic. The Danes, says the Chronicle, "raided (geridon)1 the land of the West Saxons, and occupied it; many of the folk they drove over sea, and the greater part of the others they 'raided' (geridon) and subdued, except King Alfred, and he with a little band (lytle werede) went forth, uneasily, into the woods and the moor-fastnesses." Asser adds that the Danish army wintered at Chippenham, that Alfred retreated to Somerset, and that he lived there on what he could get, by open or secret forays, from the heathen, and also from "the Christians who had submitted to the lordship of the heathen."

It is, then, clear that the West-Saxon resistance to the vikings collapsed for some weeks at the beginning of 878. The suddenness of the attack, and the overwhelming numbers of the enemy, who "covered the land like locusts," are sufficient to account for this brief demoralisation, without attributing any particular disloyalty or cowardice to Alfred and his people.

Three facts stand out from the authentic narratives: a West-Saxon migration from England, the reduction of a large part of Wessex by the Danes, and the stand made by the King and his immediate followers behind the forest-screen of Selwood and the marshes of Somerset. It was reserved for later ages to explain these events by baseless theories of Alfred's early arrogance and tyranny, of a revolt of his subjects against his oppressive government, or of civil dissensions between the West-Saxons and the Celtic populations whom they had conquered.

The West-Saxon fugitives fled, according to Ethelwerd, across the English Channel to "Gaul," that Frankish country which had just bought peace from the vikings of the Seine. They seem to have come mainly from Hampshire, for in the following spring only those Hampshire men who had not "sailed beyond sea for fear of the heathen" joined Alfred at "Egbert's Stone." Many of them, doubtless, would be clergy; later chroniclers turned them into bishops, followed by their flocks, carrying with them the relics of the saints and the treasures of their churches. Whether this be literally true or no, such sad little processions of monks and priests, flying before the storm of viking persecution, must have been a familiar sight in the last quarter of the ninth century.

The guardians of St. Cuthbert's body were still wandering over northern England with their sacred burden in 878, and it was at this time also that the shrine and precious things of St. Columba were removed from Iona to Ireland, to protect them from the "Strangers." It is, perhaps, more than an interesting coincidence that Dado, who was Bishop of Verdun from 880 to 923, is said to have hospitably welcomed certain learned Britons, refugees from their island home, "where all the inhabitants had been either killed or put to flight."

The remaining West-Saxons, who submitted to the Danes, have been accused of treachery and servility for bowing their necks to the foreign yoke, but they appear to have had little choice in the matter. Experience had shown that the only two ways of stopping a viking invasion were heavy tribute or a decisive victory, and time was needed both to collect money and to organise an effective army.

Three months later the King was ready for action, but for the moment he was powerless, and the people had to make the best terms they could. Alfred's writings show that there was harrying and burning south of Thames, as well as scattering of books and treasure, and exile of learned men. Though there is no definite record of the sacking of any of the great religious houses of the south and west, the succession of the abbots of Malmesbury and of Glastonbury becomes uncertain from the middle of the ninth century, and there may be a good deal of truth in Gaimar's account of the destruction of monasteries and churches.

From Chippenham the way was open to South Wiltshire, Hampshire, and Dorset, but Devonshire and at least part of Somerset seem to have rallied round their ealdormen, and to have supported the King when, an earlier Hereward, he withdrew to his camp of refuge in the western fens. The legendary Alfred skulks by highways and hedges, through woods and fields, to be scolded by peasants and comforted by saints in an exile which lasts for three years. The historic Alfred passed some four months in consolidating his forces for a final crushing blow at the main body of the Danes, while he held the west country against Guthrum's outposts, and carried on a skirmishing warfare from his stronghold in the Somerset "moor-fastnesses."

Between the Quantocks and the Polden Hills stretches a wide tract of marshland, where wooded knolls of higher ground rise like islands from the watery plain. Straight rows of grey-green willows now mark the course of the "rhines" or dykes, and cattle graze on the reclaimed water-meadows which in Alfred's day were all waste swamp and fen. Yet it is a wild country still, lonely and beautiful, with the level lines of its grassy flats, its shining reaches of mere and stream, and its clear pale tints of rush and sedge, withy-bed and alder thicket. It is a historic country, too, rich in seventeenth-century memories of Sedgemoor and "King Monmouth," and looking northward towards a land of old romance, Glastonbury, and King Arthur's "island valley of Avilion." Here, in the middle of the seventh century, the Britons took refuge, when they "melted like snow" before Cenwalh, King of Wessex. Here, in 845, the ealdormen of Somerset and Dorset defeated the Danes at the mouth of the river Parret. But it is King Alfred's name which is most closely associated with the district where he toiled and suffered till the day when he returned to his people as one risen from the dead.

For about ten weeks, from the early January to the late March of 878, he sheltered in the fens, guarding the "gate into Devonshire," the Taunton gap between the Quantocks and the Blackdown Hills. It was, no doubt, as Asser says, an unquiet life, full of privations and dangers, but Alfred was not in reality the forsaken outcast of popular tradition. There were royal estates at hand, such as Lyng, Somerton, and Langport, owing dues to the King, and all loyal Devon was behind him. His hardships were shared, too, by the lytel werod, the little company which had followed him into Somerset, a band of picked men to whom Asser gives the Frankish name of "vassals" (faselli). There were, apparently, a few great nobles among them--Ethelwerd definitely mentions Ethelnoth, ealdorman of Somerset--but they were chiefly thegns and king's retainers and personal followers, those, says Ethelwerd, who were maintained by the King's pastus, or "farm," the food-rents which were specially appropriated to the upkeep of his household and his dogs and horses. In the eleventh century a particular garden in Langport had still to render fifty eels a year to the king's farm, and the Somerset manors of Cheddar and Somerton were joined in a common obligation to provide a yearly "farm of one night" or to feed the court for one day a year.

Alfred, then, was neither solitary nor destitute in his weeks of waiting, but the tales which give him his mother--dead years before--for a companion, or bring his wife and children to the camp, are pure invention, though it is, of course, probable that the women of the royal family had been placed in safety in the west country, out of reach of the vikings.

In happier days, writes William of Malmesbury, Alfred himself would relate his adventures, in merry mood, to his friends. Many of the legends of the great King belong, indeed, to this period. They are to be found in the lives of St. Neot and St. Cuthbert, and in the pleasant discursive pages of William of Malmesbury,--the famous story of Alfred and the cakes, the story of Alfred's visit to the Danish camp in the disguise of a minstrel, the appearances of St. Neot and St. Cuthbert, and the miraculous draught of fishes from the frozen river,--some of them, perhaps, genuine local traditions, others floating folk-tales, others, again, the product of a pious fancy, but all of them showing the abiding human interest of the Athelney episode.

Legend does not distinguish the six weeks' stand at Athelney from the ten weeks' wandering in the marshes, but history marks more clearly the succession of events. The Chronicle and Asser agree in putting the wandering in the marshes first, then, the defeat of the Danish fleet in Devonshire, and lastly, the building of the fort on the isle of Athelney, and the six weeks' skirmishing which preceded the battle of Ethandun.

While the army of the three kings had been concentrating its efforts on south-western England, another viking force, under "the brother of Inwaer and Healfdene," presumably Ubba, was engaged in harrying the coast of Wales. The Welsh King, Roderick Mawr, son of Mervyn, after defeating the Danes in two battles, was forced to fly to Ireland, and Ubba wintered in South Wales, and ravaged the country with great cruelty, sparing neither convents, women, nor children.

Early in 878 he appeared off the north-western coast of Devonshire with twenty-three ships, acting it may be in concert with Guthrum, who was now master of southern Wessex and pressing hard on Somerset. A band of English king's thegns (ministri regis), with their men, had entrenched themselves at a place called "Cynwit," in a rude fort which could only be approached from the east. Here the Danes besieged them, but the garrison, lacking water, made a bold sally, led apparently by Odda, the ealdorman of Devonshire, and cut the viking army to pieces. Ubba himself fell, and with him from eight hundred to twelve hundred of his host. Only a small remnant reached their ships in safety, and escaped.

Such is the outline of the story as told by Asser, who had seen the fort at "Cynwit," and, as a Welshman, and Bishop of the western diocese of Sherborne, may have had access to special sources of information. The Parker Chronicle simply states that in the same winter the brother of In waer and Healfdene was in Wessex, in Devonshire, with twenty-three ships, and there was slain, and eight hundred and forty men of his army with him. Ethelwerd supplies Odda's name, and Gaimar says that Ubba was slain in "Pene wood," and buried under a great "how" (hoge) or mound in Devonshire, which was called Ubbelawe. Most of the later manuscripts of the Chronicle add the picturesque detail of the capture of the Danes'

"Raven" standard, a banner which, according to the Annals of St. Neots, had been woven by the three sisters of Ragnar Lodbrok in a single morning, so skilfully, that in time of war, if the vikings were marching to victory, the raven on the flag appeared with outstretched wings, in full flight, while when defeat was impending, it hung drooping and motionless. The raven was the messenger of Odin, the raven-god, and when the great war-banner was taken, the English might well feel that Alfred's Christian soldiers had avenged the blood of the blessed king and martyr Edmund.

Some of the twelfth-century historians make Ivar and Healfdene fall in the battle of Cynwit, no doubt from a misunderstanding of the Chronicle's description of the Danish leader as "Inwaer's brother and Healfdene's." But if, as a seventeenthcentury writer says, the battle has as many sites in Devonshire as Homer has birthplaces in Greece, the sad stories of the deaths of these Danish kings, the sons of Ragnar Lodbrok, would fill many volumes. Ivar, Inwaer, or Hingvar, whom the later authorities turn into two distinct persons, is killed by the Northumbrians, or falls at Cynwit; or, again, he dies in 870, immediately after the murder of St. Edmund, or in 872, in Ireland. Healfdene may be the "Alband, king of the Black Strangers," who was slain in 877 in a battle with the Irish Norsemen at Strangford Lough; but in English tradition, he is afflicted by heaven-sent madness, and, driven out by his Northumbrian army, he sails from the Tyne with three ships, to meet his death at sea.

The commonly accepted identification of "Cynwit" with "Kenwith Castle" or "Hennaburgh" near Bideford in North Devon is, apparently, a figment of the antiquarian imagination. There is nothing beyond the statements in the Chronicle and Asser that the fight took place "in Devonshire," to fix its site, or the burial-place of Ubba. Yet, though deprived of its local habitation and its legendary associations, the battle of Cynwit remains a most important victory for the West-Saxons, as important in its relation to the later battle of Ethandun as the Swanage shipwreck had been in its effect on the siege of Exeter. The Christian army was no longer caught between two heathen forces. Relieved of the danger in his rear, Alfred was free to concentrate his whole strength on Guthrum's host, and it was, perhaps, a direct result of the Cynwit victory that in the last week of the March of 878 he took up an actively aggressive attitude.

It was at Easter-tide that King Alfred with his little band (lytle werede) wrought a "work" (geweorc) or fort at Athelney (Æthelingeigge), and from this fort strove without ceasing against the army (here) with the help of those men of Somerset who were near at hand. In the twelfth century William of Malmesbury described Athelney as "not an island of the sea, but so inaccessible from flooded swamps and marshes that it can only be approached by boat." All overgrown with alder, it was full of game, stags and goats and other wild animals. The stags and goats have given place to the pigs and sheep of Athelney farm, but even now the description is faithful enough in the winter season, when, in spite of dykes and drainage, the country is almost submerged by floods, and Athelney is reached from East Lyng by a causeway raised above the level of the swampy fields. The tidal river Parret, turbid and sluggish, crawls westwards past muddy banks to Boroughbridge, where it is joined by the silvery waters of the Tone, which flows northwards from Taunton. Between the two streams, on the left bank of the Tone, about halfway from Taunton to Bridgewater, lies the isle of Athelney, a low rise crested with trees, not the highest ground in the neighbourhood, but well suited for a camp, communicating easily with Lyng in one direction, and with Langport and Somerton in the other, and keeping watch over the river-way to Taunton to the south. The Parret and the Tone are now artificially embanked, much of the surrounding land has been brought under cultivation, and both the old coachroad and the Great Western Railway pass within sight of Athelney. But still, when the evening mists have blotted out the modern features of the view, the rushing train, and the red, slate-roofed houses, fancy may restore the scene on which Alfred's eyes rested--the vast expanse of fen glowing like fire under the winter sunset, or gleaming white in the cold light of the moon--the little hills, uncrowned as yet by their stately church towers, swimming in a sea of mist.

It may be that the break-up of the winter frosts had rendered the marshes uninhabitable by the Easter of 878, and that Alfred was compelled to retreat to higher ground, or the building of the "work" on the isle of Athelney may have been due to purely military reasons, the first move in the offensive campaign against Guthrum's army.

Of the fort, as of the monastery which succeeded it, no vestiges remain, though a Georgian monument in the field above Athelney farmhouse commemorates the King's sojourn in the island. About a mile and a half to the north-east, at Boroughbridge, just beyond the junction of Tone and Parret, is a higher, steeper outcrop of rock, now called Borough Mump, or King Alfred's Fort, a natural fortification, on which may still be traced a triple line of terraces, partly, perhaps, due to artificial formation. This grass-grown mound, now, with its deserted church tower, a striking landmark in the wide plain, is often taken for the very "work" which King Alfred "wrought" in 878, and though it is too far from Athelney for this to be probable, it may quite possibly have been used by Alfred in his guerilla war with the Danes.

The words of the Chronicle: " KingAlfred . . . was fighting against the army (here) from the fort (weorc)" show that he was in touch with the enemy during the Athelney period, and though no authentic details of the events of those weeks have been preserved, it is likely that there were many petty engagements and skirmishes, "raids" ridden by ealdormen and king's thegns, and by the King himself, as in the spring of 871, when the West-Saxon and Danish forces faced each other in the Thames valley.

Easter Day fell early in 878, on March 23d, and it was in the seventh week after Easter, about Whitsuntide, in the second week of May, that Alfred made the next move in his plan of campaign. "He rode to Egbert's Stone (Ecgbryhtesstane) on the east of Selwood, and there came to him all the men of Somerset and of Wiltshire, and those of the Hampshire men who were on this side the sea, and they were fain (glad) of him." They welcomed him, says Asser, "as one restored to life after many tribulations." From Egbert's Stone the King marched with the army of the three shires to Iglea, where he encamped for a night, and thence, in the course of another day, to Ethandune, where a great battle was fought with the main body of the Danes.

The difficulty of locating Ecgbryhtesstane, Iglea, and Ethandune has led to wide divergences of opinion as to the line of march taken by the West-Saxon army and the site of the final battle. Eddington and Yattenden in Berkshire, Yatton Keynell, Heddington, and Edington in Wiltshire and the Somerset Edington, on the Polden Hills, have all been suggested as the Ethandune1 of the Chronicle, while corresponding sites have been found for Iglea and Ecgbryhtesstane. In a case of this kind--the location of a battlefield without direct historical evidence--"tradition" is a dangerous guide, and the only tests which can be applied are philological and strategic. The argument from strategy yields at best a probability; the argument from philology may at least prove the continuity of a place-name, and eliminate the fantastic identifications of unscientific antiquarianism. Tried by this test, the Wiltshire Edington alone gives satisfactory results.

Alfred, then, may be supposed to have ridden forth from Athelney as a king coming to his own again, mounted and equipped for war, at the head of his bodyguard of thegns, with the men of Somerset gathering behind him, and the men of Wiltshire and Hampshire pouring in from east and south to the appointed place of meeting at "Egbert's Stone," a boundary-stone, probably, at the point where the three shires met, on the east of the great forest of Selwood.

Though Sir John Spelman's identification of Brixton Deverill in South Wiltshire with Ecgbryhtesstane is apparently based on an erroneous derivation, it seems likely that the West-Saxon forces met in that neighbourhood, perhaps, as Mr. Stevenson suggests, near Penselwood, at the spot where old maps mark a "Bound Stone" at the junction of Somerset, Dorset, and Wiltshire. Penselwood is about eighteen miles from the Wiltshire Edington, and an easy day's march would bring Alfred's army to Southleigh wood in Warminster parish, where in former days there was a boundary tree called Iley Oak, which may represent the Iglea of the Chronicle, where Alfred encamped the second night, some seven miles from Edington. "Thence, on the following morning, moving his standards with the dawn," writes Asser, "he came to the place which is called Ethandun."

From Warminster, which in the eleventh century was a royal burh, a road now curves round a bold shoulder of down, and runs through four miles of hilly country to Westbury, also on the later royal demesne, and so north by the undulating valley of the Bristol Avon, to the king's "hams" of Melksham and Chippenham, a distance of between fifteen and sixteen miles. At Westbury, the Market Lavington road branches off to the east, skirting the downs, which here drop abruptly to the low-lying village and fine old church of Edington. The West-Saxons may have followed this route, or they may have climbed the downs above Warminster, and struck straight across their rolling slopes to Edington Hill, repeating, to some extent, the operations of the Ashdown campaign.

Difficult as this ground would be for marching, it was, perhaps, in those days, easier than the thickly wooded and swampy lowlands, traversed by narrow miry roads. There, was, at least, room for the troops to expand, and to advance in open order. The rounded spurs of the downs, where they fall away to the valleys on the north and west, are crested with camps and earthworks. Beneath one such entrenchment, Bratton Castle, about a mile to the westward of Edington, is the white horse cut on the chalky hillside which is locally supposed to commemorate Alfred's victory over the Danes.

Guthrum may have seized this point of vantage, commanding the road to Chippenham and the royal lands at Ethandun, or his troops may have been stationed more to the eastward, on Edington hill itself. But this is pure hypothesis. The Chronicle dismisses this famous fight, undoubtedly one of the decisive battles of English history, in a couple of sentences, and Asser, though he adds a few details, says nothing of the relative positions of the opposing forces, or the tactics of the two great leaders.

Of the numbers and constitution of the armies which now faced each other on English soil it is equally difficult to form an idea. The original here of the three kings must have been much reduced by the heavy loss in the Swanage shipwreck, but it had probably since received considerable reinforcements from the Continent. On the other hand, it does not follow that the entire host had left Mercia with Guthrum, or even that all the invaders of Wessex were with him in Wiltshire, though the Chronicle's use of the phrase "all the here" seems to imply that the Danish King had done what he could to concentrate his troops. Warned, perhaps, by the rally of the men of Hampshire and Wiltshire to Alfred's standard, he may have called in the outposts which had been harrying Somersetshire, and have prepared for a crushing blow at the West-Saxons before they could get past him to his base at Chippenham.

Alfred, too, had all the available men from the three shires of Somerset, Wiltshire, and Hampshire. Gaimar adds the men of Dorset, but they, with the men of Devon and Berkshire, may well have been exhausted by their previous efforts, or unable to leave the defence of the south-western coast and of the Thames.

The document called the "Burghal Hidage," which apparently shows fairly accurately the military strength of the West-Saxon kingdom at the beginning of the tenth century, gives Wessex, exclusive of Kent, but inclusive of Surrey and Sussex, about twenty-two thousand five hundred hides, or, at the rate of one man for five hides, a well-equipped field army of about five thousand men. Alfred's force from the three shires, at this same rate, would be about two thousand seven hundred or three thousand men, or about three thousand five hundred including Dorset. Adding something for the popular element, which was probably present in some strength in the Ethandun fyrd, this makes a respectable army for days of scanty population and hand-to-hand warfare. Some of the best modern authorities only allow William the Conqueror six or seven thousand men at the battle of Hastings, nearly two hundred years later.

Of the proportion of footmen to mounted infantry on either side, also, nothing is known, though the English pursued the defeated enemy on horseback. "They fought against all the here, and put them to flight, and rode after them to the fort (geweorc), and sat there fourteen nights," says the Chronicle. Asser further notes that the English fought in a solid mass (cum densa testitudine), not, as at Ashdown, in two divisions, that they fought "bravely and long," and that they followed the flying Danes to the fort (arx), and slew all the men they found without the gates, and carried off the horses and cattle. Simeon of Durham elaborates without improving. He makes the King and the flower of his people rise with the limpid dawn, and arm themselves with the triple breastplate of faith, hope, and charity: the king's face shines with angelic brightness: the shouts of the combatants and the clash of weapons are heard afar: God looks down from heaven and awards the victory.

Many historians, from the days of Camden onwards, have thought that the fort to which the Danes fled after their defeat was Bratton Castle, the great camp on the heights above the figure of the white horse. This seems, however, a barren and waterless stronghold for a fortnight's siege, and it is more probable that the geweorc of the Chronicle was Guthrum's base-camp at Chippenham, and that the pursuit straggled over the fifteen or sixteen miles of low intervening country, the broken Danish forces making for their fortress much as the fugitives from Ashdown made for Reading, with the mounted victors pressing them hard.

The very fact that the West-Saxons had taken to their horses implies that the fort was at some distance. Chippenham, like Reading, is on a river, the Avon, and is fertile and well-watered. Asser's story of the capture of the horses and cattle outside the ramparts applies much better to a permanent camp in a pastoral district than to the high wind-swept earthworks of Bratton Castle. Ethelwerd, too, in his account of the battle, speaks of the Danish host as "the army that was at Chippenham," and it was to Chippenham that Guthrum returned after his baptism in Somerset.

After a fortnight's siege, compelled, says Asser, by "hunger, cold, and fear," the Danes in the fort came to terms with the West-Saxons. The stereotyped alliterative phrase fame, frigore, seems rather ill-suited to a summer siege, but the conditions of surrender were so favourable to Alfred as to suggest that the vikings were desperate. "Then the here gave [the King] distinguished hostages, and swore mighty oaths that they would depart from his kingdom. They promised, also, that their king would receive baptism, and that they accomplished." Never before, according to Asser, had such a peace been concluded, for Alfred chose as many hostages as he liked, and gave none in return.

About three weeks later, Guthrum, with twentynine picked men from his army, met the West- Saxon King at Aller (Alre) near Athelney, and Alfred was his sponsor at his baptism, "and the 'chrism-loosing' was at Wedmore, and Guthrum was twelve nights with the King, who honoured him and his companions with many gifts (feo)." The little village of Aller still cherishes with pride the memory of the royal baptism of more than a thousand years ago. By a curious coincidence, the tiny ancient church contains a font, apparently of Anglo-Saxon workmanship, which was discovered in a pond in the rector's garden, and has now been restored to its original use.

Guthrum received the Christian name of Æthelstan or Athelstan, a name found in the West- Saxon royal family. In some of the chronicles of the twelfth century his companions and many of his people are said to have been baptised with him, but this is a gratuitous addition to the contemporary sources. Half a century earlier, in 826, a similar ceremony had taken place in the Empire, on a much larger scale, when Louis the Pious stood godfather to the converted Danish King Harold, the Empress Judith was godmother to Harold's queen, and hundreds of pagan Danes of both sexes followed the example of their rulers.

From the choice of Aller for Guthrum's baptism, it would appear that, after the peace of Chippenham, Alfred had withdrawn to his base-camp at Athelney. Ethelwerd, indeed, erroneously puts the baptism in "the marshy island of Alnea." After the ceremony the two kings and their retinues went to another Somerset royal "vill," Wedmore, between the Polden Hills and the Mendips. Here, on the octave of the baptism, the "chrism-loosing" took place. This was the removal of the chrismale, the linen cloth or band which was worn on the head for a week, to protect the sacred baptismal chrism, or anointing oil. On the eighth day it was laid aside with the white robes of baptism, and Ethelwerd seems to imply that it was Ethelnoth, the ealdorman of Somerset, who performed the service of unbinding the chrismale for Guthrum. The "chrism-loosing" was probably succeeded by royal feasting and carousing, and the Danish King returned to Chippenham laden with costly offerings.

In translating the passage from the Chronicle which describes these incidents, Asser renders the Anglo-Saxon feo, the gifts or wealth which Alfred bestowed on the Danes, by the curious word ædificia. This has been taken as a scribal error for beneficia, and elsewhere Asser makes pecunia, quite accurately, the equivalent of feo. On the whole, the reading beneficia may probably be accepted, but it is just possible that Asser uses ædificia in a general sense, for things wrought or made, and it has even been suggested that the word, throughout Asser's Life of Alfred, has the peculiar meaning of shrines, reliquaries, or articles of goldsmith's work.

The conditions of the compact made at Chippenham between Alfred and the Danes are only known from the entry in the Chronicle, with Asser's translation. In accordance with them Guthrum was to leave the West-Saxon kingdom, and to become a Christian. It was, perhaps, natural that the connection of Wedmore with the carrying out of the second part of the agreement should have caused what was really the treaty of Chippenham to be commonly called, by modern writers, the treaty of Wedmore, while even in later mediæval days, Guthrum's settlement in East Anglia came to be regarded in the light of a feudal grant from Alfred of "the province of the East-Anglians and of the Northumbrians."

From Wedmore Guthrum returned to Chippenham. Thence, in fulfilment of his pact, he moved across the West-Saxon border, and took up winter quarters in the territory of the Hwicce, the ancient Mercian under-kingdom. Here he remained for a year, and then, in 880, "the army (here) went from Cirencester into East Anglia, and settled the land, and divided it."

It was in 879, while Guthrum was still at Cirencester, that the Anglo-Saxon Chronicle notes the landing at Fulham, on the Thames, of "a band of vikings (hloth wicenga)," the first appearance in the Parker manuscript of that dread name. They wintered in Danish Mercia, but in the next year they crossed the sea to "Frankland," and took up winter quarters at Ghent.

It is now that the scribe of the English annals shows special knowledge of the movements of the Northmen on the Continent, though he often puts these movements a year later than the corresponding entries in the foreign chronicles. This may be due to dating each viking "wintering" from its conclusion rather than from its beginning, but the whole chronology of the period is involved in great obscurity.

Asser, also, is well acquainted with the Continental history of the time. Not content with following the Chronicle, he adds touches of his own which suggest that he may have been in "Frankland" during these troubled years. In particular is this the case with his account of the eclipse of the sun in 879, where he omits the statement in the Chronicle that it lasted for an hour, but fixes the time of its appearance with curious precision, "between None and Vespers, but nearer to None." It is probable that Asser is here alluding to the total solar eclipse of October 29, 878, not to the small partial eclipse of March 26, 879, but the Chronicle, in the annal for 885, dates the death of Louis the Stammerer, which took place in 879, "in the year when the sun was darkened."

There was some reason for associating these solar phenomena with the deaths of kings and with public disaster. If Wessex enjoyed comparative peace, the ravages of the Northmen in the Empire had never been more terrible and persistent than in the years which immediately followed the death of Louis the Stammerer, King of the West Franks, the son of Charles the Bald. The incessant dynastic quarrels and selfish intrigues of the Carolingian princes and their nobles offered an irresistible opportunity to the more restless and adventurous vikings, who still preferred piracy to colonisation. Flanders was harried, all the country between Scheldt and

Somme was ravaged, while the ships of the Northmen sailed up the Elbe and Rhine, and the imperial palace at Nimwegen was burnt to the ground. In spite of occasional successes, the Franks of both the eastern and western kingdoms were forced to bow before the storm. "Fear and trembling fell upon the inhabitants of the land." By day and by night the flames from burning churches and monasteries lit up scenes of desolation, wasted fields, and flying bands of monks and nuns, laden with relics and ecclesiastical treasures, and of homeless men of all sorts and conditions, with their wives and children.

It was, perhaps, the imminence of the danger which lent an exaggerated importance to the battle of Saucourt, in the August of 881, when Louis III., the new King of the West Franks, intercepted the Danes on their return from a predatory expedition in the Somme valley, and defeated them with great slaughter. Those who escaped took to their horses, and rode back to their camp. The victory, which inspired the fine contemporary vernacular poem, the Ludwigslied or "Song of Louis," in praise of the young King, is recorded in the Anglo-Saxon Chronicle, and was worked into the later legendary history of the viking wars. Yet in reality it did but little to check the plunder raids.

In the winter of 881 the northern leaders Godfred and Sigfred fortified themselves in a strong position at Elsloo on the Maas. From this centre they devastated the surrounding district, burnt Cologne, and, a last humiliation for the Carolingian house, set fire to the palace of Charles the Great at Aachen, and stabled their horses in the chapel. In 882, after the death of the king of the East Franks, another of the short-lived descendants of Louis the Pious, fresh Danish incursions led the Emperor Charles the Fat, son of Louis the German, to intervene in person. He besieged the fort at Elsloo, but just when success was in sight, he concluded what was regarded as a shameful treaty with the viking leaders. Godfred submitted to baptism, and received a grant of the Frisian and Flemish fiefs once held by Rorik. Sigfred and the other chiefs were bought off with a heavy tribute, for which the remaining treasures of the Church were laid under contribution. Two hundred ships, laden with spoil and captives, it was said, sailed for Scandinavia, while the Elsloo army took advantage of the sudden death of the young victor of Saucourt, Louis III., to harry the land of the West Franks, from their new base at Condé, a nunnery on the Scheldt. Hincmar,

Archbishop of Rheims, fled with the body of St. Remigius and other treasures to Épernay, where, towards the close of the year 882, he ended his long and stormy life. The Condé vikings spent the spring of 883 in harrying Flanders, and went into winter quarters at Amiens on the Somme, while another host wintered at Duisburg, on the Rhine.

The West Frankish magnates and their King, Carloman, brother of Louis III., now called on the Christian viking Sigfred to negotiate a peace with his former comrades. Twelve thousand pounds of silver induced the army to break up their camp at Amiens. A detachment of the host went eastwards to Lorraine; the remainder made a descent on the coast of Kent.

"The aforesaid army (here)," says the Anglo- Saxon Chronicle, "divided into two; one part went east, the other went to Rochester, and beset the city (ceastre), and built a fort (fæsten,geweorc), about themselves." In Latinising this passage, Asser makes the English ceastre into civitas, and renders fæsten by castellum, and geweorc by arx. The distinction is perfectly clear between the old Roman town and the temporary Danish earthwork at its gate. It is also clear that the men of Kent, who in 865 had ignominiously bought off the vikings, were now, twenty years later, able and ready to defend their country, while a West- Saxon fleet and army were prepared to support them.

Already, in 882, Alfred had "fared out to sea with ships," to fight "four shiploads of Danish men." He had taken two of the enemy's vessels, and slain their crews, and had forced the remaining two to surrender. Now, in 885, when he hastened to Rochester with the fyrd, the Danes forsook their fort (geweorc), their prisoners, and the horses they had brought with them, and fled over sea to the land of the Franks.

It is probable that Guthrum-Athelstan was in league with the invaders, for in this year he broke his peace with Alfred, and as soon as Rochester was safe, the West-Saxon fleet sailed for East Anglia, "for the sake of plunder" according to Asser. At the mouth of the river Stour, which divides Suffolk from Essex, they encountered sixteen viking ships, and, after a sharp fight, slew the crews, and captured the boats. As they returned with their booty, however, they were met by a "great fleet of vikings," and were, in their turn, defeated.

The document known as the treaty of Alfred and Guthrum probably marks the conclusion of this struggle, and its provisions are sufficiently favourable to the West-Saxons to justify the assumption that the East-Anglian Danes felt themselves beaten It lays down the boundaries between the kingdoms of East Anglia and Wessex: "up on the Thames, and then up on the Lea, and along the Lea to its source, then straight to Bedford, then up on the Ouse to Watling Street." Norfolk, Suffolk, and Essex remained to Guthrum, with the modern counties of Cambridge and Huntingdon, and parts of Hertfordshire and Bedfordshire. But Alfred gained the remainder of Bedfordshire and Hertfordshire, Buckinghamshire, and, above all, Middlesex, with London.

The Chronicle states that in 886 King Alfred "settled" Lundenburg, and all the English (Angel cyn) turned to him, save those who were in captivity to the Danish men, and he then committed the burg to ealdorman Ethelred, to hold. Asser, who misunderstood the passage in the Chronicle, makes Alfred "restore" the city, and render it habitable, "after burning of towns, and slaughter of people." Ethelwerd and Henry of Huntingdon definitely mention a siege, perhaps misled by the likeness between the words gesette, ("settled," "restored," and besætte, "besieged." Henry of Huntingdon even adds that the greater part of the Danish garrison had joined the vikings on the Continent. Whether by direct conquest or by treaty, however, it is certain that the city now passed into Alfred's hands.

Twelve years later, the fortifications of this important strategic position were still a matter of anxiety to the great King and his advisers, and the fact that one of Alfred's new mints was established there shows that it was recognised as a valuable trading centre. Henceforward Mercia ceases to be an independent English kingdom, though the great Mercian ealdormanry or earldom had its own witan, and retained a large measure of autonomy under Ethelred, who is sometimes even called rex, and his wife, Alfred's daughter, Ethelflæd, the "Lady of the Mercians."

The further clauses of the treaty between Alfred and Guthrum regulate the relations between the adjacent West-Saxon and Anglo-Danish populations. It is a formal treaty, sworn by King Alfred and the English witan on the one part, and by King Guthrum and the people (theod) in East Anglia 1 on the other, for themselves and for their descendants. It fixes the wergild of a noble, English or Danish, at eight half-marks of gold, probably equalling the twelve hundred shillings of the thegn's wergild in West-Saxon law. The English ceorl is equated with the Danish liesing or freedman; each has a wergild of two hundred shillings. The king's thegn who is charged with a serious offence must clear himself by the oath of twelve king's thegns: a lesser man may purge himself by the oath of eleven of his peers and of one king's thegn. Finally, every man is to "know his warrantor, for men, and horses, and oxen "--to have, that is, some one who will answer for his honesty if he gets into trouble in buying slaves or stock; while in commercial transactions between East Anglia and Wessex, the trader is to give hostages as an earnest of upright dealing.

Criminal law and merchant law, border-feuds and trade, thus form the staple of the first written treaty between Danes and Englishmen. A later ordinance on ecclesiastical and religious matters, which was issued by Edward the Elder, professes to recapitulate the decrees of Alfred and Guthrum, "when English and Danes fully accepted peace and friendship."

The peace of 886 lasted, indeed, for seven years, and when Guthrum-Athelstan died in 890, the Anglo-Saxon Chronicle treated his memory with respect, and recalled the facts that he was Alfred's godson, and the founder of the East-Anglian kingdom. It remained for Ethelwerd to dismiss him to the lower regions, and for William of Malmesbury to dilate on the pride and tyranny of his rule, and to compare him to the Ethiopian, who cannot change his skin.

Alfred was now, for the first time, really at liberty to give himself, with an undivided mind, to the government of his kingdom, and it is likely enough that many of his reforms were carried out in the quiet years when the West-Saxon chronicler found little to record save foreign politics, the deaths of distinguished men, and the English missions to Rome.

The intimate connection between Wessex and the Papal court, broken in the troubled times that followed the death of Ethelwulf, was resumed when, in the winter of 882, the "good Pope Marinus" succeeded the murdered John VIII. He freed the English School in Rome from tribute, at the request of King Alfred, say the contemporary authorities, and sent the West-Saxon King many gifts, and a piece of the cross on which Christ suffered.

Four missions from England to Rome are mentioned in the Anglo-Saxon Chronicle, after the death of Marinus, which occurred about 884. In 887, Æthelm, the ealdorman of Wiltshire, in 888, the ealdorman Beocca, and in 890 the abbot Beornhelm, carried "the alms of the West-Saxons and of King Alfred," to the Eternal City. In 888, Ethelswith, Alfred's sister, may have accompanied the envoys, for her death at Pavia is recorded in that year. In 889 the Chronicle notes that no formal embassy was despatched, but that Alfred sent two couriers, with writings.

It appears, then, that an annual mission to Rome was regarded as normal, but whether the "alms" were looked on as tribute, or as a voluntary offering, cannot be determined, for with the change of scribes after 891, the entries in the Chronicle stop as abruptly as they began. The darkness lifts for a moment, only to fall again with tantalising suddenness on the gleam of undiscovered country thus revealed. When the new scribe begins his work, all other matters are lost in the absorbing interest of the second Danish war.

Still more obscure, but of great interest, is an entry which is found, under the year 883, in most manuscripts of the Anglo-Saxon Chronicle, though it is omitted in the ancient Parker manuscript, and by Asser and Ethelwerd. Sighelm and Æthelstan [it states], took the alms to Rome which King Alfred promised to send thither, and also to St. Thomas in India and to St. Bartholomew, when they besieged the Danish army at London, and there, thanks be to God, they were very successful, according to the promise.

The doubtful authority of this ambiguously worded passage has been commonly taken as a proof that England was in direct relations with India in the time of King Alfred. The annal, however, seems rather to imply that Alfred promised to send alms to India than that he actually sent them, and the whole incident of the vow is suspicious, since there is no evidence for a West- Saxon siege of London before 883. Moreover, the clause about Pope Marinus and the gift of the true cross, which recurs under 885, in connection with the Pope's death, is also inserted here, and the relic is called by its technical Latin name, lignum Domini. The journey from Wessex to Hindustan, too, though not impossible, would be so great an achievement in the ninth century that some further record of it might be expected. Yet Alfred is content, in his translation of Orosius, to follow the account of India in the original text, without comment or expansion, while in his independent explanation, in the Boethius, of the terms "India" and "Thule," he simply treats "the Indias" as the south-eastern limit of the earth, "the outermost of all countries," as a contemporary Anglo-Saxon life of St. Bartholomew calls it, with "dark land" on one side, and on the other side "the sea Oceanus."

William of Malmesbury's twelfth-century version of the story hardly adds to its credibility, for he turns Sighelm, who was probably the Kentish ealdorman of that name, into the tenth-century bishop of Sherborne, and says that he "penetrated into India" and brought back gems which were still to be seen in the church at Sherborne.

But if Alfred's mission to India can only be accepted with reservations, it is not unlikely that he vowed alms to St. Thomas and St. Bartholomew, or that his envoys went on from Rome to Palestine and the East. The legendary association of St. Thomas and St. Bartholomew with India was well-known in the ninth century, and is found in sources which would be easily accessible to Alfred, such as the contemporary Anglo-Saxon Martyrology, Bede's Martyrologium, or Aldhelm's poem on the Twelve Apostles.

" India," as the plural form of the name in Anglo-Saxon shows, was used in a wide sense in the early Middle Ages, and the relics of St. Bartholomew had been translated to Italy in the ninth century3 while the famous shrine of St. Thomas was at Edessa. He suffered, writes the Anglo-Saxon martyrologist, at Calamina, a city (ceastre) in India, and his body was brought away from India, to the town called Edessa, where he is buried in a silver chest, suspended by silver chains.

Asser is probably speaking the truth when he says that he had seen gifts and read letters sent to Alfred by Elias, patriarch of Jerusalem. A begging letter from the Patriarch Elias III., addressed to the rulers of Western Europe, was delivered by messengers to the Emperor Charles the Fat in 881, and a tenth-century book of Leechdoms contains medical prescriptions which Dominus Elias (Domne Helias), patriarch of Jerusalem, ordered to be repeated to King Alfred.

A stream of Christian pilgrims was, indeed, at this time, passing incessantly from West to East. About 865, a Frankish monk, Bernard, even drew up, from his own experience, an itinerary for the use of pilgrims to Jerusalem, and the mingling of adventure with devotion which made the pilgrimage movement so popular in Western Christendom would have a peculiar attraction for Alfred's active and enquiring mind. The last entry in the Alfredian Chronicle before the change of hand in 891 breaks with imaginative extravagance into the monotonous series of sober facts: Three Scots came to King Alfred from Ireland (Hibernia) in a boat without any oars. They had stolen away because they would be on pilgrimage for the love of God, they recked not where. The boat in which they voyaged was wrought of two and a half hides, and they took with them meat for seven nights. And in about seven nights they came to land in Cornwall, and they went straightway to King Alfred. Thus are they named, Dubslane and Macbeth (Maccbethu) and Mælinmun.

They went, adds Ethelwerd, on to Rome, and then to Jerusalem, and one or more of them may have returned, with news of far countries, to the hospitable West-Saxon court which had speeded them on their way.

The peace of England in these years formed a striking contrast to the confusion and distress on the Continent, where, after the sudden death of the young West Frankish King Carloman, Charles the Fat, grandson of Louis the Pious, had once more gathered the divided kingdoms into a semblance of union, a parody of the mighty Empire of Charles the Great. He ruled, writes the English chronicler, over all the land which his great-grandfather, the old Charles (Charlemagne) held, except the country of the Bretons. He was, the scribe continues, the nephew of Charles the Bald, whose daughter Judith married King Ethelwulf, a recurrent note in the English sources, which shows that the connection with Judith of Flanders was not forgotten.

Signs of disintegration appeared at once in the newly consolidated Empire. The Old-Saxons and Frisians won a great victory in 884 over the vikings from Duisburg, but the advantage thus gained in the north was more than counterbalanced in the west when Sigfred's fleet sailed up the Seine, entered Rouen, compelled the fort at Pontoise to surrender, and in November, 885, began the famous siege of Paris, which lasted till October, 886.

The events of those eleven months stirred the whole of Western Europe. Paris, which flourished like the Paradise of God, shining like a queen among lesser cities, now saw from her island citadel the viking ships lying in the Seine, covering, says Abbo of St. Germain, the poet of the siege, more than two leagues of the stream. In the long struggle which followed, the city was splendidly defended by its heroic Bishop Gozlin, and by Odo, Count of Paris, the ancestor of the Capetian kings of France. Both sides showed themselves masters of the art of war, and the offensive operations of the Northmen, supported by siege-engines and mines, were at least as scientific as the Frankish defence.

When at last the incompetent Emperor Charles the Fat came to the relief of the beleaguered garrison, he sealed his own doom by concluding a disgraceful treaty with the invaders, and paying a heavy tribute of seven hundred pounds of silver. The vikings, permitted by this treaty to winter in Burgundy, only changed the scene of their depredations. They besieged Sens, and in the spring of 887 they again appeared in the Seine, and sailed up the Marne to Chézy; here, and in a camp near the river Yonne, they spent the two following winters.

"The army (here)," writes the well-informed English chronicler under the year 887, "went up through the bridge at Paris, and then up along the Seine, to the Marne, to Carici (Chézy), and sat there and within Yonne, two winters in the two places." With a perhaps unconscious feeling for cause and effect, he goes on to describe the deposition of Charles the Fat, in November, 8871:

Then was the Empire divided into five, and five kings were hallowed, Arnulf, who dwelt in the land east of the Rhine, and Rudolf, who took the middle kingdom (Burgundy), and Odo, who had the western part (the kingdom of the West Franks), and Berengar and Witha (Guido of Spoleto), the land of the Lombards, and the lands on that side of the mountains.

To be strong to withstand the "heathen men" was the essential condition of acceptance for the rulers of Western Christendom in the ninth century. Here the Carolingians had failed, and they were ruthlessly supplanted by the men who knew how to meet the popular need. But the flood which submerged the house of Charlemagne bore the house of Egbert on to fortune. There is no "Song of Alfred" to set against the Ludwigslied, yet the ephemeral triumph of Saucourt is far less deserving of such a tribute than the great deliverance of Ethandun, and the winning back of London.

NOTE ON THE SITE OF THE BATTLE OF ETHANDUN

For this site Yattenden and Yatton may be rejected without question, as impossible derivations from the West-Saxon Ethandun. Domesday Book shows that the Berkshire Eddington comes through Eddevetone from Eadgife-tun, "Eadgifu's town," and the Somerset Edington from Edwinetune, "Edwin's town." Heddington is written Edintone in Domesday Book, but in other early documents it has an aspirate, and seems to represent "Hedding's town." The Wiltshire Edington alone consistently appears as Edendone, a Norman form of Ethandune, in Domesday Book, and as Ethendun in the thirteenth century. It was granted to Romsey Abbey by King Edgar in the tenth century, and is probably the royal manor or "ham" which Alfred bequeathed to his wife. This philological evidence for the identity of Ethandune and Edington in Wiltshire is the more valuable since the military arguments, though pointing on the whole to a like conclusion, are not altogether convincing.

The theory2 that Ethandun is the Berkshire Eddington, near Hungerford, and that Iglea is in the Berkshire hundred called Eglei in Domesday Book, has very little to recommend it. This Eddington could only be reached in two days from the borders of Somerset by long forced marches, and Berkshire, which had borne the brunt of the campaign of 871, stood rather noticeably aloof from the struggle of 878.

Heddington in Wiltshire is a more plausible suggestion. Taking Brixton Deverill near Warminster as Ecgbryhtesslane, Iglea is identified with Highleigh Common near Melksham, and the site of the battle is placed on the Roman road from Marlborough to Bath, on the Downs, opposite Chippenham. The chief objections to this theory are the distance of Heddington from Somerset, and the implied presence of the Danish army as far north as Chippenham. It is true that, as subsequent events show. Chippenham continued to be used as a base-camp by Guthrum until he withdrew to Cirencester. But it is equally clear that Alfred's base was at Athelney, and since there had been skirmishes between West- Saxons and Danes in the spring of 878, it is improbable that in May the main Danish force was stationed some fifty miles from the Somerset fenland. This difficulty would be avoided by accepting the location of Ethandun at Edington on the Polden Hills, but this leaves no obvious site for Iglea, and involves a backward movement on the part of Alfred, after he had met the shire-forces at Ecgbryhtesstane, and a long and strenuous two days' march, through Selwood Forest to Butleigh or to Edgarley, which is supposed to be Iglea, at the foot of Glastonbury Tor, and so up the northern side of the Polden Hills, and along the ridge to a point above Edington. This theory also carries with it the assumption that the fort to which the defeated Danes fled after the battle was either Bridgewater or the Downend earthworks on the Poldens.

If, on the other hand, Camden's old identification of the battlefield of Ethandun with Edington in Wiltshire be accepted, it gives a site roughly half-way between Chippenham and the meeting-place of the West-Saxon army on the Somerset border, situated on the royal demesne, and suited by the conformation of the ground to the Danish tactics, recalling, indeed, somewhat remarkably, the conditions at Ashdown.

The early antiquaries may have been influenced in their choice of this site for Alfred's victory by the fact that the face of the chalk down, below Bratton Castle, about a mile from Edington, bears the figure of a white horse, modernised now out of all primitive semblance, but apparently akin to the white horse of the Berkshire Ashdown, and popularly connected with the defeat of the Danes.

THE VICTORIES OF PEACE

I. The Alfredian State

ALFRED had saved England for the English. A harder but more congenial task now lay before him: the administration of the land which he had won. As far as can be gathered from the scanty contemporary records, the country had been thoroughly demoralised by the Danish wars. The monasteries and churches were, in the King's own words, "all harried and burnt"; the land was wasted and impoverished; the coming generation was growing up in ignorance and lawlessness. The army, too, lacked organisation, the Church needed endowment, the law required re-enactment.

That Alfred set himself to solve these various problems in a practical and statesmanlike spirit, that he had a definite and well-considered policy, may be inferred from the whole tenor of his later life and from the avowed aims which appear in his writings. His conception of the State and of the meaning of public obligation was not original. His standards were those of his age. His political philosophy came to him from the Fathers, as explained by the theorists of his own time. His one great merit, for which he is worthy to be held in remembrance, was that he stood forth, first as the defender of his people, and then as the interpreter to them of the mysteries of the House of Life. It was not books alone that he translated into the language which all could understand, but ideals and theories of conduct.

In unaffected simplicity and sincerity he strove to be a perfect king, as the ninth century understood the virtues of kingship. Alfred's oftenquoted words in his translation of Boethius on the Consolation of Philosophy will bear repetition.

I desired tools and materials [he said, expanding the original text] to carry on the work which I was set to do, which was that I should virtuously and fittingly steer and direct (steoran and reccan) the authority committed unto me . . . it has ever been my will to live worthily while I lived, and after my death to leave to them that should come after me my memory in good works.

In his choice of the phrase "steer and direct" to describe the work of administration, the King may have remembered a passage in his earlier translation of Gregory's Pastoral Care which pictures rule and authority as a storm of the mind, tossing the ship of the heart on the waves of thought, driving it hither and thither in narrow straits of words and works, and well-nigh wrecking it on great rocks from which the skill of the steersman alone can save it. In another passage in the Consolation, Philosophy speaks of God as "a steadfast Ruler and Steersman, and Rudder and Helm," who directs and rules all creatures as a good steersman guides a ship2; Asser, too, compares Alfred to a good steersman, guiding the treasure-ship of the State to the quiet haven, in spite of a wearied crew, and the stormy seas of life.

The favourite mediæval image of the "ship of state" or the "ark of the Church," riding on the troublesome waves of this world, would come home with a special force to the sea-loving West-Saxon King, who accepted the guidance of his people as a divinely appointed responsibility, and regarded his royal authority as a trust to be used for the benefit of humanity. Here, again, Alfred was but echoing the current teaching of Christian political philosophers, as they, in turn, handed on a more ancient tradition.

The connection of the Latin substantive rex, a king, with the verb regere, to rule, and its forms rexi, rectus, and with the adjective rectus, right, or straight, had, doubtless, helped to give rise to the idea that the true king is the righteous ruler, which is one of the commonplaces of mediæval political thought. The poet Horace, writing before the birth of Christ, tells how boys in their play would repeat the proverb: Rex eris . . . si recte facies (Thou shalt be king, if thou do right), a saying which somewhat loses its point in Pope's eighteenth-century English version:

Yet ev'ry child another song will sing: Virtue, brave boys! 'tis Virtue makes a King.

Christianised and elaborated by St. Augustine and St. Gregory, this theory of kingship became familiar to mediæval students through its inclusion in those most popular seventh-century books, the Origins or Etymologies and the Sentences of St. Isidore of Seville. Kings, Isidore explains, are so called because they rule, (reges a regendo vocati), but he does not rule who fails to correct (non regit qui non corrigit). The king who does right keeps his name, the evil king loses it. The chief virtues of a king are justice and "piety" or "pity," (pietas), but of these two "piety" is especially praiseworthy, for justice by itself is severity. From the Etymologies and Sentences Isidore's definitions passed to the political theorists of the eighth and ninth centuries, Alcuin, the friend of Charles the Great, Hrabanus Maurus, the author of a comprehensive work on the Universe, Jonas of Orleans, Sedulius Scotus, and Hincmar of Rheims, all of whom wrote treatises on government, "Mirrors of Princes," for the young rulers of the Carolingian house. These books were new when Alfred became King. Hincmar, Archbishop of Rheims, a man who was the oracle of his time, only died in 882, and the child Alfred must have seen him in Paris in 856 when he married Ethelwulf of Wessex to Judith, the daughter of Charles the Bald.

Imperial Capitularies and the canons of Church Councils and synods repeated the political teaching of these learned and powerful ecclesiastics, for whom Church and State were indissolubly connected, and the king or Emperor was the Vicar of God, ruling by divine sanction. They looked back to the Western Fathers, especially to St. Isidore, St. Gregory, and St. Augustine, and behind them, again, to St. Peter and St. Paul, and the writers of the Old Testament. The theory of kingship thus evolved was high and austere. God's Vicar must govern justly; he must rule himself if he would rule others; he must give peace to his people, protect the weak, comfort the poor, and be a terror to evil-doers. Eight columns, says Sedulius Scotus, support the power of a just king-- truth, patience, munificence, eloquence, correction of the wicked, encouragement of the good, light taxation, equitable justice for rich and poor.

The influence of this reasoned theory of monarchy was strong upon Alfred, but mingled with it was another conception, borrowed from early Germanic tradition, the conception of the king, the cyning, a word which suggests origin rather than function, and recalls the political significance of the kindred group in the days when kingship was more patriarchal than official, an inherited authority and dignity, based on nobility of birth, and deriving its title from divine descent.

The Germanic cyning was the lord of his people, the hlaford, or loaf-giver, the theoden, head of the theod or folk, the drihten, a term afterwards restricted to God, the Lord of all. Hence he was in close personal relation with his subjects, their tribal chieftain, their natural leader and protector, as they were his natural followers and supporters.

Both elements entered into Alfred's view of the royal power and responsibilities. If he translated rex by cyning, he enriched the Germanic term with deeper meaning drawn from Roman, Judaic, and Christian sources. He felt that authority had been entrusted to him by God, and that he had been set to do a special work in the world. He recognised, as Cicero had recognised before him, that the unrighteous ruler was like a wild beast, "recking no more of friend or foe than a mad dog." He saw the vanity of external pomp and show, and knew that the bad king, when stripped of the trappings and power of royalty, was much like one of the thegns who served him, if, indeed, he were not "still more base." "Every one knows," he wrote, "that all men come of one father and one mother. . . . True nobility is of the mind, not of the flesh."

Yet echoes from older creeds mingled with these philosophic and Christian utterances. Though Alfred could call the Greeks a "foolish folk" for believing that Jove was the highest god, because he was of the royal kin, and in those days they knew no other god, but worshipped their kings for gods, he does not seem to have questioned his own descent from the heroes and gods of his race, for the West-Saxon royal genealogy which traces his ancestry to Woden and "Geat" is not only found in the Parker manuscript of the Chronicle, but is copied by Asser, while the regnal table which gives his descent from Cerdic is appended both to the Chronicle and to the English translation of Bede's history.

The preface to Alfred's Laws illustrates the continuity of tribal custom and the force of the traditional reverence for antiquity:

I dared not set down much of my own in writing, for it was not known to me which would please those who should come after us. . . . I then, Alfred, King of the West-Saxons, showed these (laws) to all my wise men (witan), and they then said that it pleased them all to hold them.

Even the outward signs of royalty which Alfred scorned as philosopher, he assumed without hesitation as king--the crown or "head-ring," the lofty throne, the glittering robes of state, the bodyguard of thegns, in their war-equipment, with "belts and golden-hilted swords," the hoarded treasure of gold and gems, the spacious hall, the rough plenty and primitive splendour of the homely West-Saxon court. Much of the secret of his strength lay, indeed, in this quiet acceptance and idealisation of the actual, the calm good sense and sanity of judgment which prevented him from attempting impossibilities, the faith and sympathetic imagination which widened for him the bounds of the possible.

Closely related to the mediæval theory of kingship was the corresponding theory of the meaning and sanction of law. Here, again, there was a conflict of principles, the Roman imperial conception of law as the voice of a sovereign authority, the Hebraic belief in the revealed will of a divine Lawgiver, the Germanic reverence for traditional custom. Here, too, mediæval political philosophers of Germanic race, Roman training, and Christian creed were groping after a system which should unify and consolidate these heterogeneous materials, and bring pagan custom into a vital relation with the law of the Christian God.

In England, the direct influence of Roman law was slight, but in the seventh century, after the adoption of Christianity, some part of the ancient custom-law of Kent was apparently written down in Roman fashion, though in the vulgar tongue, by the clerks who came over with St. Augustine. What King Ethelbert and his advisers thus did for Kent, King Ine, Alfred's reputed ancestor, did for Wessex, and when Alfred in turn set himself to the task of stating and interpreting the law of his kingdom, there were already precedents for him to follow, in the written "dooms" (domas) of his predecessors,--themselves but a small portion of the still unwritten custom,--in the canons of the Church, the "dooms" of ecclesiastical synods, and, above all, in the Scriptures, the books of the Hebrew law, and of its fulfilment in the law of Christ.

There is a striking passage in the Consolation of Boethius, in which, when Alfred translated it, he may have seen the reflection of his own thoughts of God and the law. God, says Philosophy or "Wisdom," is Himself "king and lord and wellspring and beginning and law and wisdom and righteous judge." In the English version the Latin lex is rendered by æ (law)2 and the Latin arbiter by dema (judge), the "deemster" or declarer of "dooms," and in his "Code" of law the King wrote of the "dooms" of Moses, and of Christ's, æ even as Ine had set down æ or law and "kingly dooms" (cynedomas).

Alfred, then, clearly thought of law, æ as the principle of good, the will of God, which was essential righteousness. If instinct and early habit made him revere the custom-law as a sacred impersonal deposit from the inherited wisdom of the past, he would derive from his study of the Bible the idea of a personal lawgiver, a human instrument, by whom the knowledge of God's will might be conveyed to man. Such a lawgiver was Moses; such in his degree was Ine of Wessex; such would Alfred himself be--the interpreter of eternal truth and justice to his generation.

This attitude towards abstract law and its concrete expression goes far to explain the significance of Alfred's own "dooms," which have come down to us in a tenth-century manuscript, in intimate connection with the "dooms" of Ine, and with an original West-Saxon version of the Ten Commandments, and of other Biblical passages.

If from one point of view Alfred's dooms may be classed with his literary works, from another they belong to the administrative history of his reign. They are, indeed, closely bound up with his whole theory of government, and with the educational policy which is involved in it. They are no mere enunciation of tribal custom, but a compilation from many sources, selected with system and method. A great body of unwritten custom-law still lay behind them. They no more covered the whole field of political and social life than the King's translations from the Latin covered the whole field of knowledge, but, like those translations, they were inspired by a conscious purpose, and, like them, too, they gave the people, in the tongue that they could understand, the things that were most "needful" for them to know. More fully even than the Frankish capitularies to which they have been compared they fall into line with an ordered scheme of administration, and seek to bind together the scattered threads of Kentish, Mercian, and West-Saxon law, to add, reject, amend, and harmonise, and to reconcile Germanic tradition with the law of the God of the Hebrew and the Christian.

The short personal introduction with which Alfred makes the transition from the biblical and historical sections of his Code to the English laws shows the King in his literary workshop, with his scribes about him, collecting materials, judging, selecting, dictating, organising, or in consultation with his witan, deciding how best to enforce and "hold" the venerable customs of his forefathers.

I then, Alfred king [he writes] gathered these (old "dooms") together, and bade that they should be written down, many of those which our forerunners held, those which pleased me, and many of those which pleased me not I rejected, with the counsel of my witan, and bade that they should be held in another fashion. For I dared not be so bold as to set down much of my own in writing, for it was not known to me which of these would please those who should come after us. But of those which I found either from the days of Ine my kinsman, or Offa the Mercian king, or Ethelbert, who first of the English people received baptism, I gathered together here such as seemed to me the most worthy, and the others I rejected. I then, Alfred, king of the West-Saxons, showed these to all my witan, and they then said that it pleased them all to hold them.

The Code opens with the Ten Commandments, the words which the Lord spake to Moses, followed by extracts from the Mosaic law, as contained in the book of Exodus, and from the gentler, more humane teaching of Christ, who came not to destroy the law, but to fulfil it. This introductory portion ends with the Christian golden rule in a negative form: "What ye will not that other men should do unto you, that do ye not unto other men." "From this one doom," comments Alfred, "a man may bethink him how he should judge every one rightly: he needs no other doombook." Yet he did not ignore the "other doombooks" to which he had access, "synod-books," or the collections of canons and ecclesiastical laws which "the holy bishops and other noteworthy witan of the English" had issued after the conversion of the land to Christianity, and the dooms which remained from the days of his Christian predecessors, Ine of Wessex, Offa of Mercia, and Ethelbert of Kent. Behind the first Christian King he did not go, for with him began the era of written custom-law.

Alfred's Code may thus be divided into four main parts:--an ethical and historical introduction, derived from the Bible and from the history of the

Church; his personal introduction, or preface; his own collection of dooms, including a table of wergilds; and the dooms of Ine, distinguishable as a separate document by the opening clause: "I, Ine, by God's gift king of the West-Saxons . . . took counsel concerning the salvation of our souls and the state of our kingdom."

Though Alfred's legal work was sufficiently important to become the foundation of later compilations, and to be referred to as "the doombook," an acknowledged authority, the arrangement of his Code suggests rather a juridical treatise than a manual of practical law. Beginning with the divine sanction of all law, as he understood it, he was specially concerned to show how Christian mercy had softened and humanised the stern justice of the Mosaic dispensation. Finding the death penalty in the Jewish law, where Germanic law only demanded a money fine, he assumed, quite unhistorically, that the change was due to the influence of Christianity. The bishops and witan, runs the historical preface,

set down for the sake of the mercy, the "mild heartedness," which Christ taught, for most misdeeds, that by their leave secular lords might without sin take a money fine (bot) for the first offence . . . they set down then in many synods the fines (bote) for many human misdeeds, and wrote them in many synodbooks, here one "doom," there another.

Thus Alfred linked his own dooms, with their money fines, to the penal enactments of the book of Exodus on the one hand, and to the older law of the West-Saxon kingdom on the other. It is even possible that he translated, or caused to be translated, the Ten Commandments and the passages from the Bible which precede his dooms, with the deliberate intention of teaching his illiterate secular ministers, as he translated the Pastoral Care for the instruction of his ignorant clergy.

Asser[1] paints a somewhat highly coloured picture of the King, insisting on his officials--ealdormen, reeves, and thegns (comites, praepositi, ac ministri)--fitting themselves by education for their judicial duties, and describes how those who were too old or slow-witted to learn to read for themselves would get younger men to read "Saxon books" aloud to them.

Dr. Liebermann has suggested[2] that these "Saxon books" were the dooms of Alfred and Ine, and though this is, of course, only a guess, it is worth noting that Ine's preface expressly states that his object is to establish "right law," and to prevent its perversion by his "ealdormen and subjects." The underlying motives which actuated the drawing up of Alfred's Code may throw light on its peculiar arrangement. The doombooks of the three lawgivers, Moses, Alfred, and Ine, are juxtaposed, not amalgamated, and they do not follow each other in chronological order, for Alfred's own dooms are placed between the archaic law of the Jews and the archaic law of the West-Saxons.

Of the dooms of the days of Offa and Ethelbert, which Alfred mentions in his preface, there is no clear trace in his code, though the table of wergilds for injuries to various parts of the body evidently corresponds to the similar table in the Laws of Ethelbert, if with many changes and modifications, due to the different tariffs in use in Kent and in Wessex. Kentish and Mercian elements may also have been taken up into the Code from the canons of church synods, such as the famous Legatine Council of 787, where, in the presence of King Offa and his witan, the decrees were read both in Latin and in the vulgar tongue. The text of Alfred's dooms need not, however, be forced into conformity with the preface at every point, nor is there any reason to suppose, with Sir Francis Palgrave, that a separate code was issued for Mercia, with Offa's Laws appended, in the place occupied by the Laws of Ine in "the statute for the West-Saxons."

The West-Saxon code, as it stands, is, no doubt, both self-contradictory and redundant. It would be impossible to work it as a whole, for not only is much of the Mosaic portion inapplicable to ninthcentury Wessex, but Ine's dooms conflict in several instances with the parallel sections of the dooms of Alfred, while both collections present a strange medley of ecclesiastical decrees, public and private law, and rural custom, in which the only unity is a unity of principle.

Still, in spite of inconsistency and obscurity, Alfred's vernacular dooms, with their core of ancient custom, form a unique and invaluable record of early English law. Curt, elliptical, disjointed, their very heterogeneity is characteristic. They show a State in the making, inchoate still, and weak, but reaching out towards centralisation, and finding it, to a certain extent, in the person of the King. They show, moreover, the King gathering up the broken fragments of the older tribal society, and fitting them into some sort of coherent whole.

Strong as was the force of custom, Alfred at least was able to rearrange the custom-law, to decide in what way one or another part of it should be observed, and to frame new rules to meet new cases. If he did not dare to set down much of his own in writing, it was no small matter that he dared to innovate at all, for it meant that the king was powerful enough to be a constructive statesmen.

To speak of "statesmanship" in the ninth century may, indeed, seem absurd. It would be futile to attempt to separate legislation from administration, or to distinguish the different "organs of government" in the rudimentary West- Saxon kingdom. But those organs existed already in germ, and much depended on the way in which they were developed. In Alfred's reign the lines were laid down on which development should proceed, and in the work of political organisation the King took the leading part. To Alfred himself, government seemed a very personal thing. To rule men well was to him, as to St. Gregory the Great, the "art of arts," the "craft of crafts." Nowhere has he revealed himself more fully than in his additions to the reflections of Boethius on earthly possessions and authority.

The sixth-century philosopher spoke of authority as to be desired only as a means of developing natural talents for government, which otherwise would perish without fulfilling their proper function. Alfred's mind seized on this suggestive thought of the natural ruler, played round it, expanded it, probably with the help of the current commentaries on the text of the Consolation, and adapted it to the conditions of Christian kingship.

No man [he wrote] can prove his full powers, his "craft," nor "direct and steer" authority, without tools and materials. . . . These are a king's materials and the tools with which he governs:--he must have a well-peopled land; he must have men of prayer (gebedmen), "bedesmen," and men of war (fyrdmen), and men of work (weorcmen) . . . without these tools no king can prove his full powers (crœft). For his materials, also, he must have sustenance for the three orders, his tools . . . land to dwell in, and gifts, and weapons, and meat, and ale, and clothes, and whatever else the three orders need. Without these he cannot keep the tools, and without these tools he cannot do any of those things which he has been bidden to do.

Here is a clear recognition of the art of government as the essential function of the true king, and a distinct conception of the king as a craftsman, carrying out the commands of a Divine Master by means of human tools. The idea of the three orders of men, the oratores, bellatores, and laboratores, was, in itself, not new. It went back, perhaps, to the Guardians, Warriors, and Husbandmen of Plato's Republic, as it went forward to the doctrine of the Three Estates of the Realm. But, even if Alfred derived it from a commentary, or from one of his learned clerks, his use of it was quite original, and he made it his own by translating it into terms of his everyday life, and finding in it an expression of his administrative difficulties and problems.

Wessex, in the last quarter of the ninth century, was still a tribal State, Germanic in spirit and institutions, full of crude barbaric survivals from the days of heathenism, but Christianised, and, in some degree, centralised, by the efforts of a long succession of churchmen and kings. The machinery of administration had already been elaborated, the links between central and local government had been forged, when the rude shock of the Danish wars came to expose the latent defects of the system, and to hasten the slow process of social disintegration which often accompanies a period of political transition. The legal myth which makes King Alfred the founder of the English constitution originally sprang from a dim perception of the truth that England owes her peculiar form of government in large measure to the two facts that in the ninth century Wessex was nearly conquered by a foreign power, and that it was saved by the representative of the line of Cerdic.

As the deliverer from the Danish peril, the West-Saxon King won a position of unquestioned supremacy over the shattered remnants of rival royal houses, while the destruction of ancient landmarks by the vikings obliterated local traditions, and left him free to experiment in new directions. The ties of blood and race, on the other hand, tempered his reforming zeal with reverence for the past, and made him content to build on the old foundations.

The emphasis laid by Alfred on the individual responsibility of the king was, doubtless, due rather to his sense of the weakness of his "tools," the three orders, than to any personal ambition, but his absolute power was none the less real for being unsought.

It is interesting to compare the preface to his "dooms" with the earlier prologue to the "dooms" of Ine. Whereas Ine only legislates with the advice and teaching of his father, the sub-king Cenred, and of the bishops, ealdormen, and distinguished witan and clergy, Alfred does all the preliminary work himself, makes his own selection from the "synod-books," and has his own opinion as to what is best for his purpose. He apparently consulted his witan chiefly about the advisability of excluding certain "dooms" from the written collection, and decreeing that they should be "held in another fashion." When his "Code" was drawn up, indeed, he submitted it to the approval of the magnates, and received their assent to its provisions, and he was chary of introducing novelties which might be displeasing to those who came after him, but if he respected his witan he evidently managed them, and in the whole transaction there is no hint of popular co-operation.

The government of the West-Saxon State at this time seems, in fact, to have centred in the court and household of the king, the little knot of confidential officials, widening sometimes into the larger group of the witan, who formed the ruling class of the country, from whose ranks the public servants were drawn. "King's ealdormen" and "king's thegns," "king's reeves," and "king's clerks," gathered about their royal lord and master in the "king's hall" of Anglo-Saxon documents, the "court" or curtus regius of Asser's biography, the "palace" or palatium of contemporary Latin charters. From the king's hall they went forth to act as presidents of the local courts of justice, captains of the local military forces, or collectors of local dues, always, if Asser may be believed, under the strict personal supervision of the king himself.

Some of them, perhaps, would be ministers of the household in the narrower sense, the king's marshal or "horse thegn," his seneschal or "dish thegn," his butler or pincerna, his chamberlain or "rail thegn."The Chronicle mentions the death of "Ecgulf the king's horse thegn" in 897, and Alfred's grandfather Oslac had been butler or pincerna at the court of Ethelwulf, but only faint traces of these offices appear in the reign of Alfred, nor did he claim any new or extraordinary privileges for the monarchy. If he issued decrees in the first person, and spoke of "my witan," he was only following the example of Ine.

Like his predecessors, too, he usually styled himself "king of the West-Saxons" (rex Occidentalium Saxonum) or "king of the Saxons" (rex Saxonum). In his literary works, and in the opening sentences of the personal preface to his dooms and of his will he calls himself simply "king Alfred" (Ælfred cyning); in the concluding passage of the preface to the laws and in the body of his will he is "king of the West-Saxons" (Westseaxna cyning), and though there are indications that after 886, when he acquired London, he used the title of "king of the Anglo-Saxons" (Anglorum Saxonum rex, Angul-Saxonum rex), the evidence for this is slight, and somewhat untrustworthy. Unlike his father and brothers in their Kentish charters, he never describes himself as "king of the West-Saxons and of the men of Kent" (Cantuariorum), but this may be because only one of his extant grants relates to lands in Kent, for in a private Kentish land-grant which he confirms, he is so styled.

In Alfred's laws, again, the fine for breaking into the king's burh, or fortified house, was, as in the days of Ine, a hundred and twenty shillings, the fine for infringing the royal protection, or borh, an offence not mentioned in the laws of Ine, was five pounds of fine silver. Fighting in the king's hall was still, as in the seventh century, a capital crime, which left the life and property of the offender at the mercy of the king. High treason, too, plotting against the king's life, or harbouring outlaws, was accounted by Alfred a capital offence, the one crime, as he says in the preface to his laws, to which Christian judges dared not show mercy, the Judas crime of betrayal of the lord. Yet even here, the same penalty is assigned to treason against lords of lower rank; the horror with which the deed is regarded is chiefly due to the conception of the sacredness of the personal tie between lord and vassal, though it is probably also influenced by the decrees of church synods, and the ecclesiastical reverence for "the Lord's Anointed."

If Alfred, moreover, formed his own judgments independently, the records of the meetings of the West-Saxon witan during his reign are sufficiently numerous to warrant the inference that they were habitually consulted by the King in matters of moment. They approve his laws, they advise him about his father's will. They witness his early arrangements with his brother concerning his inheritance, and his own later will. They attest the royal charters and share in the conclusion of the sworn treaty of peace with Guthrum and the East-Anglians in 886. The Mercian council, also, was practically independent under the powerful ealdorman Ethelred, while there is some evidence in the signatures to charters of the persistence of a separate council for Kent.

Alfred, then, reformed through restoration. He revived the ancient institutions, and gave them new life and meaning. If he made the royal power a reality in England, and established the tradition of a strong personal monarchy, this was due to his own active and competent intervention in the work of administration, rather than to any deliberate centralising policy. But in an age when the maintenance of public order was the one crying need of the State, strength was the first quality demanded of the government, and it was because the West-Saxon kingship of the ninth century possessed this quality, that it was able, like the Tudor despotism in the sixteenth century, to tide the country over a difficult period of transitionsition sition, to retain as well as to reject, to preserve the more sound and wholesome elements of the older society, and to give them an opportunity of tranquil development.

Alfred's "Code," holding within it the earlier "dooms" of Ine, and expanding them with provisions designed to meet present emergencies, is typical of the way in which the customs of Wessex were handed down from generation to generation, and historical continuity was secured.

Next to the king in social and political importance stood the great lay nobles, the ealdormen and king's thegns, and the ecclesiastical dignitaries. The ealdorman, though as a rule nobly born, was essentially a royal official, the head of a shire, the president of the shire-court, the leader of the shire forces. The usual Latin equivalents of ealdorman in the signatures to charters are dux, comes, and, occasionally, princeps.

Asser translates the ealdorman of the Anglo- Saxon Chronicle by dux, comes, or consul, while Alfred in his literary works uses ealdorman somewhat generally to render the Latin dux, princeps, rector, satrap, subregulus, or other terms denoting authority. If Moses, the leader and lawgiver of the people of Israel, refuses ealdordom or sovereignty in the Pastoral Care, in the Consolation the two sons of Boethius, who were senators and magistrates, are described as ealdormen and getheahteras, or councillors, the precise terms applied to the witan in their capacity of royal advisers. In the Orosius the military side of the office is emphasised, and the ealdorman Arpelles, or Harpalus, leads the Median fyrd against the Persians. In the English version of Bede, patricius is translated "high ealdorman," and the judge (judex) who tries the British martyr St. Alban is the dema or "doomsman," and ealdorman. The Alfredian Chronicle even describes Cerdic and Cynric, the founders of the royal house of Wessex, as "two ealdormen."

The West-Saxon ealdorman seems to have been appointed by the king, possibly with the sanction of the witan. The office was, apparently, not hereditary, but was held for life, or during good behaviour. It involved heavy responsibilities and duties, balanced by considerable privileges. The ealdorman may have been endowed with official estates. He probably received a proportionate share of the profits of justice. By Alfred's laws, if his fortified house or burh were broken into, he was entitled to the same compensation as a bishop, a fine of sixty shillings, as against the thirty shillings of the ordinary thegn, the ninety shillings of the archbishop, and the hundred and twenty shillings of the king.

A special fine of a hundred and twenty shillings was paid for fighting before the "king's ealdorman" in the "moot," or court of justice, and he had also a right to a fine of a hundred and twenty shillings if the "folk-moot" were disturbed by the drawing of weapons. The infringement of his peace, protection, or borh, was valued at two pounds, where the archbishop took three pounds, and the king five pounds. With this high position went corresponding obligations. The Chronicle shows the ealdorman fighting against the Danes at the head of his local troops, and giving, if needful, his life for his country, like Ethelwulf of Berkshire, who fell at Englefield.

In Alfred's laws, again, the ealdorman is seen presiding in the "folk-moot," where he was assisted by a subordinate, "the king's ealdorman's junior." It was his place to authorise the transference of a dependent to a new lord, in another district (boldgetœl), and it was to him that the man applied who was too weak to beleaguer his foe for seven nights before proceeding to active vengeance, in accordance with the new restrictions on private feuds laid down in the laws of Alfred.

"Let him ride to the ealdorman," runs the doom, "and ask him for help. If he will not help him, let him ride to the king, before he fights."

Captains, justices, policemen, and members of the great council of the realm, the ealdormen thus bound together central and local government in the days of Alfred, as in the days of his father. Yet they were never a very numerous body. Eight is the highest number of duces signing a royal West-Saxon charter in Alfred's reign, and more often there are only three or four.

The names of ealdormen, comites, or duces which occur in the ninth century, so far as they can be assigned to localities at all, are connected with Dorset, Somerset and Devonshire, Hampshire, Wiltshire and Berkshire, Surrey, Kent (where the ealdorman's office was probably an innovation), Essex, and Mercia. It appears fairly certain that each of the West-Saxon shires was normally under the rule of one ealdorman, while Kent was perhaps divided into two ealdormanries, and in Mercia there seem to have been from three to five ealdormen under the great prince Ethelred, subregulus and patricius, Alfred's son-in-law.

Alfred's ealdormen, at least in the earlier years of his reign, have no special personal distinction. Of the names which have survived, only three stand out with any marked individuality--Ethelred the "Lord of Mercia"; Ethelnoth of Somerset, according to Ethelwerd the companion of the King in his Athelney exile, the signatory of charters in 880 and 894, and one of the leaders in the campaign of 894; Æthelhelm or Æthelm of Wiltshire, his comrade in arms in 894, the bearer of Alfred's alms to Rome in 887, whose death the Chronicle records in 898.

In Alfred's will he bequeaths a hundred mancuses "to each of my ealdormen," and a like sum to " Æthelm and Æthelwold and Osferth," his two nephews and his kinsman, to whom he also left grants of land, while "Ethelred ealdorman" has a special bequest of a sword worth a hundred mancuses. It may be that Æthelhelm, the Wiltshire ealdorman, and Alfred's nephew were one and the same, and the names of Æthelwold or Æthelwald and Osferth also appear among the duces who witness land-grants in the late ninth century, and at the beginning of the tenth century. Hence it is quite possible that there were royal nobles holding official positions in Wessex in Alfred's reign, and that members of the royal house signed charters sometimes as filius regis or frater regis, and sometimes as dux or ealdorman. Alfred himself, it must be remembered, was the son-in-law of the comes Ethelred "Mucill," and the brother-in-law of the ealdorman Athulf or Ethelwulf, who is, possibly, identical with the dux Ethelwulf, who signs Mercian charters.

Beside the ealdorman, his colleague, and perhaps to some extent his subordinate, worked another official, the "king's reeve" (gerefa), or steward, the administrator of the royal estates. In his public capacity, he was particularly concerned with matters affecting trade and commerce. Merchants had to bring before him in the folkmoot the men who were to accompany them in their journeys through the country, for whose good behaviour they were responsible. Thus when the legendary "three ships" of the Vikings came to the Dorset coast, the reeve rode down to meet the strangers, and wanted to "drive them to the king's town," the royal "vill," which was his special sphere of action. The king's reeve appears further, to have exercised judicial functions of a more general character. He could receive accusations in the "moot," and it has been suggested that he may have presided over a smaller and less formal court than the shire-moot, answering to the hundred-moot of later days.

Asser speaks of the "ealdormen and reeves" (comites et praepositi) who gave judgment in their courts, or meetings, with an appeal to the king. The king's reeve, indeed, whether in his judicial capacity he acted independently, or merely as the ealdorman's assistant or substitute in the shirecourt, was primarily a royal servant, and the manager of the Crown lands, the king's agent, tax-collector, and bailiff. In some cases his functions seem to have been specialised. In the annal for 897 the Chronicle, in a list of noteworthy men who had recently died, mentions Beornulf the wicgerefa2 or "town-reeve" of Winchester, and Wulfric the king's horse-thegn, who was also Wealhgefera, or Wealhgerefa, the "Welsh companion," or "Welsh reeve," who may possibly have been the superior of the "king's horswealh" of Ine's laws, who rode on the king's errands, and, in virtue of this service, had a wergild of two hundred shillings.

The guides (ductores) who escorted Asser through Sussex on his first visit to King Alfred were also probably "riding men" and minor local officials, while the "king's geneat" Æthelferth, who, with the king's reeve Lucumon, fell in the sea-fight of 897, was, doubtless, an officer of a higher grade, a member, perhaps, of the royal household, with the thegn's wergild of twelve hundred shillings.

It is probable that all the king's reeves, geneats, and immediate followers would belong to the comprehensive class of "king's thegns." The Chronicle, in the annal for 897, seems to include bishops and ealdormen, as well as town-reeves and "horse-thegns," under the term "king's thegns," and there can be no doubt that the thegnhood was a large and heterogeneous body, ranging from the great noble to the petty official and the obscure country gentleman.

The Latin equivalents for "thegn" are miles and minister, the soldier and the servant, and the thought of service, public or private, runs through all the various uses of the word. When in his will King Alfred left directions for his ealdormen and thenigmenn, he summed up the political and official world of ninth-century Wessex, much as he summed up the social world in the "ceorl or eorl" of his laws.

Two centuries earlier, in the days of Ine, the lay nobles below the rank of an ealdorman seem to have been divided into "king's thegns" and "gesiths," and the gesiths, again, into landowners, with a wergild of twelve hundred shillings, and landless men with a wergild of six hundred shillings. The gesiths, moreover, of the seventh century apparently formed a hereditary class of "born gentry," comprising both men and women. By Alfred's time the words gesith, gesithcund, are no longer found in the Anglo-Saxon laws, though the terms twelfhynde and sixhynde are retained, probably without any essential difference of meaning, and it would appear that the word thegn gradually took the place of the older gesith as the class name of the smaller gentry, even when they were not, like the "king's thegn," in a direct personal relation to the King.

But this change did not fully come about till the tenth century, and here, as in so many other ways, the reign of Alfred is transitional. The king's thegn is not mentioned in Alfred's laws, but the treaty with Guthrum provides that a king's thegn accused of homicide may clear himself by the oath of twelve king's thegns, where his social inferior requires only one king's thegn and eleven of his own equals. The charters, too, show lists of signatures of ministri, with a few ministri regis, who often attest grants of land made by the king to one or another of his "faithful servants" or thegns. Sometimes, when ministri regis and ministri witness the same charter, both groups may be supposed to have been personal followers of the king, of varying degrees of dignity. Sometimes, when the names of ministri are afterwards found among the duces, in spite of the danger of assuming identity of person from similarity of name, it is hard to avoid the inference that the ranks of the ealdormen were being recruited from the thegnhood.

It has been suggested1 that the remarkable diversity of names among the comparatively few ministri who sign Alfred's charters may be connected with Asser's account of the system of rotation adopted by the King, whereby his "noble thegns" (ministri, satellites) were divided into three groups, each of which in turn spent one month in three at the royal court, doing many kinds of service, and returning home for the remaining two months.

There is, at least, evidence enough to show that Alfred had a small body of thegns always about him, and that the king's thegns, as a whole, while maintaining a close personal connection with the king, as their immediate overlord, were becoming a class of landed proprietors, with private houses and estates. The old personal tie of the Germanic comitatus, the tie which bound together King Hygelac and his thegn Beowulf as "board-fellows and hearth-fellows," was, perhaps, beginning to be replaced by a territorial relation. Yet the personal bond still held. If the ancient Germanic princeps gave food and lodging, a war-horse, and a "blood-stained and victorious spear" to his comites, King Alfred could bequeath two hundred pounds to the men who followed him, to whom he "gave gifts at Eastertide."

When, in his translation of Boethius, he had to treat of the pride of kingship, he broke away from his original to draw what was probably a picture of the West-Saxon court as he had seen it, with the goodly company of thegns who served the king standing about the throne, and overawing the multitude by the splendour of their elaborate war-equipment, their "belts and golden-hilted swords.". Nor had the thegns forgotten how to fight and die for their lord, as the records of the Danish wars prove.

Alfred himself saw thegns and lords everywhere, in classical history and mythology, and in the Old Testament narratives, as well as in the early annals of his own people. In his writings, Cyrus of Persia, no less than Edwin of Northumbria, or Cynewulf of Wessex, is served by thegns. The "witch" Circe, who herself has a very great band (werod) of thegns, transforms the thegns of Ulysses into wild beasts. Uriah is David's "trusty thegn," David himself is Saul's thegn, and more righteous as a thegn than as a king.

Alfred would seem, then, to have been the centre of a small circle of permanent followers, his household troops, his "men"; the recipients of his Easter gifts, his lytel werod, a term often used in early Anglo-Saxon literature for the personal following of young warriors who form the comitatus of a chief. Outside this nucleus was a wide and varying circle of king's thegns, landowners who did four months' service at court during the year, and outside these, again, a more indeterminate ring of landowning twelfhynde men, and "thegn-born," but probably landless, sixhynde men, with a fringe of twyhynde ceorls, free peasants who owed service to the fyrd, but were, apparently, only called out when there was urgent need. Each great noble, too, had, in all likelihood, his own troop of immediate followers and henchmen, and when the summons to the army went forth, the countryside would be alive with bands of horsemen, glittering with helmet and "byrnie," or shirt of mail, with sword and spear and shield, while stolid companies of plodding footmen would wend their slow way to the place of meeting, carrying, perhaps, the rude axes, forks, and flails of their daily toil, or armed with stout cudgels cut from the forest. In his translation of St. Augustine's Soliloquies Alfred has inserted a picturesque description of the gathering of the fyrd, the soldiers streaming in from all sides, along the narrow muddy lanes and straight level highroads, to join the king, all alike, from the least to the greatest, seeking the same lord, by devious paths.

The only mention of the fyrd in Alfred's laws seems to refer to a full levy, since the fine for burhbryce, an offence which touched all classes, from the king to the ceorl, is doubled "when the fyrd is out." To break the peace of a private stronghold, when the house-father had been called away to defend the community, savoured of treachery, and demanded exceptionally severe treatment.

A widely accepted theory credits King Alfred with a threefold reform of the West-Saxon army, by the extension of the thegnhood, as a class of landed proprietors owing special military service, by the division of the fyrd into a reserve and a field force, and by the organisation of a scheme of national fortification. Yet, though there are signs that the military resources of the kingdom were strengthened during Alfred's reign, the exact course of this development is singularly hard to trace. In the first place, the King is supposed to have increased the number of thegns or mounted soldiers by compelling every man who held a minimum of five hides, or six hundred acres, of land to serve in the army with the thegn's full equipment of horse and armour, "helmet and byrnie, and sword overlaid with gold." Such a specialisation of military service in relation to a definite unit of land-tenure would be quite in accordance with early Lombard and Frank precedents, and there is some evidence to show that five hides was regarded as the minimum holding of a well-armed soldier in England in the eleventh century.

Alfred's connection with this "five-hide rule" is, however, merely a matter of conjecture, an assumption based upon inferences from two eleventhcentury statements of older English custom, which give as one of the conditions under which a ceorl might rise to the status of a thegn, the possession of five hides of his own land. It would, moreover, be rash to conclude from rules framed to meet particular cases that at any period all holders of five hides were of necessity thegns. There are, indeed, instances of ceorls holding more than five hides who remained "rustics" (rustici). Nor do the archaic elements in the documents which treat of the ceorl who "thrives to thegn-right" clearly belong to the age of Alfred. The use of the old word gesithcund, and the apparent incorporation of a passage from the laws of Ine, seem rather to indicate that they may go back to the beginning of the eighth century, a date which would agree well with the frequent recurrence of units of five and ten hides in Bede's writings and in ancient land-grants.

Ine's laws, too, as preserved by Alfred, imply that five hides was the normal holding of the twelfhynde West-Saxon, for the Welshman who held this amount of land became sixhynde, and the Welsh are usually estimated at half the value of the English. That military service was early bound up with land-tenure appears from the mention of the trinoda necessitas as a burden on land from the seventh century onwards, and from the clause in Ine's laws which condemns the gesithcund landowner to forfeit his land for neglect of the fyrd.

The important part played by the thegnhood in the campaigns of 871 and 878, at Englefield and at Wilton, at Cynwit and at Athelney, shows that it was an organised, disciplined, and, to some extent, localised body, even before Alfred's accession, nor were the West-Saxon troops of the later Danish wars so far superior to those of the beginning of the reign as to suggest that any far-reaching change had taken place in their numbers or constitution. Alfred, however, may well have carried further the system which was already in working order, a system which, maintained and developed by his successors, found documentary expression in the eleventh century, when it had become stereotyped. What little evidence there is seems certainly to point to an original specialisation of the fighting force on personal lines, early modified by a gradual territorialisation of military service, apparently in the ratio of one well-equipped horseman to every five hides of land.

Alfred's second reform, for which the Chronicle makes him directly responsible, the division of the fyrd into two bodies, was neither original nor particularly successful. "The King," according to the annal for 893 (894), "had divided his fyrd in two, so that they were always half at home, half out, besides the men who had to hold the burhs." This was a recognised military expedient, practised, if Cæsar is to be believed, by the ancient Suevi, and attributed by Orosius to the Amazons, in a passage which may have caught Alfred's attention. It corresponded to the similar arrangement for rotation of service among the king's thegns attached to the court, and is often explained to mean a reduction of the field force to enable the farmer-soldiers to cultivate their land and gather in their crops.

The Chronicle places by the side of the fyrdmen, as a separate military group, "the men who had to hold the burks." Field service is associated with the building and repair of bridges and fortifications in the triple military obligation of the trinoda necessitas, fyrdung, brycgbot and burhbot. The Latin terms for these services, expeditio, pontis structura or restauratio, arcis constructio, munitio, restauratio, and so forth, occur constantly in early charters, but it is not easy to discover exactly what the duty of burhbot or its equivalent involved before the Danish wars.

The idea of organised defence, of strongholds and cities of refuge, was, of course, familiar enough in ninth-century England. The ancient earthworks,

British, Roman, or Anglo-Saxon, which still crown the English hills, were already old in the days of Alfred. The crumbling walls of many a Roman city, too, must have witnessed to former strength and security. There was a West-Saxon camp at Wareham, there were defences at Exeter, and an earthwork at Cynwit, before the peace of 878 gave Alfred leisure to devise any new scheme of fortification. These, and such as these, were doubtless the arces which even privileged landholders were bound to maintain by burhbot or fæstengeweorc.

The Anglo-Saxon word burh or burg, the borough of later times, seems always to have carried with it the thought of protection, enclosure, fortification. The burh of king or ealdorman or thegn was his strong house, guarded by palisade and gates, earthworks or ditch; the enclosed or walled town was a burh. In the early Anglo-Saxon literature, and in Alfred's own writings, burh and ceaster, the Latin castrum, are used indifferently for a city or town, as equivalents for the Latin civitas, urbs, oppidum. To Alfred, Troy, Athens, Rome, Constantinople, and Jerusalem were burhs, as well as Lundenburg, or Canterbury, the burh of the men of Kent. But though the burh, as opposed to the unprotected tun or ham, was a house of defence, or a fenced city, this was only one of its functions. If Alfred saw the "burh of the mind" in St. Gregory's mœnia mentis, the mind's fortifications, he could distinguish between a "strong city," a fæste burh, and an "open burh, which is not surrounded by a wall." The fortress pure and simple, the Latin arx, appears in the Alfredian Chronicle up to the year 893 (894), not as burh, but as geweorc, "work," or fæsten, "fastness," whether the "work" is wrought by the Danes, as at Nottingham and Chippenham, or by the West-Saxons, as at Athelney;--whether the "fastness" is the old Roman town of Exeter, or the earthwork from which the vikings blockaded Rochester in 885.

Alfred renders arx, as applied to the Capitol, by fæsten, while Asser consistently uses arx to translate the geweorc of the Chronicle, and mentions the Danish arx and vallum at Reading, the West-Saxon castellum of Wareham, and the arx at Cynwit. Towards the close of his work he waxes eloquent over Alfred's activity in restoring and founding cities and towns, and in urging his negligent people to build forts, castella or arces; to carry out, in fact, the duty of fæstengeweorc or burhbot. He describes, further, how the forts which the King had ordered to be built were unfinished, or not even begun, when the Danes invaded England by land and sea, and how the workmen repented of their carelessness when their kinsmen were slain and their goods carried off, and did their utmost to repair their error, by constructing fortresses (arces) and doing other works of common utility for the common realm.

Asser probably wrote this passage about 893, and it is interesting to recall that in 892 Haesten's vikings had stormed an unfinished fort, a geweorc or fæsten, in the Andredsweald. Still more significant is it that in the year 893 (894) the word burg or burh appears for the first time in the Anglo- Saxon Chronicle as the equivalent of geweorc, with the primary meaning, it would seem, of a fortress. When, in that eventful year, Haesten's army "went up the Thames till they came to Severn, and then up the Severn," the ealdormen of Mercia, Wiltshire, and Somerset marshalled their forces, with "the king's thegns who were at home in the forts (at thæm geweorcum), from every burh east of Parret, both west and east of Selwood, and also north of Thames and west of Severn, and a part of the North-Welsh people."

It can hardly be doubted that these king's thegns were identical with "the men who had to hold the burhs," of whom the same annal speaks, and that the burhs from which they came were the forts or "works" in which they were "at home." This is confirmed by the chronicler's description of the situation of the burhs whence the king's thegns gathered for the blockade of Buttington in 893. They lay along the natural lines of defence of the country threatened by an army invading England by way of the upper Thames and the Severn. The burhs to the east of the river Parret and the west of the forest of Selwood would guard northern Somerset, those on the east of Selwood would shield Wiltshire, and those north of Thames would protect Mercia, while the burhs west of Severn would hold the Welsh frontier, and co-operate with the loyal North Welsh.

It is worth noting, too, that the leaders of the English forces were the ealdormen of just these western districts of Mercia, Wiltshire, and Somerset. The whole passage in the Chronicle may be compared with the annals for 918 and 921, when the men of the "nearest burhs" came from Hereford and Gloucester in the one case, from Kent, Surrey, and Essex in the other, to help the shire forces against the Danes.

There are, then, signs of an organised system of fortification in Wessex and English Mercia in the year 893, of the enforcement of the obligation of burhbot, in the form of the building and repair of strongholds, and of the performance of regular garrison duty by the king's thegns. The work of "bettering" the burhs was supplemented by the work of "holding" them.

The statements of Asser and the Chronicle are borne out by the evidence of the document known as the "Burghal Hidage," which probably belongs to the early years of the tenth century. It gives a list of burhs, principally in Wessex, and connects a round number of hides with each. If, as seems likely, it represents a scheme of military fortification, in which the land was grouped round burhs for purposes of home defence, the system may, quite possibly, have originated with Alfred, for many of the burhs in the list figure in his wars with the Danes.

Starting in Sussex, the Burghal Hidage works round to the west by Hastings and Lewes, Chichester and Porchester, Southampton and Winchester, Wilton and Shaftesbury, Wareham and Exeter, Pilton near Barnstaple, Watchet and Axbridge, to Lyng and Langport on either flank of the isle of Athelney, Bath and Malmesbury, and so to the Thames with Cricklade, Oxford, and Wallingford, and back to Surrey and the south. It thus includes strongholds of many different types. If the burks "west of Severn" were, perhaps, mere earthworks, arces, geweorcas, others were great camps, like the castellum of Wareham, which had a nunnery within its enclosure, seaports, or ancient Roman cities. What was new, was apparently not the building of fortifications, but their co-ordination in a definite scheme. The old burhs seem to have become units in a system of national defence, intended to guard the frontiers, while the new burhs, military, it may be, in origin, became in their turn units in a system of national commerce, and the word burh, supplanting geweorc, as thegn supplanted gesith, added to its wide significance that specialised meaning of a fortress in which it is used in the Chronicle during the Danish wars of Edward the Elder.

The need of an organised defensive policy had, doubtless, been impressed on Alfred by the successes of the vikings in their earlier invasions. In 839 they slew many men in London and Rochester. In 851 they "broke" Canterbury and London. In 860 they sacked Winchester before the fyrd could come to its help. Nottingham, Thetford, and Reading, Repton and

Cambridge, Wareham and Exeter, all important strategic points, fell easily into their hands. Chippenham seems to have been undefended until they fortified it. But in 878, the sally of the king's thegns from the fort at Cynwit, and the building of the "work" at Athelney, marked a new departure in West- Saxon tactics.

After the peace with Guthrum, Alfred appears to have used his leisure in applying the lessons of the past struggle. By 885 the defences of Rochester were sufficiently strong to enable it to stand a blockade. In 886, the newly acquired burh of London was given to Ethelred of Mercia to "hold," and twelve years later, in 898, a conference is recorded, in which Ethelred and his wife Ethelflæd took counsel with King Alfred and Archbishop Plegmund concerning the "restoration" (instauratio) of the city. In the campaigns of 893, 894, and 895, too, the citizens or burhware of London were active, while the vikings were forced to raise the siege of Exeter, and were driven away from the Sussex coast by the burhware of Chichester.

Alfred's military reforms were completed by the establishment of a small fleet of warships, the nucleus, it may fairly be said, of the future English navy. The constant danger of maritime invasion, the growing familiarity with the viking ships and methods of warfare, had perhaps reawakened in the West-Saxons something of their primitive instinct for seamanship. As early as 851 there seems to have been a sea-fight off Sandwich, in which the vikings were defeated, and in 875 Alfred was able to lead a few ships to victory.

Yet the ease with which the main Danish fleet sailed to Wareham in 876, and the apparent inability of the West-Saxons to guard the Channel and the Irish Sea with a sufficient force, show that their naval strength was far inferior to that of the invaders. In 882, and again in 885, it is true, Alfred defeated the Danes at sea, and in the latter year the Chronicle says that he sent a ship here2 to East Anglia, implying that he had already a fleet. It must, however, have been small and inadequate, for though it was victorious in its first encounter with sixteen Danish ships, it could not stand the assault of the "great fleet of vikings" which intercepted it on its homeward voyage. In 893 and the two following years, when the Great Army took ship for England, and the vikings brought large fleets into action, Alfred was content to check them with his land forces, without attempting to meet them at sea.

It was not till 896 (897) that he made the original experiment in shipbuilding on which his popular reputation as "the founder of the English navy" chiefly rests. He "caused long ships to be built against the æscas." "the ashes," or Danish vessels;

they were fully twice as long as the others, some had sixty oars, some more. They were swifter, steadier, and also higher than the others. They were fashioned neither in the Frisian nor in the Danish manner, but as it seemed to him that they might be most useful.

If these figures are to be taken at all literally, Alfred's fine vessels would seem to have been actually about twice the size of the ordinary Danish warship. The Gokstad boat had thirty-two oars, almost exactly half as many as Alfred's long ships, while the accounts of the battle of Cynwit give the Danes a fleet of twenty-three ships, and a loss of from eight hundred and forty to twelve hundred men. As some of the vikings escaped, this makes a probable average of about fifty men to a ship, a likely enough crew for a thirty-oared vessel.

Though in their only recorded action Alfred's new ships proved somewhat unwieldy, they seem to have created a precedent, for in the Danish wars of the tenth century there is good reason to believe that the typical English ship had sixty oars, with, of course, many variations in size and capacity. Edward the Elder, moreover, appears to have carried on his father's naval policy, since in 911 he could gather together a fleet of a hundred sail.

It is pleasant to think that the building of the long ships, one of the last achievements of Alfred's arduous life, was a labour of love. The spirit of the sea breathes through his writings. He is interested in ships and shipping for their own sake, and can seldom resist the temptation to expand and elaborate a nautical simile in the book he is translating. The idea of his "long ships," higher than the others, may even have been suggested to him by his study of the chapter in Orosius where Antony's ships are said to have made up in size what they lacked in number, since they stood ten feet out of the water. "They were so wrought," adds Alfred, "that they could not be overladen with men." If the English translation of Boethius dates from about 897, it is specially interesting to note Alfred's addition to the description of the Golden Age, when "no man had heard of a sciphere" or pirate fleet, and to read in his expansion of the story of Ulysses and Circe, how Ulysses, after losing ninety-nine out of his hundred ships in the ten years' siege of Troy, sailed out into the "Wendelsea," or Mediterranean, with a single three-banked galley, a trireme, or thrirethre scip. In the metrical version the Greek ships become "beaked keels," and "sea-horses," and Ulysses, in his foam-girt trireme, faces the storm-wind and the roaring brown waves, as Alfred himself may have faced them when he "sailed out on the sea with ships" against the Danish men.

If the scantiness of contemporary records and the luxuriant growth of later tradition make it difficult to trace Alfred's military and naval reforms in detail, this is still more the case with his judicial system. Yet the very extravagance of his popular reputation is suggestive--the legendary haze may be only the smoke from the smouldering fires of truth. The King who has been credited with the institution of trial by jury and judgment by peers, with the division of England into shires, hundreds, and tithings, and the first issue of original writs, must have won so high a place in the imagination of his people by an honest zeal for justice, and a determined effort to ensure its impartial administration.

Asser has described King Alfred's judicial work in the interesting chapters with which his book abruptly closes. After noting the King's painstaking thoroughness in examining judicial cases in the interests of the poor, who found in him almost their only helper, he explains more fully that the ealdormen and reeves (comites et praepositi) could not enforce their decisions in the courts, owing to the constant quarrels among the litigants, noble and non-noble. In consequence of these differences of opinion, both parties to a suit would pledge themselves to submit to the King's judgment, though coercion had to be used to induce those who were conscious of a weak cause to appear before such a judge.

The King, indeed, in matters of justice, as in all other business, was a most clear-sighted investigator. It was his custom to revise almost all the judgments which were given in his kingdom, when he was not present, and if he found any injustice in them, he would gently ask the judges (judices), either in person, or by one of his faithful ministers, why they had judged so wrongly, whether through ignorance or malice, or from love or fear or hate of any man, or from greed of gain. If they confessed to ignorance, he would say: I greatly wonder at your presumption in assuming the office and rank of witan (sapientes), conferred by the gift of God and by my gift, when you have neglected the study and practice of wisdom. Wherefore I command you either straightway to resign your public offices, or to apply yourselves much more earnestly to the study of wisdom.

Asser seems here, in his pedantic fashion, to show Alfred trying, with characteristic directness, to realise in everyday life that ideal of the just king which was one of the favourite themes of mediæval political philosophers. Justice, and mercy or pity, the two scales of St. Isidore's judicial balance, were, indeed, recognised as the essential virtues of the Christian king, who swore in his coronation oath to "ordain equity and mercy in all judgments." The picture of the good king drawn by Jonas of Orleans in the days of Louis the Pious might be the portrait of Alfred, as Asser knew him, more than half a century later--the just and equitable ruler, the defender of churches, of God's servants, of widows and orphans, and of all the poor and needy; quick to prevent or suppress injustice, ready, as "judge of judges," to hear the cause of the poor, and to protect them against unjust dealing or oppression at the hands of his ministers.

That Asser's somewhat grandiloquent account is more than a fancy sketch is seen by its close agreement with Alfred's Code of Laws, which had probably been compiled two or three years earlier. Thus, in the preface to his laws, Alfred inserted the Mosaic warning against taking gifts, "for the gift blindeth the wise and perverteth their words," and expanded the injunction, "thou shalt not wrest the judgment of thy poor in his cause," into: "Judge righteous and equal judgments; judge not one judgment for the rich and another for the poor, nor one judgment to friends and another to foes." These Hebrew precepts became approved maxims of later English law, and were incorporated in a little vernacular tract on the duties of the ideal judge, which was probably drawn up towards the close of the tenth century, or early in the eleventh century. When King Alfred asked his ealdormen and reeves if they had failed in their duty "from love, or fear, or hate, or greed," he was simply applying this teaching to practical purposes, and traces of an ancient official oath may even be detected in the formal wording of his question. The laws of Alfred and Ine, moreover, reflect an administrative system which is quite in accordance with Asser's statements.

Ealdormen and king's reeves appear as active and responsible ministers of royal justice, holding "folk-moots," receiving accusations, restraining private feuds, and, in the case of ealdormen, at least, liable to forfeit office through misconduct, unless pardoned by the king.

Ine's dooms seem to have been written down with special reference to the needs of ealdormen and other officials, and Edward the Elder, in later days, referring probably to Alfred's "Code," exhorted all "reeves" to judge such right judgments (domas) "as they know to be most righteous, as it stands in the "doombook." The reeves were evidently expected to be diligent readers of the law, and Asser, when he wrote of the ignorant judges whom the King drove to study "Saxon books," may have actually seen harassed ealdormen and their subordinates wrestling with the intricacies of the newly codified "dooms," sighing deeply, and lamenting that they had not applied themselves to such studies in youth, thinking the young men of that time happy, in that they could easily obtain instruction in the liberal arts, but counting themselves unhappy, since they had neither been taught when young, nor were they able, now that they were old, to acquire the knowledge which they earnestly desired.

Curiously enough, Asser's concluding chapter has been regarded both as supporting[1] and as controverting[2] the accredited theory that in the Anglo-Saxon law-courts, "the suitors were the judges." If decisions on questions of fact were obtained by a direct appeal to God through the ordeal, or by a solemn process of compurgation, the declaration of the custom-law applicable to each particular case was the function of the whole court. This theory would make the ealdormen and reeves mere "presiding magistrates," but the laws of the tenth and eleventh centuries hold them responsible for unjust judgments, on pain of fine and dismissal, and it is probable that even as early as the ninth century their personal and official influence was sufficiently strong to endanger the even-handed course of justice.

Perhaps the conditions under which Alfred was called on to govern have not been fully taken into account in estimating the value of Asser's evidence. In or about 893, when Asser is supposed to have written his book, the codified custom-law had been very recently issued, and was both novel in arrangement, and difficult to grasp in its variations and inconsistencies. Wessex had been disturbed and shaken out of accustomed grooves by the long war, and a new factor had entered into the problem of administration, with the incorporation of English Mercia and London. There may well have been disputes over wergilds and penalties and titles to land, in which the suitors would neither agree among themselves nor accept the ruling of the ealdorman, while the ealdorman himself was at a loss for want of expert knowledge. In such cases it would only be natural to turn to the king for a decision, just as a man needing help in the prosecution of an authorised blood-feud was bidden by Alfred's laws1 to "ride to the ealdorman," and, failing him, to "ride to the king." It does not seem necessary to treat the appeal to the king which Asser describes, as a formal appeal from a lower to a higher court, a much later legal conception.

The doctrine of the equitable jurisdiction of the king, on the contrary, may have as one of its roots the early attribution of the virtues of justice and mercy to the ideal ruler. There can, at least, be little doubt that Alfred himself looked on God as the supreme judge, the arbiter and lawgiver, on the king as his vicegerent, and on the ealdormen and reeves as the king's servants and instruments, or that he laid stress on the importance of legal knowledge as a qualification for judicial office.

The exhortation to the sapientes or witan to make themselves truly wise, which Asser puts into his mouth, is quite in harmony with the tone of his laws and writings. The illiterate ealdormen, reeves, and thegns, who preferred the "unaccustomed discipline" of laboriously learning to read to the loss of their official positions, were possibly drawn from life.

It may further be pointed out that most of the questions referred to the king would probably be now, as later, civil cases concerning the ownership or possession of bookland, where resort to arbitration was both easy and usual. This is admirably illustrated by an apparently genuine document, an anonymous Anglo-Saxon petition or letter to the King, which dates from the reign of Edward the Elder. The petitioner sets forth how Helmstan, his godson, having been convicted of theft, a certain Æthelm Higa appeared as a claimant of his five hides of land at Fonthill in Wiltshire, and would have obtained them, had not the petitioner interceded for Helmstan with King Alfred: "God rest his soul." The King referred the case to arbitration, and the arbitrators met at Wardour in Wiltshire, on the royal demesne. Among them were Wihtbord and Ælfric the hræl (rail) thegn, and Byrhthelm and

Wulfhun the Black of Somerton, and Strica and Ubba, and many more,"
including the petitioner himself. Helmstan's landbook or charter was "borne
forth," the signatures of its witnesses, King Alfred and others, were
examined, and it was decided that Helmstan might prove his claim by
means of oath-helpers. Æthelm Higa, however, would not consent to this,
so the arbitrators appealed to Alfred in person. "We went in to the King,
and explained how we had decided, and why, and Æthelm himself stood
there with us, and the King stood and washed his hands at Wardour in the
bower. When he had done, he asked Æthelm why our decision did not
seem right to him, and said that for his part he could think of nothing
better."

So the King appointed a day for a trial by oath, or compurgation, and the
petitioner promised to be one of Helmstan's oath-helpers, on condition of
obtaining the reversion of the land in dispute. The trial took place; the oath
succeeded; Helmstan recovered the land, and all went well till he again
yielded to temptation, and stole some oxen. Tracked, and caught with a
great bramble-scratch on his nose, which was taken as evidence of his
flight, he was convicted, and sentenced to banishment by King Edward,
who had now succeeded his father. The petitioner, however, interceded
with the new King at Chippenham, and the culprit was allowed to return,
while the petitioner secured his reversion. Finally, as the endorsement of
the document shows, Æthelm Higa gave up his claim in the presence of the
King and before witnesses at Warminster. "How indeed," writes the
petitioner, "can any plea be ended if neither money nor oath end it, and if
every 'doom' which king Alfred gave may be set aside?"

The general impression left by this most instructive letter is of a patriarchal
justice, homely, simple, and informal. But it should be observed that
Helmstan's two trials for theft were carried out without the king's
intervention, though the criminal eventually obtained the king's pardon; that
Alfred was first called in, perhaps as overlord rather than as sovereign, to
protect the interests of Helmstan, one of his own "men," that he referred
the case to arbitration, only gave his personal decision when the arbitration
broke down, and even then was content to leave the final judgment to the
ordinary method of trial by compurgation.

Dimly, but with a certain consistency, the outlines of Alfred's judicial

154

organisation thus rise from the confusion of the contemporary records. The king was already the "fount of justice," as lord of his men, sovereign of his subjects, and rightful defender of all the oppressed. His jurisdiction was exercised, either directly, in the full national assembly and in the royal court in the narrower sense, or indirectly, through his delegates in the local courts held by ealdormen and reeves.

In all cases the suitors of the court could declare the custom-law if necessary, but considerable discretionary powers remained with the president, a royal official, while in the central courts the suitors were themselves witan, men of good birth or high position. In Alfred's laws1 the judges who award and modify penalties are called "wise men" (witan), and "world lords," lay or secular lords, as well as doomsmen (domeras).

The constitution of the local courts seems to have been more popular, but here the sources are "certain only in uncertainty." That there was a "folk-moot" in Alfred's day, presided over by an ealdorman, or possibly by a king's reeve, can be asserted with confidence, but beyond this it is hardly safe to venture, though it is highly probable that the folk-moot under the ealdorman was the court of the shire, and it is possible that there was also a court for a smaller district, meeting more frequently, under the king's reeve, and corresponding to the later hundred court.

It is quite likely that both hundred and shire are ancient territorial units. All the West-Saxon shires are mentioned in the Alfredian Chronicle before the first change of hand in the year 891, and it is reasonable to suppose that, whatever their origin, they were used in the ninth century as administrative units. Some systematic division of the country into fiscal areas would early be rendered necessary by the collection of the royal revenues. These were drawn in large part from the king's demesne land, and from the dues or "farm" levied by him on his progresses, supplemented by an occasional gafol or tribute. Payments were, no doubt, still often made in kind, but the process of commutation for money had begun long before the time of Alfred.

Asser gives a circumstantial account of Alfred's careful appropriation of his revenues, half to secular purposes, half to religious objects. The secular fund, he says, was subdivided into three sections: the first devoted to the maintenance of the warrior thegns who served by turns at court, "according to each man's proper office and dignity," the second, to the artificers whom the King collected from many nations, the third to the strangers who flocked to his court. The ecclesiastical fund was similarly divided into four parts. One went to the poor, one to the King's new religious houses of Athelney and Shaftesbury, the third to his court school, and the fourth to the monasteries of Wessex and Mercia, with contributions to those of Wales and Cornwall, "Gaul," Britanny, and Northumbria. Alfred is said, also, to have sent alms to the patriarch of Jerusalem, and even to India, and the Chronicle in several annals records the bearing of the alms of "the West- Saxons and King Alfred" to Rome.

Without attaching too much weight to the details of the financial scheme set forth by Asser, there is no need to doubt that Alfred made a wise and businesslike distribution of the royal funds, and there is some evidence to show that a regular financial system based on the local territorial units was in existence before the close of the ninth century—ines due from the lord who lured away a dependent from his own shire, without the ealdorman's witness, were paid to the king, half in the shire whence the dependent had fled, half in his new shire. There seems therefore to have been a royal financial centre in each shire, while the king's reeves had as their paramount duty the financial and economic supervision of the king's estates, the collection of food rents, and the provisioning of the royal household.

Side by side with Alfred's administrative reforms, inspired by the same deep sense of personal responsibility and Christian principle, went that revival of learning and religion for which the King gave thanks to God in his preface to the Pastoral Care. When, in that preface, he looked back to the happy past of the English people, before the Danish ravages, he pictured a strong and virtuous king, ruling a Christian community of learned and godly clergy and laity.

This was the Golden Age which he sought to restore. "I often called to mind," he wrote, "what wise men (witan) there were of old among the English (Angel cynn), both of the clerical and of the lay estate." First among the instruments or "tools" of government he named the "men of prayer," gebedmen, oratores. If he urged the lay witan to read "Saxon books," he looked to the clerical witan to provide a vernacular literature. Church and State were, to the political thinkers of the ninth century, living parts of one organic whole, and in England, at least, their separate functions were not, as yet, very clearly differentiated.

In his laws Alfred hardly discriminates between ecclesiastical and lay assemblies, synods and secular councils, or between the bishops and the other "distinguished witan." Ine's dooms open with an injunction to the clergy to observe their canonical law, their "right rule," and Ine and Alfred alike legislate for ecclesiastical persons, places, and seasons, and issue decrees affecting baptism, Sunday observance, church taxation, and rights of sanctuary.

To this close connection between Church and State may perhaps be attributed the absence of records of special ecclesiastical councils or synods in Alfred's reign, though this may also be due to the general meagreness of the documentary evidence for the period. Circumstances doubtless contributed to strengthen the royal power over the Church. The Danish wars had impoverished the West-Saxon prelates and clergy, both regular and secular, by the destruction of books and treasures, and had thinned their ranks by death and exile. Whatever the theory of episcopal election may have been, in practice Alfred, probably with the approval of the witan, seems to have appointed bishops and abbots, and to have looked on them as his ministers and officials. He mentions "Plegmund, my archbishop, Asser, my bishop, Grimbald, my mass-priest, and John, my mass-priest," in the preface to the Pastoral Care, and Asser says that the King gave him Exeter with all its diocese (parochia).

There was room, too, for Alfred's personal intervention in matters of ecclesiastical discipline. Viewed from the standpoint of Continental Catholicism it may well be that English churchmanship appeared lax, and English monasticism scarcely worthy of the name.

The English clergy, to judge by the letters of Pope John VIII., written during the first ten years of Alfred's reign, were careless and worldlyminded. They married, wore secular dress, and lived as laymen, heedless of their sacred calling. At a somewhat later date, Fulco, Hincmar's successor in the archbishopric of Rheims, wrote in a similar strain, though he did full justice to the efforts of King Alfred and Archbishop Plegmund to raise the standard of piety and learning. In the letter in which he recommends Grimbald to Alfred, in reply to the King's application for helpers in the work of reform, he alludes to the decline of the Church in England, due, as Alfred had himself explained, to the frequent attacks of the pagans, to the lapse of time, the negligence of prelates, and the ignorance of the people. Asser, too, says that in the course of years the monastic rule had come to be neglected in England, and the desire for the monastic life had waxed faint, by reason of the constant attacks of the Danes by land and sea, or from the great wealth of the people, which led them to despise the life of the convent.

The days of the Benedictine revival had not yet dawned, and King Alfred's own interests were rather educational than monastic, but he founded monasteries at Athelney and Shaftesbury, and started the scheme for the building of the New Minster, at Winchester, which was carried on by his son, Edward the Elder

The Athelney house was always small and poor. Its few extant charters are probably spurious. The last traces of its buildings were destroyed in the eighteenth century. The little church, raised on piles, with its four circular apses, of which William of Malmesbury writes, has vanished as completely as the defences which in Alfred's time guarded the island sanctuary. The site, Asser says, was surrounded by a vast marshy fen, and by water, so that it could only be approached by cauticæ--a word which may possibly signify causeways, but which more probably stands for caudicæ, canoes, or "dugouts";--or by a bridge which had been laboriously constructed between two forts (arces).

At the western end of this bridge a very strong fort, of admirable workmanship, was built by the King's orders. There is nothing in Asser's account to show whether the bridge and forts were built in connection with the monastery or earlier, nor does he say if the bridge crossed the Parret or the Tone. It seems, however, likely that it was thrown across the Tone, close to the foot of the isle of Athelney, and that the forts protected the two banks of the river, and formed part of the monastery. It should be remembered that the burh of Lyng lay about a mile to the west of Athelney, and the burh of Langport four or five miles to the east, and that Athelney Farm is still approached by a causeway from East Lyng, and by a bridge over the Tone from Langport.

If the flanks of the isle of Athelney were guarded by burhs, Shaftesbury was itself a burh, included in the "Burghal Hidage." Here, on a steep hill, Alfred planted a religious house for women, and set over it as abbess his own daughter Ethelgifu. William of Malmesbury states that in his time Shaftesbury was only a village, but that it had formerly been a town, as was shown by a stone preserved in the nuns' chapter-house, which bore this inscription:

In the year of our Lord's Incarnation 880 King

Alfred built this city, in the eighth year of his reign.

There was thus an early tradition that Alfred founded the burh as well as the abbey. He is also sometimes regarded as the joint founder, with his wife Ealhswith, of the "Nunnaminster" at Winchester, and he appears to have planned the foundation and endowment of the "New Minster," and, possibly, to have chosen Grimbald for its abbot.

The early history of Athelney is associated with the curious story told by Asser of the attempt to murder its first abbot, John the Old-Saxon, priest and monk. In default of English monks, the community was made up of priests and deacons from beyond the sea, chiefly, it would appear, West Franks, with a number of foreign children who were trained for the religious life in the monastic school. Asser had even seen a young Danish boy among them. The Frankish monks apparently chafed under the yoke of their Saxon abbot, and plotted to slay him. Two of their serving-men fell upon him with swords as he prayed in the church at night. The abbot, who was not altogether ignorant of the art of war, resisted manfully, crying aloud that his assailants were demons and not men, "for he thought that no men could dare so greatly." The monks came to the rescue, the traitors among them, feigning horror, and the would-be murderers, leaving their victim half dead, escaped to the marshes, only to be caught and put to death with tortures, a fate well-pleasing to Asser, who sees in it a sign of God's mercy in not permitting so shocking a crime to go unpunished.

This tale is interesting for the light which it throws on the admixture of brutality and superstition with simple devout faith, in ninth-century Christianity, but it has won greater celebrity than it deserves from the confusion of John the OldSaxon, abbot of Athelney, with John the Scot, Johannes Scotus Erigena, the famous Irish scholar and philosopher.

William of Malmesbury repeats the current legend that after the death of his patron Charles the Bald in 877, John the Scot came to England, attracted by King Alfred's munificence, and that his pupils stabbed him to death with their metal pens (graphii) in the abbey of Malmesbury. The question has been further complicated by the supposition that John, the "mass-priest" of the Pastoral Care, who is also mentioned by Asser, is identical with both John the Old-Saxon and John the Scot.

The identification of the Scot and the Old- Saxon may be rejected without hesitation. There is absolutely no justification for connecting Asser's account of the unsuccessful attempt on the life of the abbot of Athelney with William of Malmesbury's narrative, which he is careful to give as hearsay (ut fertur), of the murder of John the Scot by his pupils at Malmesbury. The identification of John the mass-priest with John the Old-Saxon of Athelney is more probable, but it also rests on an assumption which does not admit of proof. Asser certainly seems to regard the two as identical, for though he distinguishes the abbot as "Old-Saxon by race," he first describes John the priest as a man of "quick wit" (acerrimi ingenii), and then, in almost the same words, writes of John the abbot that he rushed upon his assassins with his usual "quickness of wit" (ut solito ac semper acris ingenio). There remains the possibility that John the "mass-priest" was John the Scot, but Asser does not mention the Scot, while William of Malmesbury, who mentions both, does not connect them, and the authentic history of John the Scot stops before the death of Charles the Bald. The three Johns seem to have been first woven into one by that ingenious fourteenth- or early fifteenth-century forger, "Ingulf of Croyland.''

King Alfred's other "mass-priest" and helper, Grimbald, whose name is coupled with that of John in the preface to the Pastoral Care, was apparently a monk of the Abbey of St. Bertin in Flanders, who was sent over to England, at Alfred's request, by Fulco, abbot of St. Bertin and Archbishop of Rheims. The stories of Alfred's early meeting with Grimbald, and of the later mission of Asser and John the priest to bring him to England, may be dismissed as legends, but there seems no reason to doubt the genuineness of the letter in which Fulco commends the learned monk to the King as a spiritual watch-dog against the devourers of souls, sent in return for the "mortal hounds" which Alfred had presented to the Archbishop as a protection against "visible wolves."

The date of Grimbald's coming to the English court is uncertain. He may have arrived before 887, at about the same time as Asser himself, but if he was the same person who was actively concerned in the struggle between the Abbey of St. Bertin and Baldwin, Count of Flanders, in 892, he cannot have settled in England till after that year. The point is important, since it affects the question of the date of issue of the translation of the Pastoral Care, in which Grimbald took part.

On the whole, if Asser's confused chronology be disregarded, the recorded facts fit in very well with a date later than 892, though they come from such untrustworthy sources that they can only be accepted with caution. Asser describes Grimbald as an excellent singer (cantator), most learned in every kind of ecclesiastical discipline and in holy Scripture, and adorned with all the virtues. He is said to have been the first abbot of the New Minster, or Hyde Abbey, and he was canonised after his death in 902. He was long remembered with reverence both at St. Bertin and at Winchester, and his name was used in later days to give force to the absurd fables connected with the foundation of the University of Oxford.

In addition to these Frankish scholars, Asser names four Mercian "luminaries," whom Alfred called to his aid, Werferth, Bishop of Worcester, Plegmund, who succeeded Ethelred as Archbishop of Canterbury in 890, Æthelstan and Werwulf, "priests and chaplains." Æthelstan is probably the priest who is supposed to have carried Alfred's alms to Rome and India in 883. He may also be identical with the Æthelstan who became Bishop of Ramsbury, in 909. Priests called Æthelstan and Werwulf witness charters, several of them of very doubtful authenticity, between 898 and 909, and in 899 Bishop Werferth grants land to Werwulf the priest, "for our ancient fellowship, and his faithful friendship and obedience."

Of Werferth, Bishop of Worcester, the translator of the Dialogues of Gregory the Great, more is known. He was consecrated to the see of Worcester in 873, and held it till his death in 915, and his name occurs constantly in Mercian land-books and charters, as witness, as donor, and as grantee. It must have taken some courage to accept a bishopric in Mercia with the Danes occupying London, or threatening the kingdom from Lindsey. The peace of 873 proved illusory in the following year, but though Werferth is said to have followed King Burhred into exile, he is found signing charters under Ceolwulf in 875, while after the peace of 878 he seems to have been on excellent terms with Ethelred, "Lord of Mercia," and his lady Ethelflæd. He was present at the London conference of 898, and in that year Alfred granted land at Rotherhithe to him and to Archbishop Plegmund. He appears to have held a position of almost archiepiscopal authority in Mercia, and to have played an important part in public affairs. King Alfred left him a hundred mancuses in his will, and in the contemporary documents he is seen receiving land from the cathedral of Worcester and granting it out again to his kinswoman, disputing over the title to the possessions of his see, and winning privileges from his friends Ethelred and Ethelfæd when they build a burh at Worcester "for the defence of all the folk." He was also, apparently, a friend of Ethelnoth, ealdorman of Somerset. His established fame hardly needed the additions of the Book of Hyde Abbey, which makes him the translator of Boethius, or of "Ingulf of Croyland," who states that Alfred held St. Neot and "St. Werferth" in great veneration.

Alfred's fourth Mercian adviser was Plegmund, Archbishop of Canterbury from 890 to 914. Fulco of Rheims wrote to congratulate the English King on his choice of so good and devout a primate, and to commend the Archbishop himself for his reforming zeal. Plegmund, indeed, loyally supported Alfred in all his projects, and was one of the most distinguished of his little band of literary churchmen.

There would appear, on the other hand, to have been strained relations between Alfred and Plegmund's predecessor, Archbishop Ethelred, since Pope John VIII. wrote to urge him to stand firm as a wall for the house of the Lord, "not only against the King, but against all those who wished to act perversely," and the papal exhortations to the young Alfred to follow in the steps of his pious ancestors suggest that, as Sir John Spelman says, the King's "Life and Ways were not perfectly pleasing to the Fathers of Rome." From the general tenor of the Pope's letters it may be gathered, however, that it was not Alfred's independence of the Holy See, or his absolutism, which gave offence, as Spelman thinks, but the general secularism and laxity of the English Church, especially in relation to the marriage-law. Ethelred, too, may have had private enemies, for John VIII. promises not to believe anything he has heard against him. Asser, the friend and fellowworker of Plegmund, may best be considered apart, in relation to his Life of the King.

Of Alfred's personal piety no doubt can be entertained. Asser has recorded his dedication to God "of half the service of his mind and body," his observance of the canonical hours of worship, his reverence for those relics of the saints which he always carried about with him, his prayers and lavish almsgiving. But even without this testimony the King's writings would reveal his devout nature, and his care for the things of the mind and the spirit. It was characteristic of his practical bent, and of his own mental activity and desire for knowledge, that he should devote an eighth of his revenues to the instruction of the young. No modern stateman could see more clearly the importance of education in the scheme of government than this ruler of a half-barbarous people. His ideal is expressed in the hackneyed but memorable passage in the preface to the Pastoral Care:

Let all the free-born youth now in England (Angel-

cynne) who have the means, be set to learning, so

long as they are unfit for other occupations, until in

the first place they can well read English writing.

Let those afterwards be taught the Latin tongue who

are to be educated further, and raised to a higher

estate.

The King's attempt to realise this ideal took the form of the foundation of a court school, on the Frankish model, where the royal children and the sons of the nobles, with promising boys of humble origin, could learn to read and write both English and Latin, under competent masters, until they were physically strong enough to turn from the study of the "liberal arts" to hunting and other "human arts" befitting those of noble birth.

Thus on law and justice, on the army and the navy, on the church and the schools, King Alfred left his mark. It is interesting to ask how far in all his administrative experiments he was, consciously or unconsciously, following the example set by the Frankish emperors and kings. In his military organisation, his personal administration of justice, his patronage of scholars, and his court school, there are many striking parallels with the imperial and West Frankish system of government. Alfred himself was, throughout his life, in close and friendly relations with the Continent. His court was thronged with foreigners of all nationalities, "many Franks, Frisians, 'Gauls,' pagan Danes, Welsh and Scots, and Bretons." Frankish scholars, Frisian sailors, Northern explorers, Scots from Ireland, and Asser the Welshman were all alike welcome. There was no insularity in his outlook. As Asser says, he sought without what he could not find within his kingdom, and he would naturally turn for guidance and inspiration to the great Christian Empire of the West. At the same time, his keen intellectual curiosity led him far afield in his search for information, and Celtic and Scandinavian elements must be taken into account in estimating the influences which helped to mould the Anglo-Saxon State.

Continental analogies may also be due rather to development on similar lines than to direct imitation, and Asser's Life of Alfred is too obviously modelled on Frankish biographies to be taken as a faithful picture of his policy in all its details.

Yet, were he even less of an original statesman than he appears to have been, Alfred would still rank among the makers of England. William of Malmesbury went to the root of the matter when, in speaking of the fame of Edward the Elder, he added: "Yet the chief Glory, in my judgment, belongs to his father [Alfred], who prepared the way for all this greatness."

THE VICTORIES OF PEACE II

II. Alfredian Society

WITHIN the organised community of the West-Saxon State, king and people lived a simple country life in local village groups. Land, its settlement and tillage, its transference, and the uncertainties of title; the recording of boundaries; the alternations of crops and fallow; the gathering of the harvest; rights of pasturage; hunting and fishing, and the cultivation of waste places;--all these things made up the chief daily interests of the average ninth-century Englishman, in time of peace. His talk was of good and bad husbandry, of weather and of stock, of trespass and cattle-lifting, of sport and woodcraft, when it was not of raids and harrying, and the warhosts of "heathen men."

A growing proportion of land was held, in the second half of the ninth century, by "book," or charter, though by the side of the "bookland," "folk-land," held under the custom-law by "folkright," without written title, still persisted. The advantage of the "book" was that it gave greater freedom of disposition to the grantee, and careful precautions were taken to prevent the abuse of this freedom. An elaborate clause in Alfred's laws, an early instance of a kind of entail, or family settlement, provides that bookland shall not be granted away from the kindred of the owner, if such alienation is forbidden in the original charter. Only in the central court, however, with the witness of king and bishop, could the injured kinsmen plead their rights, or the landowner maintain his claim to alienate without restriction. Alfred himself, in his will, limited the succession to his bookland to his male descendants, his kinsmen on the "weapon side," or "spear side," as long as any of them remained alive.

Bookland was held by great ecclesiastics, religious houses, nobles and thegns, lords whose estates were worked by dependents, but there were also small freemen who cultivated their own farms, and a considerable amount of land was sublet on lease or "loan."

The Danish wars worked havoc among the titles to landed property. "Books" were lost or destroyed, and had to be replaced by fresh grants, while landowners were driven from their homes, or permanently impoverished. In particular, as might be expected, this seems to have been the case in Mercia. King Alfred must have seen many changes of ownership when, towards the close of his life, he drew a spiritual lesson from the land-law of his day, and contrasted the loghut on loan-land of this transitory life with the eternal home in the heavenly country.

Every man [he wrote in his preface to the translation of St. Augustine's Soliloquies] desires, when he has built a cottage with his lord's help on his lord's loan-land, to rest awhile therein, and hunt, and fowl, and fish, and provide for himself in divers ways on that loan, both by sea and by land, until he can earn bookland and eternal inheritance by his lord's grace.

It is, unfortunately, easier to collect and catalogue the dry bones of legal theory than to clothe them with flesh and blood. The social life of the ninth century has left peculiarly few traces as compared with either earlier or later periods. The archæological evidence, though interesting and significant as far as it goes, is somewhat meagre and inconclusive, for the custom of burying weapons, personal ornaments, and articles of domestic use, in the graves of the honoured dead, had been discredited by the triumph of Christianity over paganism. Ninth-century literature, too, has little to say of social conditions. The older poetry, and Bede's vivid Latin prose, are invaluable for their wealth of detail, and their incidental sketches of manners and customs. The homilies and saints' lives of the tenth and eleventh centuries are full of intimate touches and personal description. But the Anglo-Saxon Chronicle is eloquent only on war, Asser dresses up his facts in bombast till there is hardly any nature left in them, and Alfred's strenuous age was more concerned with producing saints and heroes than with writing about them. The charters, the laws, and the King's translations, with his original additions, furnish chance suggestions and hints, often difficult enough to interpret, but, in the main, we must rest content with imperfect knowledge. Still, by reading backwards from a near future, and forwards from a not far distant past, much may be done to reconstitute the years that lie between.

Though the land was sparsely inhabited, with wide stretches of forest and marsh, the population, at least in the agricultural districts, was gathered into villages, where the log-huts or wattle and daub cottages of the peasants clustered irregularly about the little wooden church. In the hilly districts and pasture-lands of the west the houses were, probably, less concentrated, and in many lonely forest glades and waste heaths the work of colonisation must still have been going forward.

Something, perhaps, of this primitive English society may be reflected in the pioneer life of our modern colonies. The log-cabins of western Canada, parted by miles of virgin forest, or grouped about a rough-hewn church, the lumber camps, the rude waggons, the draught oxen, the wild nature around the oases of cultivation, the daily contact with the fundamental facts of existence, may all have had their prototypes in the political infancy of the mother-country.

The vestiges of that early civilisation have been almost effaced from modern England. Even physical features have changed: forests have been cut down, and marshes have been drained; rivers have altered their direction and character; the coast-line has shifted with the encroachment or receding of the sea. The defences of Anglo-Saxon "camps" and the course of Anglo-Saxon roads may still, indeed, be traced, but the perishable wooden buildings of the Germanic settlers have passed away far more completely than the solid Roman masonry which they, in large measure, replaced.

The ordinary Anglo-Saxon house of the ninth century probably consisted of a hall or livingroom, with a "lean-to" or a separate building for sleeping, and other penthouses, huts, or sheds, for cooking, storage, stabling, and various domestic purposes. The burh of the king's thegn would often have, in addition to the principal house, a belfry, a kitchen, and a church or private chapel. The homesteads of smaller men would be much the same in design, though with fewer buildings and less pretension. The whole group, the burh, ham, or tun, would be enclosed by a low earthwork, probably surmounted by a stockade, and would look not unlike a large Scandinavian farm at the present day, or a western American ranch, with its numerous wooden "shacks," houses, barns, and stables. Even the ceorl's cottage, his "worth" (weorthig) or "town" (tun), was guarded by a hedge, and he, like his betters, was entitled to a fine for edorbryce, breaking though his edor or hedge, an offence which corresponded to the burhbryce of a thegn or ealdorman.

In the famous account of the death of Cynewulf of Wessex, which is given in the Parker Chronicle under the year 755 (757), the "bower" or sleeping apartment is far enough away from the main building for the King to be slain before his thegns, who are resting in the hall, can come to his rescue. The "bower," too, at Wardour, where Alfred heard petitions as he washed his hands, was evidently a distinct room, if not an independent structure, and it was in his "chamber" (cambra or camera) that the King was accustomed to study, and to talk and read with Asser.

An admirable illustration of the composite character of a West-Saxon royal ham is found in the English translation of St. Augustine's Soliloquies, where, after speaking of the household of wisdom, Alfred adds: Just so is every king's ham: some are in the bower, some in the hall, some on the threshing-floor, some in the prison (on carcerne), and yet they all live by the favour of one lord, even as all men live under one sun.

Here the king's ham is seen as a self-sufficing unit, a little community in itself, and it is peculiarly interesting to observe how this private unit has already been adapted to public uses. The royal prison is part of the royal palace. In like manner, Alfred's laws provide that the man who breaks his solemn oath must spend forty nights in prison (on carcerne), in the king's tun, and there must suffer what the bishop has laid on him as a penalty. If he have no means of subsistence of his own, his kinsmen must feed him. If he have neither kinsmen nor "meat," he must be fed by the king's reeve.

Outside the gates of the royal ham lay the homefarm, or demesne, the estate, managed by the king's reeve, which produced grain for the "threshing-floor." The arable land of the demesne might be in a compact block about the hall, or it might consist of scattered strips in the open fields of the village. In either case it was generally cultivated by the forced labour of the peasants, who owed tribute (gafol) and work to the king, as to their lord. Actual slaves, who were personally unfree, not merely economically dependent, would also form part of the household, and share in the work. The ceorls who tilled the demesne would usually live in the neighbouring dependent village, where their own arable acre or half-acre strips were intermixed in the open fields. So closely connected was the arable land with the open-field methods of cultivation, that in Alfred's laws the agrum of the book of Exodus is translated "acres" (œceras).

The life of the court was reproduced on a smaller scale in the hall of ealdorman or thegn. The nobles had their own demesne lands and dependent villages, scattered up and down the country, their own reeves, and their own little circles of servants and officials. The laws of Ine allow the migrating gesithcundman to take with him his reeve, his smith, and his child's nurse. The ceorl had his homestead, his "worth" (weorthig), or "flat" (flet), with its yard or garden, as well as his arable strips in the common fields, and his proportionate share in the meadows, woodland, and waste.

There can be little doubt that, by the end of the ninth century, the power of the lord had grown apace, so that, in all likelihood, the free village community had become rather the exception than the rule. Yet fragments of an older social order are embedded in Ine's laws, as preserved by Alfred, survivals, it may well be, from a time when the self-governing village group was normal, and the dependent village was exceptional. The careless ceorl who left a gap in the fence round his "worth" (weorthig) had no compensation for the inroads of his neighbours' cattle. The idle ceorls who did not finish their share of fencing the common grass-land, the "grass tun," or the arable, whereby stray animals ate up the growing hay or crops, had to make good the damage to their co-partners: there is no hint of a lord. So, too, when one ceorl borrowed a yoke of oxen from another, it was apparently the local community which saw to his fulfilment of the conditions of his contract. But such survivals of ancient custom were already archaic by Alfred's time. The vicissitudes of the Danish wars, the forced sales of land, and personal submissions, had tended to depress the peasantry, and to hasten the development of the power of the thegnhood.

In Alfred's laws and writings, the individualistic note, perceptible in Ine's day, is accentuated and strengthened. Treason to a lord is the unpardonable sin. A man may not fight for his own kinsmen against his lord, though when his lord is attacked, he must always defend him. The obligation, however, was not all on one side. If the dependent gave service, he received protection. The lord fought for his men. The ceorl might build his hut on his lord's land, with his help.

"Workmen," equally with clergy and warriors, were recognised as essential to the well-being of the State.

Asser is, probably, unduly hard on the West- Saxon aristocracy when he accuses them of worldliness and selfishness, and says that they cared more for their own interests than for the common good, and that the poor had few or none to help them, save only the king. It was for the good of the whole community that order should be maintained, and that theft should be put down with a high hand. The thegnhood took over the responsibility for the police of the country, when the old system of kindred responsibility weakened with the lapse of time and the stress of the Danish wars.

Ine had decreed that the man who left his lord without leave, and "stole away" into another shire, must return, and pay sixty shillings to his lord. In Alfred's laws this is elaborated: the man who wishes to seek a lord in a new locality2 must do it with the witness of the ealdorman whom he previously followed in his shire. If he fail to obtain this witness, his new lord has to pay a fine of a hundred and twenty shillings to the king, half in the shire whence he fled, half in the shire in which he now lives. If, again, the man had done evil in his own home, if he were flying from justice, his new lord had to pay the penalty, in addition to a fine of a hundred and twenty shillings to the king.

The right of choosing a lord, rather than absolute independence, was, then, even in these early days, coming to be regarded as the mark of freedom, but the restrictions on liberty in this respect were all made in the public interest, and the resources of the State had increased since Ine's time. The administration of the kingdom was at once better organised and more elastic, though the official and aristocratic element was also more pronounced. When Alfred in his will granted liberty to his men to choose a lord after his death outside the royal house, he could only secure this privilege to them by obtaining the confirmation of the "witan of the West-Saxons." In his translation of St. Augustine's Soliloquies, Alfred makes God the good lord, in whose righteous household the fugitive sinner seeks a refuge from the miserable service of the devil. The king was the chief of earthly lords, and his household was the model of all others.

Asser gives a graphic description of the West- Saxon court, thronged with strangers, the King himself the centre of a crowd of ministers, foreigners, scholars, ecclesiastics, handicraftsmen, huntsmen, and falconers:-- questioning, discussing, picking the brains of all with whom he came in contact, as eager to learn as to teach. Asser describes, too, the court-school, which must have been comparatively new in 893, when he wrote, for while Ethelwerd, Alfred's youngest son, was a pupil in it, Edward and Elfthryth, the second and third of the royal children, were brought up by governors and nurses, though not without such "liberal discipline" as the study of psalms, Saxon books and Saxon songs could supply. The nobly born boys who were taught with the little Ethelwerd were, doubtless, received into the King's household to be educated and trained, in accordance with mediæval usage.

Nor was the more practical side of life neglected. If Asser dwells, with a scholar's delight, on Alfred the royal student, poring over manuscripts in his chamber, he can also praise the royal sportsman, skilled in hunting and hawking, an expert in falconry and a dog-fancier, with special keepers for his falcons (falconarios), his hawks, (accipitrarios), and his hounds (canicularios). Fieldsports, indeed, were more than mere amusements when even the king's table was largely dependent on wild game for its supplies. Hunting and hawking formed a necessary part of a nobleman's education, and Alfred was a trained and skilful hunter, "incomparable," says Asser, "in that art, as in all other gifts of God, as we have frequently seen."

Alfred, who thought wolf-hounds a suitable present for an archbishop, and in whose laws the misdeeds of dogs found a place, shows a healthy love of sport and natural history in his writings. He asks with Wisdom in the Boethius2: "Do you then take your nets and your dogs out to sea, when you go hunting?" And answers for himself: "I ween that you place them up on the hills and in the woods."

The deer of Ireland and the reindeer of Norway interest him, as well as the elephants, lions and tigers of his classical studies--with "the beast which we call lynx (lox)," of which Aristotle the philosopher said that it could see through trees, and even stones. He has the quick power of observation of a true Nature-lover, and introduces country sounds and sights into his translations-- the startling crash of the forest-tree, falling when men least expect it; the swine rushing back from clean water to wallow in miry puddles; the change of seasons; the growth of plants and trees; the wonders of a starry night; the ebb and flow of tides: all have their appeal for him, and are all fraught with spiritual meaning.

One Creator there is without any doubt [he writes, adding his own song of praise to the chant of Wisdom]. He is the ruler of heaven and earth, and of all creatures visible and invisible, even God Almighty. . . . So now with spring and harvest-tide (autumn); in spring things grow; in harvest-tide they wither. And again, with summer and winter; in summer it is warm, and in winter cold. So also the sun brings bright days, and the moon shines at night, by the power of the same God.

Among the strange Norwegian customs of which Ohthere told his lord King Alfred, was the habit of ploughing with horses, instead of oxen. In England horses were used for transport, not for agricultural work, and were of considerable value. "Formerly," says one of Alfred's dooms, "the gold thief and the stud thief and the bee thief had each a punishment . . . now they are all equal," and another law gives compensation for the theft of the cow and her calf, or the stud-mare and her foal. As the mares, the equæ silvestres, ran wild in the woods, the temptation to drive them away must have been great. But there were "tame horses" also, for which the reeve had to build stalls in the burh, and the king had a "horsethegn" who seems to have been a person of some importance. There are frequent references to riding in the contemporary sources--riding to war, to the "moot," or court of justice, or on the king's errands, and a horse was esteemed a precious gift, worthy of record in a "book" or charter.

The royal court and the household of the great noble were alike migratory, and the lines of local and social cleavage must have been less sharply defined when the king was constantly moving about among his subjects, and the kingdom was governed in much the same way as a large country estate. Alfred had demesne lands in Kent and Surrey and Sussex, in every county of the older Wessex, and even in remote Cornwall. He is said to have been hunting in Cornwall when he turned aside to pray at the shrine of St. Gueriir for some alleviation of his chronic infirmity. The king's stewards, in their double capacity, political and economic, would need to be as efficient as the "wise reeve" of a later treatise, who had to know the lord's land-right, and the folk-right which the witan declared from of old, and the times of tillage, and all that belonged to the tun, to the very mouse-traps, and the pins of the doorhasps: "by town (on tune) and down (on dune), by wood and water, by field and fold, within and without."

Like many great administrators, King Alfred had a passion for detail, and took an active part in the small affairs of daily life. Nothing was too petty for him; nothing was too trivial for his keen interest in human nature and the world of men. He loved building, and, besides his fortresses and monasteries, Asser speaks of the cities and towns which he founded or restored, of the "halls and royal chambers" which were constructed of stone and wood by his orders, and of the stone-built royal "vills" which were moved at his command from their former sites to more convenient positions.

Asser also makes the curious assertion that gold and silver "edifices" (œdificia) were built by the King's instructions (illo edocente). This probably means that some of his houses were decorated with gilding and metalwork. Alfred, like Beowulf, when he approached the hall "Heorot," may have seen his royal "ham" shining from afar, "splendid and gold-adorned." There are instances of such decoration in ninth-century chronicles as well as in both earlier and later records, Frankish, English, and Scandinavian.

In another passage Asser connects building with decoration, and seems to hint that Alfred had some special knowledge of working in metal, when he describes him as teaching "his goldsmiths and artificers," his falconers and dog-keepers, and then adds that he made by his own device buildings (ædificia) "more venerable and precious" than those of his predecessors. His familiarity with the builder's craft is seen in the way in which he introduces it into his parables and allegories. Thus in the Boethius2 he writes:

Whoso will have eternal bliss, must fly from the dangerous beauty of this world, and build the house of his mind on the firm rock of humility, for Christ dwelleth in the valley of humility, and in the memory of wisdom.

And again3:

Even as the wall of every house is made fast both to the floor and to the roof, so every good thing is made fast to God; for He is both roof and floor of all that is good.

The original preface to Alfred's translation of the Soliloquies of St. Augustine is, in itself, a perfect little picture of the building of a tun or ham in the ninth century:

I gathered me then staves, and props, and beams, and helves for each of the tools that I could work with, and bough timber and bolt timber, and for each of the works which I could perform as many of the fairest trees as I could carry away. Nor did I come home with a burden, because I did not wish to bring the whole wood home, even if I could carry it. In every tree I saw something that I needed at home. Therefore I exhort every one who is able, and has many wains, to wend his way to the same wood where I cut the props. Let him then get more, and load his wains with fair rods (gerdas, or yards), that he may weave many a fine wall, and set up many a goodly house, and build a fair tun, and dwell therein with mirth and ease both in winter and summer, as I never yet have done. But He who taught me, and to whom the wood was pleasing, may make me dwell more easily both in this transitory log-hut by the road, while I am in this world, and also in the eternal home which He has promised us through St. Augustine and St. Gregory and St. Jerome, and through many other holy Fathers.

If the exterior of the "fair house" of the Anglo- Saxon king or noble were gay with paint and gilding, and sometimes, it may be, rich with carving, the interior was no less gorgeous. The walls were hung with costly tapestry, and the columns which supported the roof were turned, carved, or brightly coloured. There were no chimneys, it is true, while the windows were unglazed, and the furniture was somewhat scanty-- a "high seat" for the lord, with benches for the lowlier men, trestle tables, and beds in the burcotes cotes or "bowers" for the lord's family and the more distinguished guests--but the drinking vessels were often of gold or silver, and of beautiful design and fine workmanship, and though to modern ideas the standard of comfort was low, the artistic standard was relatively high. Beauty of form and colour probably entered more intimately into the everyday life of the mass of the people in ninth-century England than it does at the present day.

At great festivals, public or private, at Christmas and Easter, at marriages, and after victories, or when the short cold winter days made outdoor labour and recreation difficult, there would be much good fellowship and merrymaking in the homes of both rich and poor, feasting and drinking in the "mead-hall," music and song, games of chance and skill, and contests of wit. Merrymaking, no doubt, often degenerated into the drunkenness which was a constant reproach to the Anglo-Saxons, hard drinkers and heavy feeders from the beginning. Ine legislated for the case of a quarrel at a feast, or drinking-bout, and Alfred wrote severely against excess in dainty food and diverse drinks. His own marriage, however, was celebrated by a great concourse of people of both sexes, and the festivities were kept up "by day and by night."

The somewhat gross revelry at such gatherings was redeemed by a love of music which seems to have been as intuitive with the Germanic races as their love of strong drink. The young noble's education was not complete until he knew the traditional songs of his country, and could, presumably, chant them to the harp for the entertainment of his fellows. The professional bard, or scop, was often of high birth. He was received with honour and rewarded with rich gifts, whether he was permanently attached to the court, or wandered at will from hall to hall. Even kings, as the legend of Alfred's minstrel visit to the Danish camp shows, did not disdain to follow the example of David, the psalm-scop and harper. Alfred tells the story of Orpheus, in the Boethius, in his own words, with evident pleasure in the thought of the harping that would cause wild beasts to run up and stand as still as if they were tame, though men or dogs came near them: "nor did any beast feel rage or fear towards another for gladness of the music."

Jugglers and mountebanks, on the other hand, were discouraged by the Church, and Alfred faithfully reflected the feeling of his time when he wrote of Homer as "the good scop" and translated the histriones of St. Gregory's Pastoral Care by "evil gleemen."

Alfred's revival of letters appears to have been accompanied by a revival in art following on the destruction worked by the Danish army. Here, however, even more than in literature, there was a real revival, not so much a new birth as a quickening of inherited instincts and aptitudes, which had weakened without altogether perishing. Recent archaeological research has practically established the existence of a native school of decorative art in ninth-century England, a school strongly affected by Irish and Frankish example, but with a distinct individuality and a continuous tradition of its own. If the elaborate jewelled ornaments found in the graves of the præ-Christian period witness to the taste and skill of the heathen Germanic settlers, the illuminated manuscripts of the seventh and eighth centuries show the strength of the influence of the Christian art of Celtic Ireland, while the early ninth-century coinage has marked Frankish characteristics.

Yet Anglo-Saxon art at its best was constructive, not merely imitative. It combined these different elements in original fashion, and produced workmanship alike imaginative in design and delicate in execution. Fortunately, the evidence, if not very full, is highly significant and varied. Gold rings, decorated with filigree work, or inlaid with niello, silver ornaments, engraved with dainty and intricate patterns, or moulded into fanciful shapes, imply genuine artistic feeling and great technical facility in the English craftsmen of Alfred's boyhood. The repetition of the same designs in later work points to the persistence of the established tradition through the disturbed period of the Danish incursions.

Alfred may have inherited artistic sensibility from his parents. He was certainly brought up among beautiful things. His mother tempted her children to learn to read with an illuminated manuscript. His father's gold ring, shaped like a mitre, with his name, † Ethelvulf R (rex), wrought in the fabric, has survived. His sister's ring, too, with an Agnus Dei in niello on gold, and † Eathelsvith Regina scratched on the inside of the hoop, has been preserved. Another gold ring, inscribed with the name of Alhstan, probably belonged to the warrior Bishop of Sherborne, who died in 867.

The papal historian has recorded the rich stuffs and the four silver-gilt gabatæ, the hanging bowls used as church lamps, "of Saxon workmanship" (gabathe Saxisce)5 which King Ethelwulf carried with him to Rome. Alfred himself mentions the "treasures and books" which he had seen in the English churches before the Danish ravages. He shows perception in classing them together, for every manuscript, apart from its literary value, was in itself a work of art, and the urgent imagination of the ninth century sought expression almost indifferently through the pen, the needle, or the graver's tool.

"Treasures and books" had been to the young Alfred a stimulus and a delight. They had stirred his inventive fancy, satisfied his love of symbolism, and deepened his sense of colour and his appreciation of grace of line and harmony of proportion. When at last he found leisure to carry out his literary schemes, it was natural that he should also restore the artistic environment of his early years, and call goldsmiths and artificers to his counsels as well as scholars and clerks. Nor must undue stress be laid on the break with the past caused by the devastating fury of the vikings.

In Northumbria, doubtless, the former cultivation to a great extent passed away. In Mercia there was plundering and burning. But Wessex was only in the grip of the heathen army for a few months in 878, and the very desolation of the northern kingdoms would tend to concentrate the scattered talent of the country at the West- Saxon court, where all fugitive scholars and artists were welcome, and Irish pilgrims, Mercian ecclesiastics, and Frankish monks could meet and exchange ideas. Asser speaks[1] of the numerous workmen (operatores), "gathered from many nations" whom Alfred employed, and it is expressly said of John the Old-Saxon that he was not only "most learned in all discipline of the literary art," but also "skilful (artificiosus) in many other arts." The blending of Celtic and Frankish elements which distinguished the ninthcentury school of Anglo-Saxon craftsmanship may well have been strengthened and emphasised by the cosmopolitan character of the Alfredian courtcircle.

A little group of objects, differing in purpose and origin, but possessing certain common features, gives the clue to the distinctive characteristics of this English art. It includes a manuscript--the Codex Aureus, or Golden Gospels--and several specimens of metalwork--a sword-hilt from near Wallingford, in Berkshire, a knife from Sittingbourne, in Kent, various small silver articles from buried hoards of treasure, the jewel found at Minster Lovel in Oxfordshire, and, most noteworthy of all, the famous "Alfred Jewel". In all these pieces, each admirable in its way, Celtic and Frankish suggestions have been developed on independent lines. Foliage treated with an attempt at naturalism, in the manner of the Carolingian Renaissance, is combined and interwoven with animal forms twisted and contorted into decorative patterns after the Irish fashion, with modifications which seem to be peculiarly Anglo- Saxon.

The connection between the ornamentation of West-Saxon metalwork and the illuminations of the Codex Aureus is of special interest. This splendid manuscript contains the Vulgate version of the Gospels, written in fine Latin characters, and magnificently illuminated with full-page figures of the Evangelists. The introduction of Anglo- Saxon decorative and palæographical details makes it probable that it was the work of an English artist, and resemblances have been traced between it and the Psalter of St. Augustine, a Canterbury manuscript of the early eighth century, in which Celtic and Latin elements are already blended. On the margins of the opening page of St. Matthew's Gospel the Codex Aureus bears, moreover, an inscription in Anglo-Saxon, setting forth how "Ælfred aldorman" and Werburg his wife bought the manuscript with "clean gold" from the "heathen army,"--"for God's love, and for our soul's behoof, and because we would not that these holy books should remain longer in hethenesse,"-- and how they presented the costly gift to Christchurch, Canterbury. This was the Kentish ealdorman, King Alfred's namesake and contemporary, whose will, written in Anglo-Saxon, is still extant. His name and the names of his wife Werburg and their daughter Alhthryth appear at the side of the same page of the Codex, while at the top, in an English hand, is a Latin petition to pray for Ceol heard the priest, Ealhhun, and Wulfhelmaurifex, a goldsmith with an Anglo-Saxon name.

The Codex Aureus, then, was certainly in Kent in the second half of the ninth century, and was seen and handled by nobles, clerks, and artificers. This enhances the importance of the similarity which has been observed between the treatment of zoomorphic motives in its illuminated letters, and the animal forms on the metalwork of the same period, in particular on the Wallingford sword-hilt.

The guards of this exquisite piece of work are inlaid with silver on a background of niello, in delicate patterns, divided into compartments. On the upper guard, nearest the pommel, are the symbols of the four Evangelists, the man, the eagle, the ox, and the lion. On the lower guard are twisted animal designs akin to the zoomorphic illumination in the Codex Aureus, while on both guards the foliage is of the naturalistic Carolingian type. The pommel is ornamented with animal heads in relief and a beaded border, and a small fragment of gold plate, which doubtless once adorned it, recalls "the golden-hilted swords (hiltsweordas)" which the king's thegns wore when they stood around their royal lord. Such a noble weapon was, perhaps, the sword worth a hundred mancuses which King Alfred bequeathed to Ethelred of Mercia. Such, too, may have been that "Saxon sword," with a golden scabbard, with which Alfred is said to have invested his little grandson, Athelstan.

If these works of art may, not unfairly, be connected with the Alfredian revival, others go back to the opening years of Alfred's reign, and to still earlier days, before the Danish wars. The Sittingbourne knife, which has the maker's name in silver, and the owner's name engraved in brass, is inlaid with silver and brass, in scroll patterns like those on the silver and niello bands and the silver strap-tabs discovered near St. Austell in Cornwall. These were probably hidden not long after 871, since they were found in company with a silver cup containing coins, of which only two were as late as the year of King Alfred's accession.

The mixture of silver and niello, in these objects, the panelled decoration, the pearled or beaded borders, the peculiar zoomorphic ornament, and the terminal animal heads in relief, all characterise the Anglo-Saxon art of the later ninth century. Animal forms of the same description, moreover, are inlaid in Ethelswith's ring. A pattern on Ethelwulf's ring is repeated on a strap-tab belonging to the northern Cuerdale hoard, which seems to have been deposited about 910. Niello is used in Ealhstan's ring, and cramped animals fill the lozenge-shaped compartments which alternate with circles to form its hoop. Thus the style is carried back to the first half of the ninth century, while the connection with the Codex Aureus and the Psalter of St. Augustine suggests the continuous and gradual development of both ecclesiastical and secular art in southern England, under the influences, direct or indirect, of the Irish, Northumbrian, and Frankish schools.

From the first, however, the native designers seem to have shown a power of original adaptation, which was fostered by the stimulating atmosphere of Alfred's enlightened court, where the King in person directed his goldsmiths, and an ealdorman was willing to give great sums to save an illuminated manuscript from desecration.

Among the many remarkable ninth-century specimens of metalwork, the skill of the southern English craftsmen is, perhaps, seen at its height in two enamelled jewels, which may well be associated with the West-Saxon revival of art. Of these, one, found at Minster Lovel in Oxfordshire, has a cross in cloisonné enamel2 on gold, in green and opaque white on a blue ground, in a circular setting of gold filigree, which slopes outwards from the enamel, and is finished by a scalloped border. A narrow gold cord surrounds the enamel, and between it and the outer border are two bands of filigree-work, in a zigzag pattern, filled in with raised dots, which crust the surface, and give a very rich effect. A hollow projecting socket of gold, in which a pin and rivet still remain, show that the jewel was originally the head of some kind of small rod or staff.

Of the same character, but far more elaborate and beautiful, is the "Alfred Jewel" which was dug up in 1693 in Newton or Petherton Park, near Athelney. This jewel has often been described, but it must be seen, for the harmony of its colouring and the delicacy of its workmanship to be fully appreciated. Though larger than the Minster Lovel specimen, it is a little thing, not quite two and a half inches in its extreme length, an inch and a fifth in width, and about half an inch in thickness. An oval slab of rock-crystal protects the enamel; the edge of it curves outwards so that the front, or obverse, of the jewel, is smaller than the back, or reverse, which consists of a flat gold plate, engraved with a foliated design, and secured by the overlapping, in a succession of small triangles, of the border of the filigree frame. The central enamel, cloisonné on gold, shows a half-length figure, apparently in a sitting posture, in a green robe, with touches of red, a foliated wand or sceptre in each hand, and a lily-like design in gold on either side. The background is blue, and the flesh-tints are of an opaque white. The drawing is rude, but the colouring is bright and pure. The whole is surrounded by a frame of exquisite gold filigree. A beading encloses the front of the crystal. Around the curving sides runs the legend:

+AELFRED MEC HEHT GEWYRCAN

(Alfred bade me be wrought)

in golden open-work letters, through which the crystal can be seen. Two narrow beadings, producing a corded effect, separate the legend from the solid band of filigree-work which completes the setting. This is decorated with a pattern resembling the ornamentation of the Minster Lovel jewel, but somewhat more complicated--a sinuous line of gold filament is broken by foliated ornaments, on a ground thickly encrusted with raised gold dots. The oval of the frame is broader at the top, corresponding to the head of the enamelled figure. The bottom of the setting is prolonged into an animal-head terminal, also covered with gold dots, and with gold filaments marking the contours of the head. The back of the terminal is flattened, and engraved with a scale pattern. The open mouth of the monster, which has been regarded both as a wild boar and as the "dragon of Wessex," holds a pin and rivet which prove it to have been the socket of a stem or handle, probably of some perishable material, wood or ivory, which has rotted away, leaving the metal intact. The eye-holes of the animal may once have been filled with garnets, crystal, or blue glass, as in the case of similar terminals, and the empty gold cells at the points of the ears look as if they, too, had held vitreous paste or crystals.

It is satisfactory to be able with some confidence to reject the theory of the Eastern origin of the enamel of the jewel, which was supposed to have been brought from Constantinople, and set by an English goldsmith. Too little is known of early mediæval enamels to admit of a positive conclusion, but whereas the oldest certain examples of Byzantine enamel date only from the beginning of the tenth century, specimens of Celtic enamelled work of a much earlier period can be produced both from Britain and from Ireland. The opaque white flesh-tints and the translucent green which appear on the Alfred Jewel may also indicate a Celtic derivation, and the roughness of the enamelwork as compared with the finish of the gold setting may imply an industry in a primitive stage of development. Although, then, nothing can be definitely asserted, the evidence favours Irish influence and an English source for the enamelled figure.

Another magnificent example of the same school is the circular cloisonné enamel brooch set with gold filigree and pearls, which was discovered in London in 1839. This represents a crowned head and bust, in blue, green, and opaque white. It has been assigned both to the ninth century and to a later period, and it is certainly superior in drawing and in finish to the Minster Lovel specimen, and even to the Alfred Jewel.

The figure in the Alfred Jewel has always been a puzzle to antiquaries. It has been taken for a king enthroned, for Alfred himself, for St. Neot or St.

Cuthbert, the saints connected with his legendary history, for the Pope, with the symbols of earthly and heavenly authority, and for the glorified Christ. It is most probably intended to represent the Saviour, in the manner of the miniatures in the manuscripts of the seventh and eighth centuries. A two-sceptred Christ appears in the Irish Book of Kells, and the St. Luke in the Gospels of St. Chad bears a cross in one hand and a foliated wand or sceptre in the other.

An English origin may be still more confidently assumed for the gold setting of the Alfred Jewel than for its enamel. In conception and execution it is thoroughly in keeping with well-authenticated examples of late ninth-century Anglo-Saxon work. The filigree has parallels, not only in the Minster Lovel jewel, but in several late Anglo-Saxon brooches. The animal-head terminal is also a recognised characteristic of the metalwork of the period. Ornaments decorated with these heads have been found with coins which enable them to be dated with some precision, and it is further possible to connect some of them very closely with the Alfredian "monster," by the recurrence of its curious ears, shaped like "commas," on the St. Austell silver bands, and on other ninth-century relics, including a strap-tab from Sevington in Wiltshire, which was buried with an engraved silver spoon and fork, and with coins ranging from about 806 to 890. In the Alfred Jewel, moreover, the eye-socket is of the same character. The striking coincidence in general form between the Alfred Jewel and the earlier Irish pins, with pendant, "kite-shaped" heads, and animal terminals, is a further sign of Celtic influence. The engraved design on the gold back of the jewel apparently represents a tree, conventionally yet freely treated, on a hatched ground, after the fashion of the Carolingian manuscripts.

The survival of these fine products of the English goldsmith's art gives life to Asser's account of Alfred's patronage of goldsmiths and craftsmen, and to the king's own rendering, in the Boethius, of "the bones of Fabricius" (ossa Fabricii) by "the bones of the famous and wise goldsmith Weland.""I call him wise," writes the artloving Alfred, in one of his characteristic comments on the text, "because the skilled craftsman can never lose his craft, and can no more be deprived of it than the sun can be moved from his place." Then, the legends of his childhood returning to his memory, he asks again: "Where now are Weland's bones, or who knoweth now where they are?"

It was Weland, the magic smith, who forged the sword with which Beowulf slew the monster Grendel, and as Alfred wrote of his "wisdom," he may have thought of such wonderful pieces of craftsmanship as the Wallingford sword-hilt, or the lovely little gold-panelled dagger-pommel which was found near Windsor, not very far from the spot where tradition has located "Wayland's Smithy" in an ancient dolmen on the Berkshire downs. The Anglo-Saxon goldsmith might, indeed, be an armourer, decorating the weapons of war, or an ecclesiastic, lavishing his skill on the ornamentation of the rich covers of sacred manuscripts, such as Wulfhelm aurifex may possibly once have wrought for the Codex Aureus, or a professional artificer, working to order, like Alfred's aurifices. In any case, the nameless maker of the Alfred Jewel must have been a master of his craft, an inspired artist, with a true creative gift.

The archœological and historical evidence for placing the production of the Alfred Jewel in the Wessex of the late ninth century is so strong that it may be allowed to override certain philological considerations which seem to indicate either a northern source, or an earlier date. These are based chiefly on the archaic forms of some of the letters in the inscription, notably the square C and G, and on the occurrence of the Anglian mec and heht in the legend. The square letters prove little, for they are also found on Alfred's coins, and in the Worcester manuscript of the Pastoral Care. Heht is both an Anglian and a West-Saxon form, which is employed in the prefatory verses to the English translation of Gregory's Pastoral Care, but the use of the northern mec for me is a more serious difficulty, since it is unknown to the written and spoken language of Wessex in the ninth century. If the jewel is to be regarded as a product of the Alfredian revival, this form can only be explained on the supposition that the goldsmith either copied a northern model, or was an Anglian, working on traditional lines;-- no improbable contingency, with Mercian and Northumbrian refugees flocking into Wessex, and artificers of all kinds seeking the patronage of the king. That very skilful handicraftsmen could be quite poor scholars is shown by the blundered inscription on a finely worked ring in the Ashmolean Museum: Sigeric mea heth gewyrcan (Sigeric bade me be wrought). Perhaps the Anglian element in the Alfred Jewel may be connected with the noticeably Celtic features of its form and workmanship, but as yet the mystery of its true origin and purpose remains impenetrable.

At the same time, if the attribution of the jewel to King Alfred cannot be proved, at least it cannot be disproved. The name Alfred is not, it is true, followed, as in the rings of Ethelwulf and Ethelswith, by the regal title, and this has been taken to imply that the work was executed before Alfred's accession in 871, or that it was made for some Alfred other than the King. Alfred was a fairly common name in Wessex in the second half of the ninth century. It was borne, among others, by a bishop of Winchester, and by the purchaser of the Codex Aureus, the ealdorman of Kent. Still, the King was more likely to order such a costly masterpiece than any of his subjects however wealthy or distinguished, and the fact of its discovery on ancient crown land, near Athelney, is also not without weight. The ascription, moreover, is sanctified by use and sentiment, and by the unhesitating belief of generations of scholars, and until more decisive evidence can be brought forward, the beautiful little jewel may be permitted to retain its time-honoured association with King Alfred.

As to the purpose which the "Alfred Jewel" was intended to serve, speculation has been busy since the beginning of the eighteenth century, without arriving at any entirely satisfactory explanation. The connection with Athelney led to the idea that it was a personal ornament, or a symbol of royalty, a relic of the King's exile, an amulet, the head of a sceptre, or a jewel worn in a crown-encircled helmet. A more plausible theory was advanced by Dr. Clifford in 1877. He saw in the jewel the handle of a baculus Cantorum, a pointer or book-staff, such as are found among the treasures of mediæval churches. These pointers, which were often made of costly materials, were sometimes fastened into the binding of ecclesiastical books, and Dr. Clifford further suggested that the Anglo-Saxon œstel, which is glossed stylus in the eleventh century, was such a book-staff, and that the jewel is the remnant of one of those œstels worth fifty mancuses which Alfred sent to his bishops, with copies of the English translation of Gregory's Pastoral Care. He pictures John the Old-Saxon, one of the collaborators in the translation, receiving a "presentation copy," as abbot of the new foundation of Athelney, and it would be pleasant to think that the skilful artist, "John, priest and monk," had a hand in the decoration of the œstel, as well as in the translation of the text. But this identification with a particular book-staff is too fanciful to be admitted, though it is quite possible both that œstels were pointers, and that the Alfred Jewel and the Minster Lovel jewel were the handles of such pointers.

Alfred may even have been influenced in the devising of his œstel by the remembrance of the shrine which his father Ethelwulf gave to Malmesbury Abbey, to hold the bones of St. Aldhelm. It had, according to William of Malmesbury, a crystal cover, on which the King's name might be read in letters of gold. On the front were figures in solid silver, and on the back were representations of St. Aldhelm's miracles, in what appears to have been some kind of repoussé work (levato metallo). Thus the jewel, with its mingling of Irish, Anglian, and southern characteristics, may be the fine flower of an artistic revival which had its roots deep in the past, and its fruits in the immediate future.

Alfred, like his father, had a great reverence for the saints, and prayed daily before the relics which he always carried about with him. It is in relation to these relics that Asser gives a long account of the King's practical skill and "wisdom," in designing a horn lantern. Anxious to devote half his time to the service of God, he found it difficult to measure the hours in the sunless days of rain and cloud, and the dark nights. He therefore caused wax candles to be made, each twelve inches long, of the weight of twelve pennies, and calculated to burn for four hours before the relics of the saints. In this way six candles exactly marked the twenty-four hours of a day and night. He soon found, however, that it was necessary, if they were to burn evenly, to shield them from the draughts which blew through the doors and windows, and the chinks in the masonry of churches, through the cracks in walls, and the slits in tents--a lively, though unconscious, commentary on the inconveniences of Alfred's shifting quarters. He devised, then, a lantern of wood and horn, with a door. In this the candles, renewed every four hours, were placed, and, shielded from the wind, burnt steadily, and gave a fairly accurate measure of time.

Asser's enthusiasm over this simple contrivance, with the space which he allots to it in his book, may imply that it was a new thing, at least in this particular form. It is typical of much in Alfred's history that where important matters have been forgotten, this homely instance of his mechanical ingenuity should be remembered. At a period when the general standard of artistic production was so high, it is rather surprising to find the coinage comparatively poor in design and execution, distinctly inferior to the eighth-century issues of Offa of Mercia, which were influenced by the Carolingian Renaissance, and the Frankish reform of the currency. Though this does not of necessity imply a decline in prosperity, the shock given to English commerce by the Danish invasions may be inferred from its revival and expansion after the peace of 878, when large quantities of coins were issued, and trade regulations were inserted in the West-Saxon laws. If, indeed, the viking raids checked commercial development in England, the viking settlements stimulated it, for the Northmen were keen traders and merchants.

The West-Saxons do not appear to have had a coinage till late in the reign of Egbert, Alfred's grandfather, who seems to have been the first independent West-Saxon King to coin money at the ancient Kentish mint of Canterbury. Ethelwulf and his three elder sons followed the example thus set. It was reserved for Alfred to adapt the old machinery to new conditions, and to organise not only the internal and Continental trade of his kingdom, but also the commercial relations between Wessex and the Danelaw.

Picturesque sidelights are thrown by Alfred's laws on the industrial side of West-Saxon life. Merchants or "chapmen" (ciepemen) are bidden to bring the men whom they wish to "lead tip country" before the king's reeve in the folk-moot, to state their numbers, and to hold themselves responsible for their good behaviour. If, on the road, they find it necessary to engage more followers, they are to notify the fact to the king's reeve, with the witness of the "moot."

Ine's earlier decrees are also retained: the merchant who buys "up country" must have witnesses, though if he is caught in the possession of stolen goods, he is somewhat lightly fined, and if he can prove that he acquired the goods in ignorance, he goes scot-free. Under the brief businesslike phrases, may be divined the small beginnings of great movements, the internal traffic in cattle and agricultural products, the import trade in silks and spices, in precious metals and jewels, of the tenth and eleventh centuries. The travelling merchant, with his train of men and waggons or pack-horses, wanders "up country" from town or port, eagerly welcomed in hall and village and outlying farmstead. There is chaffering and bargaining as the goods change hands, sometimes paid for in kind, sometimes with Alfred's silver pennies, coined at one of the great trade centres, the towns on the highways of commerce, to which, his rounds ended, the merchant would return, to replenish his empty bales.

The West-Saxon courts and reeves might be trusted to look after local trading interests, but with the formation of the Danelaw a new factor had entered into commercial intercourse, which could only be dealt with by the central authority. When Alfred acquired London, he made provision, in his treaty with Guthrum-Athelstan, for trade in "cattle and goods," between the Danes of East Anglia and his own subjects. Hostages were to be given by the trader, Danish or English, who crossed the border into alien territory, as pledges of peace, and a proof of honourable intentions.

In connection with the Danish settlers, too, came in new measures of value, the Scandinavian halfmark of gold1 side by side with the West-Saxon shilling2 and mancus. These were all, at this time, used as units of account, representing weights of gold or silver. The only actual coins issued by Alfred were silver pennies, and the halfpennies which he seems to have originated. These coins were struck at seven or eight mints: the ancient Roman cities of Canterbury and Winchester, the "head burhs," ecclesiastical and civil, of the West- Saxon kingdom; Exeter, Bath, and Gloucester for the newly settled west country; Oxford, on the Mercian border; London, commanding the river highway of the Thames, where Healfdene had coined before; and, unless the monogram on the pennies bearing this mint-mark has been misread, the northern town of Lincoln, in the next reign a stronghold of Danish power.

The archbishops of Canterbury had also the right of coining money, and a curious series of silver pennies was issued in East Anglia, in honour of St. Edmund, without a mint-mark, but bearing the saint's name and the names of many moneyers, some of them of unquestionably foreign stock, Scandinavian or Frankish. Independently of these, Guthrum-Athelstan struck coins in East Anglia, copied from one of the Alfredian types. He, too, employed moneyers with foreign names, many of them, apparently, Franks. The names of more than a hundred moneyers appear on the various coins which bear the superscription of King Alfred, but it is practically certain that a large number of these were Anglo-Danish imitations of Alfred's coins, not really issued by his authority.

Among Alfred's genuine coins, twenty-three types have been distinguished, of which thirteen fall within the period before 878, and the remaining ten, including the great majority of extant specimens, belong to the latter years of the reign, after the first peace with Guthrum. The earlier types are copied from coins of King Ethelred of Wessex, of Archbishop Ethelred of Canterbury, and, in one case, from a curious penny apparently struck by Healfdene, the viking leader, during his brief occupation of London after the peace of 871. This type, which was also imitated by Ceolwulf II., the puppet king of Mercia, has a monogram of London on the reverse. Healfdene, then, working from Continental models, probably inaugurated the monogram coinage, to which several of Alfred's types conform. They have the mint name in monogram form on the reverse, while in other types the reverses bear the mint name, the moneyer's name, crosses and ornaments. The obverses of the various issues have the mint name, or, more frequently, a cross or a rude bust of the King, with his name and title. Canterbury, as might be expected, appears to have been the most prolific mint. Next to it come Oxford and London. The title Rex Saxonum on the rare Winchester and Exeter coins links the later coinage of Alfred to the first issues of his son and successor, Edward the Elder.

That the West-Saxon coinage was far from pure is evident from the care taken to specify that important payments shall be made in unalloyed metal. Thus Alfred's laws mention the "five pounds of pure pennies" which constitute the fine for breaking the king's borh or protection, and the noble's wergild is fixed in Alfred's treaty with Guthrum, for Englishman and Dane alike, at eight half-marks of refined gold, "cooked gold," that had been tried by fire. In the Boethius, too, Alfred compares the union of many forms of goodness in the Highest Good, to the melting of metal into an ingot, and speaks of the cleansing and refining of men by the heavenly fire as like the refining of silver. Already, then, some system of "blanching" or assaying gold and silver had been established. Already the foundations were laid for the elaborate organisation of the later Exchequer. Rustic still, and simple, primitive even to barbarism, Alfred's England yet held within it a mighty force of life, the youthful promise of a splendid maturity.

THE VICTORIES OF PEACE III

III. Alfredian Literature

IN literature as in politics, in the life of thought as in the life of action, King Alfred stands at the opening of a new era in the development of England. The keynote of that era he himself unwittingly struck when he wrote in the preface to the translation of Gregory's Pastoral Care:

Formerly . . . foreigners sought wisdom and learning in this land . . . now we should have to get them from abroad if we would have them.

The earlier English literature, Latin, Anglian, and Saxon, had been native to the soil, monastic and ecclesiastical in form, yet popular and spontaneous in spirit, the outcome of an enthusiastic acceptance of the Christian faith. Cædmon and Bede, Aldhelm and Cynewulf, though they drew their ultimate inspiration from Rome and the East, were the immediate fruits of English Christianity. The later literature was more exotic in character. It was the result of a deliberate policy, a royal boon, given to the people with a didactic intention. If the English Alcuin had carried to the court of Charles the Great something of the learning of the monastic schools of Northumbria, Frankish culture reacted on England in the ninth century, when the court schools of the Carolingian emperors served, in all probability, as models for the educational system of the West-Saxon kings.

It is only in relation to Alfred's political theory as a whole that his literary work can be fully appreciated. Seen in isolation, it appears somewhat crude and disjointed, but as a part of a system of education which was itself part of a wider scheme of government, it becomes both intelligible and admirable.

Alfred was no cloistered scholar, studying for the pure joy of learning, but a student and teacher, with an eminently practical aim. There is conscious utilitarian purpose behind all his writings. They are designed for the education and training of the citizens of a Christian State. His translations from the Latin of Gregory the Great, Orosius, Bede, and Boethius popularised the books which seemed to him most needful for every man to know, famous books on theology, ancient and modern history and geography, and philosophy. By his English work in the Chronicle and the Laws he preserved all that was best and most stimulating in the annals, the customs, and the beliefs of the past, all that was most worthy of record in the political and social experiences of the present.

He recognised the value of "men of prayer" as instruments of government, and he deliberately set himself to raise up a succession of learned and godly men in Church and State, by educating the clergy and fitting them to become in turn the teachers of the laity, and by diffusing sound and useful knowledge in the vulgar tongue among free men of every rank. In the decline of learning in Wessex, the King called scholars to his help from far and wide, the four Mercians, Werferth, Bishop of Worcester, Plegmund, afterwards Archbishop of Canterbury, and the priests Æthelstan and Werwulf , Grimbald the Frank, Johnthe Old- Saxon, and Asser the Welshman. He heaped rewards and preferment on these men, and kept one or other of them in constant attendance on him, to read and interpret the Latin books which he could not as yet translate for himself. Even Asser's turgid rhetoric cannot altogether hide the artless simplicity of Alfred's zeal for knowledge, a zeal akin to the ardour of the early Renaissance scholars of the sixteenth century, or of the nineteenth-century pioneers of the movements for the higher education of women and of working-men. The King seized every moment of the rare leisure of his busy manhood to gratify the long-suppressed desire for learning of his childish years.

One day, when he and Asser were talking and reading together, Alfred drew from his bosom a little Book of Hours, psalms and prayers, and asked to have a passage which had struck him copied into it. Failing to find space, Asser fetched a clean quire of parchment and started a new volume of translated extracts. Thus arose the Encheiridion, Manual, or Handbook, so-called because Alfred had it at hand "by day and night," a collection of flowers of thought (flosculos), culled from the Bible and the great masters of literature, which grew to be almost as large as a psalter. It seems to have been known in the twelfth century both to Florence of Worcester, who calls it Dicta regis Elfredi, and to William of Malmesbury, and from it came the pretty tale of St. Aldhelm winning the half-civilised West-Saxons to listen to his teaching by singing to them in their native tongue on the bridge at Malmesbury, a story which would please the King who loved the fable of Orpheus, and was himself engaged in a gallant struggle with the forces of ignorance and barbarism.

If, as Asser states, the Handbook was begun in 887, Alfred's definite scheme of translation would be started shortly after the second peace with Guthrum-Athelstan, when five peaceful years lay before him. To this period most authorities agree in attributing the Laws, the first section of the Anglo-Saxon Chronicle up to 892, and Asser's Life of the King, which was apparently written about 893.

On the question of the time and order of production of the four great translations, the Pastoral Care, the Orosius, the Bede, and the Boethius, opinion is more widely divided. In the absence of evidence, conjecture and imagination have been busy, and each of Alfred's works has become the centre of a circle of controversy. It is, at least, safe to assume that the renewal of the Danish invasions in 892, with the war, pestilence, and murrain that clouded the following years, would leave little leisure or energy for literary interests, and that the translations were probably completed either before 893, or after 896.

Since Asser, who wrote his Life of Alfred about 893, and himself took part in the English version of the Pastoral Care, only mentions the Handbook and Werferth's rendering of St.Gregory's Dialogues, some critics would place all the books which are directly due to the King in the last few years of his life. Others, again, think with Professor Wülker that the Pastoral Care, the Bede, and the Orosius followed each other in quick succession between 889 and 893, while the Boethius, the Soliloquies of St. Augustine, or "Blooms", and perhaps the translation of the Psalms, were written in the years between 897 and 901.

The first theory seems to compress Alfred's literary activity into an unduly short space of time, more especially if 899 or 900 rather than 901 be taken as the year of the King's death. The second theory leaves unexplained the silence of Asser on the subject of Alfred's original work, a silence possibly due to the obviously imperfect and unrevised form of Asser's biography, which may have been written at different periods. It should always, moreover, be remembered that Alfred's method of composition was slow and careful, and that each book was the fruit of a long process of thought and preparation, which may have been spread over several years.

In the preface to the Pastoral Care the King himself describes how he turned the Latin into English, "sometimes word for word, sometimes sense for sense," as he learned it from Plegmund and Asser, Grimbald and John, and how he began his task "amid the various and manifold troubles of this kingdom." Even if none of the four translations appeared in its final shape before 896, it does not follow that they were not begun earlier, and brought to perfection in the face of almost insuperable difficulties and hindrances. In any case, the Pastoral Care, the Orosius, and the Bede belong in the order of thought to Alfred's earlier literary period, and, as far as subjectmatter is concerned, his works fall naturally into two groups, the one practical, the other more speculative in character. Law, history, and pastoral theology may well have occupied the laborious days of educational and administrative organisation, while the study of philosophy, the "heavenborn Wisdom," of Boethius and St. Augustine, would fill that brief time of "stillness" which crowned the strenuous reign with peace.

The Laws of Alfred the Great deserve a place among his literary works, both because they are intimately connected with his general educational policy, and because they bear the clear stamp of his mind and thought, in the original preface, in the passages translated from the Bible, and in the whole sequence and arrangement of the material.

William of Malmesbury's rhetorical statement that the King issued laws "amid the blast of trumpets and the clash of arms" need not be taken literally. Alfred's "dooms" were evidently designed for the government of the country in time of peace, and were drawn up, as the preface shows, with care and deliberation, after consultation with expert advisers. They may have preceded the completion of the first section of the Chronicle, in or about 892. Their latest editor, Professor Liebermann, dates them tentatively" after 890." Dr. Turk, who has made them his peculiar study, places them in 890, but thinks that they followed the translation of the Pastoral Care. It seems probable, at least, that they ought to be assigned to the opening years of Alfred's literary career, and that they form part of that constructive policy which he elaborated in the first peaceful interval of his reign.

The Code has been preserved in several manuscripts, of which none are earlier than the tenth century. The most ancient, which was probably copied straight from an Alfredian original, is now bound up with the famous Parker manuscript of the Anglo-Saxon Chronicle, and, like it, seems to have come from Winchester. It is in the West-Saxon dialect, and is supposed to have been written about the middle of the tenth century.

The first part, or historical introduction, recalls Asser's statement that the King began to study "the rudiments of Holy Scripture" on St. Martin's Day, 887. The passages from the Bible are rendered into English with an ease and vigour which imply a practised hand. These passages are taken from the Vulgate, St. Jerome's Latin translation of the Bible, and it is possible that some of them may have been copied into Alfred's Handbook before they were incorporated with his dooms.

In the Decalogue, the second and parts of the fourth and tenth commandments are omitted, in accordance with current ecclesiastical usage, but a tenth commandment is added from the book of Exodus2: "Ye shall not make with me gods of silver, neither shall ye make unto you gods of gold." In the ninth commandment, now the second, "God wrought heaven and earth" is turned into "Christ wrought heaven and earth," while in the fifth commandment, "Honour thy father and mother, that thy days may be long in the land which the Lord thy God hath given thee," the last clause is transposed and made to refer to the parents "whom the Lord gave thee," instead of to the land, a grammatical mistake of a pleasant suggestiveness, for Alfred had good cause to thank God for the gift of his mother Osburh, and Ethelwulf, whatever his failings, had been a tender and indulgent father to his youngest son.

In the extracts from the Mosaic law, the book of Exodus is followed somewhat freely from the twenty-first chapter to the thirteenth verse of the twenty-third chapter. The adaptations which the King deemed suitable, if slight, are significant. Explanations are given, to bring Hebrew custom into harmony with Germanic ideas. The "Hebrew slave (servus)" becomes the "Christian theow." The place to which an involuntary manslayer may fly for sanctuary is, like the cities of refuge in the translation of the Pastoral Care,I a frithstowe, a place of peace, and the manslaughter may be atoned for according to "folk-right." The owner of an ox which has killed a man or woman is to be put to death or to pay a money penalty as the witan find right. For the offering of the first-born son are substituted "the first fruits of all that go and grow." "Thou shalt not wrest the judgment of the poor in his cause," is expanded into: "Judge righteous and equal judgments: judge not one judgment for the rich and another for the poor, nor one judgment to friends and another to foes."

More striking than any of these changes is the fact itself that Alfred could accept, and work into his Code with so little alteration, the laws that had been designed for the guidance of an Oriental people more than two thousand years earlier. Like the Puritans of the seventeenth century, he identified the English with the children of the promise, and took over without question the Mosaic law as applicable to ninth-century Wessex. This was, perhaps, less strange for Alfred than for the Puritans. He too, like Moses, had to give laws to a tribal society, based on slavery, monotheistic, respecting the rights of the family and kindred, with a rude idea of a retributive justice, "an eye for an eye, a tooth for a tooth," a life for a life, where even animals taking life were punished with death, where fines were exacted, oaths of purgation sworn, and witnesses called in, where tithes were paid to the Church, and the poor, the widow, and the fatherless were protected by the State.

Yet if, in his political outlook, Alfred stood as near to Mosaic Israel as to Christian Rome, if his love of truth and justice made him admire the rigid impartiality of Hebrew ethics, his tender nature was irresistibly drawn to the mercy and charity, the "mildheartedness," to use one of his favourite English words, of the Christian dispensation. He passes from the law which God gave to Moses to the law which Christ gave to his Apostles, and translates the Apostolic letter from Jerusalem, which explains in a tolerant spirit how far the old law need be observed.I The letter closes with the Golden Rule, which in several old Greek and Latin versions of the Acts of the Apostles was added to the text, and was thence transferred to some manuscripts of the Vulgate.

Turning, then, from the primitive Judaic and Christian law to its later application, Alfred comes to the decrees of the "synods" held by the "holy bishops and other noteworthy witan of the English (Angel-cyn)." He includes the bishops among the witan, and makes no distinction in kind between ecclesiastical and secular law or between lay and clerical assemblies. Church and State to him are one: a united body, with different organs and functions, but a single aim.

Most interesting is the brief autobiographical introduction which ushers in the English dooms. Here, in his own words, Alfred recognises both the traditional customary character of English law, with its threefold tribal and local division, West-Saxon, Mercian, and Kentish, and its personal character, as to some extent the work of the three great royal lawgivers, Ine, Offa, and Ethelbert. He strikes the same note as in the preface to the Pastoral Care. He is an adapter and an interpreter rather than a creator, one who dares not set down much of his own, but regards himself as a trustee, using the heritage of the past for the good of the generations to come.I The haphazard arrangement of these English dooms contrasts with the comparatively logical order of the biblical sections which precede them. Thrown together almost at random, with little attempt at classification, and with many repetitions and seeming inconsistencies, they yet show Alfred careful of detail, scrupulous, just, and thoughtful for his people's welfare. If in their technical aspect they belong to legal and administrative history, the principle that underlies them gives them educational and literary value.

It was a happy chance that brought together in one cover the best manuscripts of the Laws and of the Anglo-Saxon Chronicle, which may almost be regarded as complementary parts of Alfred's scheme of national education, the ancestral customs which were "good to hold" illustrated by the tribal history, the annals of the deeds of men who "wrought a goodly example for those who came after."

The searching criticism to which the so-called Anglo-Saxon Chronicle has been subjected by English and German scholars has done much to establish the relative historical value of its different parts, without impairing its claim to be considered a unique vernacular record of the history of a primitive Germanic people. There are, as Professor Earle and Mr. Plummer have explained, four main Chronicles, contained in seven manuscripts, all based on a common original, an Alfredian Chronicle, ending with the year 891.I In or about that year copies were probably made, and sent to various religious houses, where they were carried on as independent local annals. The oldest of the seven manuscripts, which the Elizabethan Archbishop Parker bequeathed to Corpus Christi College, Cambridge, extends from the birth of Christ to the year 1070, and was apparently a Winchester book, transferred to Canterbury in the eleventh century. It is now bound up with the Latin Acts of Lanfranc, the Laws of Alfred, certain lists of popes and bishops, and that Carmen Paschale of the poet Sedulius from which Asser quotes in his Life of Alfred.

The association with the laws and papal and episcopal lists may be ancient. Gaimar, the Anglo-Norman twelfth-century poet, seems in one passage to connect the laws with the Alfredian Chronicle, as in another passage he distinctly connects the Chronicle with Winchester. Alfred, he says, caused an English book to be made, of adventures and laws, and battles and kings:

Il fist escrivere un livre Engleis, Des aventures, e des leis (laws) E de batailes de la terre, E des reis ki firent la guere.

And again he tells how the "great book called the Chronicle," in which was written the true history of the kings, was due to Alfred, and was kept chained at Winchester:

Croniz ad hum (name) un livere grant: Ka Wincestre, en l'eveskez, La est des reis la dreite estorie E les vies e la memorie. Li reis Elfred l'out en demaine, Fermer i fist une chaine.

Thirteen or fourteen different handwritings can be traced in the Parker manuscript, and it may be divided into thirteen chronological sections, of varying age. The first four sections, which end with the year 912, and cover the life and death of Alfred, appear to date from the late ninth or early tenth century. The opening section goes to 892, and seems to have been copied from a copy of the Alfredian source, for it contains certain errors in chronology which are almost certainly to be attributed to the carelessness of a copyist, since they are not found in the Annals of St. Neots, a compilation derived from the same original. As the scribes of the four main Chronicles follow this copyist, and repeat his errors, modern critics trace these four Chronicles, at least in their common section, up to 892, to a hypothetical faulty transcript of an original manuscript, ending with that year, in which the chronological errors did not occur.

This original manuscript, the fount and source of the whole series of Chronicles, may be safely attributed to the direct initiative of King Alfred. Mr. Plummer believes that "the idea of a national Chronicle as opposed to merely local annals" was Alfred's own idea, "carried out under his direction," even if he did not actually dictate some of the annals, a view which is borne out by Gaimar's testimony, and by the fact that the genealogy of the West-Saxon royal house prefixed to the Parker manuscript is only brought down to the accession of Alfred. The affinity in expression between the Chronicle and Alfred's translation of Orosius, to which attention has been called by Mr. Plummer, points in the same direction, while the distribution of copies of the Alfredian Chronicle among the different religious houses would be quite in accordance with that transmission of the English version of the Pastoral Care to the bishops of which Alfred speaks in his preface.

The King's own relation to the Chronicle, also, his work of selection and compilation, is not unlike his connection with the Laws. Here, too, he borrowed from foreign sources, worked up the native traditions, and added something of his own. Here, too, his circle of ecclesiastical advisers may have lent efficient help. It has even been suggested, though there is no means of proof, that the original Alfredian Chronicle was written by Archbishop Plegmund.

The question of the sources from which the original Chronicle was drawn is somewhat easier of solution. In all probability Alfred found ready to his hand ancient annals of the tribal kingdoms, either in Latin or English, preserved at Canterbury or at Winchester, with lists of kings and archbishops, and royal genealogies, like the one prefixed to the Parker manuscript. From about the year 597 the legends and traditions of the English people, in common with their laws and customs, would be written down under the influence of Christianity, in imitation of the Roman fashion. There must also have been many floating folk-tales and ballads, "Saxon songs," such as Alfred loved to learn by heart, while Bede's Ecclesiastical History and other Latin records were, of course, easily accessible. From all these materials, the King and his helpers may have compiled the Chronicle, in much the same way as, about the same time, they compiled the Laws.

Alfred would appear to have dictated or suggested the written vernacular record of the events of his own reign up to 892, with the immediately preceding reigns of his three brothers, and to have welded this on to an already existing Chronicle, ending with the reign of his father Ethelwulf. A distinct break occurs in the Parker manuscript at the year 855, after the mention of the death of Ethelwulf, when an elaborate royal pedigree is inserted. Here, says Professor Earle, "the termination of an ancient Chronicle is plainly seen, like the lines of some ancient seacoast high up in the mainland." To make the work complete, the prefatory annals would be translated from Bede, and other historical Latin sources, or borrowed from old English traditions, legends, and songs, and the story would thus be carried back to the birth of Christ. To the whole, finally, was prefixed, as a sort of introduction, the accepted genealogy of the West-Saxon royal house, with the regnal table, down to the year of Alfred's accession. The last entry in this early Chronicle is the notice under 891 of the death of the learned "Scot" or Irishman, Suibhne or "Swifneh." The scribe then wrote the number 892 ready for the next year, but did not fill in the annal. Then the book was, apparently, transcribed, with several errors in chronology, and copies of the transcript were sent to the various monasteries, to be developed on independent lines. One such copy remained at Winchester, and formed the nucleus of the Parker manuscript. A second scribe wrote as far as 894, a third finished the annals for 894 and 895, and a fourth continued the story till 912, some years after Alfred's death.

If the "Anglo-Saxon Chronicle" can no longer be treated as a homogeneous consecutive historical narrative, the full realisation of its composite character has emphasised the individual value of each of its parts. Though modern scientific research often shatters old beliefs, their fall may reveal unexpected truths and hidden beauties.

Few would probably now accept the early annals which describe the settlement of the Germanic tribes in Britain as a direct basis for sober history; but as a subsidiary source, full of literary and archaeological suggestion, the Chronicle has never ranked higher than in the present century. Nor must scepticism be carried too far. From the accession of Ethelwulf, at least, the Chronicle may be treated as history rather than myth, while for the reign of Alfred the Parker manuscript is an almost contemporary West-Saxon authority.

Yet it must be owned that in many ways the Alfredian Chronicle is a most disappointing collection of documents. Opening with a series of brief disconnected notices of events, taken from biblical or classical history,--the birth of Christ, the coming of the Magi, the Massacre of the Innocents, the accession of Roman emperors, the sack of Rome by the Goths, and the withdrawal of the Roman legions from Britain,--it proceeds with a confused and self-contradictory account of the Jutish and Saxon invasions and settlements, evidently based on legend and tradition, fanciful and unsubstantial as a dream, but, like a dream, interesting for its relation to a subconscious reality. The annals of the "Heptarchic" kingdoms follow, mere notes of military and ecclesiastical affairs, and of such natural and social phenomena as eclipses of the sun, appearances of comets, or outbreaks of pestilence. The deaths of popes, kings, and prelates are entered, and the ancient genealogies of the various royal houses are carefully preserved, but the whole effect is meagre and disjointed.

Not until the ninth century, and the triumphs of Egbert, does the narrative begin to widen and deepen and to grow more trustworthy, until with the entry of Alfred on the scene in 853 and the description of his "hallowing to king" by the Pope, it becomes a vivid, if concise, record of the long Danish wars and the ravages of the vikings on both sides of the Channel. Alfred's birth is not mentioned, but marginal crosses mark his consecration by Pope Leo IV., his share in the struggle with the Danes in 868, his victory at Ashdown, his accession, the critical year 878, and his death in 901.

The works of peace, administrative, educational, and literary, have left no direct trace on these annals. The original Alfredian Chronicle, which may be regarded as beginning after the mention of Ethelwulf's death in the entry under 855, is chiefly concerned with the fortunes of war and with the deaths of kings and great men. The first section seems to have broken off at 891, leaving the space for 892 blank. When another hand took up the tale, the years of peace were nearly over, and the history of Alfred's reign closes with that splendid succession of war-annals, extending from 893 to 897 (892-896), which Professor Earle described as "the most remarkable piece of writing in the whole series of Chronicles." The freedom and swing of the prose, the life and freshness of the narrative, belong to the ripest period of Alfred's intellectual development. The victories of his past wars inspire these fine annals, themselves a victory of peace. They may rank with the

Boethius and the Soliloquies as the last and noblest expression of the great King's genius, and it is fitting that they should end the Chronicle of his reign. After 897, for the few years that remain, there is silence, save for the notices of the deaths of Ealdorman Æthelm and Bishop Heahstan in 898, and of Alfred's own death in 901.

The annalistic character of the Chronicle gives continuity to its influence. It links together the active and contemplative sides of Alfred's life, and translates action into literary form, while the more purely literary works reflect the light of thought on action.

The first of these literary works to be produced seems to have been the English version of the Dialogues of St. Gregory the Great. There is no need to reject Asser's explicit statement that this translation was made by Werferth, Bishop of Worcester, by the King's command, though he may have had collaborators, as the brief characteristic preface, probably from Alfred's own hand, suggests.

I besought my trusty friends [wrote the King]

that out of God's books of the lives and miracles of

the saints they would set down for me the instruction

which follows, so that, strengthened in my mind

through memory and love, I may, amid the troubles

of this world, sometimes think on the things of heaven.

Three manuscripts of the translation survive, two of them in close agreement, the third, to some extent, a revised version by an unknown scholar. The original work was extremely popular in the Middle Ages. It recounts, in the form of dialogues between Pope Gregory and his disciple, Peter the Deacon, the lives and miracles of Italian saints, and, by its treatment of the question of a future life, it had much influence on the medi- æval doctrine of purgatory. The translation, as Asser notes, is somewhat free, not so much "word for word" as "sense for sense" (sensum ex sensu), a phrase used also by Alfred in its vernacular equivalent (andgit of andgite), in his preface to the Anglo-Saxon translation of Gregory's

Pastoral Care.

In its appeal to self-love and self-interest, its illustrations of the profit to be derived from an assiduous worship of the saints, and its elaboration of the system of future rewards and punishments, St. Gregory's book of Dialogues represents the materialistic side of mediæval Catholicism. Its more spiritual side is represented by the great Pope's Cura Pastoralis, the Pastoral Care. There are many reasons for placing the translation of the Pastoralis next to the Dialogues in order of production. The method of translation, "sense for sense," is the same as in the former book. The King's helpers were the men whom Asser enumerates, Werferth and Plegmund, Grimbald, John, and Asser himself. The translation was started under similar conditions, "amid the various and manifold troubles of this kingdom"; all the circumstances fit in with Asser's account of the beginning of Alfred's literary labours; the subject followed obviously from the previous study of Gregory's Dialogues; above all, the preface, one of the few practically undoubted pieces of Alfred's English prose composition, is, as Professor Wülker has shown, a preface to the whole of his literary work, an introduction to all his translations of "the books which are most needful for every man to know."

In this preface the King formulates his educational ideal with convincing directness. He describes the disastrous effects of the Danish wars on Wessex, the country all "harried and burnt," the churches despoiled of treasure and books, the clergy illiterate, learning so "clean decayed" that when he came to the throne he could not call to mind a single priest south of Thames who knew Latin, or could even understand the ecclesiastical offices in English, while south of Humber there were but few, and north of Humber, to the best of his belief, things were not much better. A lament for the good old days when England was in the van of progress, is followed by a sketch of the constructive policy whereby Alfred sought to restore that happy past, if "stillness" for the task were granted him. He knew that the hope of the future lay in the children of the present; his wish was to see "all the freeborn youth in England who have the means set to learning so long as they are unfit for other occupations, until they can well read English writing," while those were to proceed to Latin who were to be fitted by higher education for responsible positions. To supply material for such a course of training it seemed well to provide a series of English textbooks, and in casting about for Latin works suitable to be translated for this purpose, it was natural that the King should place in the front rank "the book that is called in Latin Pastoralis, and in English hierde-hoc (shepherd's book)," that "golden little book" which was the approved manual for the training of pastors and teachers.

The Cura Pastoralis, or Liber Regulœ Pastoralis, was, indeed, one of the most celebrated of mediæ- val theological treatises, full of wholesome doctrine and practical wisdom, inferior in authority only to the Scriptures and the Canon Law. Several ninth-century Councils had enjoined its use, and Hincmar, Archbishop of Rheims, had ordered each bishop in his province to hold the Canons and the Regula Pastoralis in his hand at his ordination, while he was exhorted to follow their precepts in his life and teaching. When, then, Alfred sent a copy of his English version of the Pastoralis to every bishop in his kingdom, he was acting in accordance with the best ecclesiastical traditions of the time.

To each bishop-stool in my kingdom I will send a copy [he wrote at the close of his preface], and in each is an œstel worth fifty mancuses. And I command in God's name that no man take the œstel from the book, nor the book from the minster. It is unknown, how long there may be such learned bishops, as now, God be thanked, are everywhere. Wherefore I wish them always to remain at that place, unless the bishop will have them with him, or if they have been lent out, or sent away to be copied.

An œstel was probably a pointer or "book-staff" of rich workmanship, and the manuscripts would doubtless have covers of costly materials, which have long since vanished."

A peculiar interest attaches to the Worcester manuscript of the Pastoral Care, a small quarto, written in several hands, now one of the chief treasures of the Bodleian Library at Oxford. It is, almost certainly, the actual copy which Werferth received from the King; the text is headed: "This Book shall to Worcester"; and the preface opens with a greeting from "Alfred king" to "Werferth bishop." The pages of the manuscript are yellow with age, and pierced with wormholes, yet the writing is still clear and black and beautiful, with its fair rounded letters, as easy to read as print, its coloured capitals, red chapter-headings, and delicately drawn and illuminated initials; here a piece of graceful interlacing or plaiting, here a fantastic dragon-headed scroll, here, again, a grotesque human mask or figure decoratively treated; the whole, alike in form and in subject-matter, a silent but eloquent witness to the artistic and literary enlightenment of the so-called "Dark Age."

An original epilogue in English alliterative metre ends the translation of the Pastoral Care, and a short verse prologue precedes it. In this the book, speaking for itself, tells how "Alfred king turned each word of me into English, and sent me to his writers, south and north, and bid them make more such copies, that he might send them to his bishops." From these words, and from the differences of hand in the contemporary Worcester manuscript, it may be inferred that Alfred employed a regular staff of scribes and clerks in his literary enterprises, but it is impossible to decide how the work was distributed, or what personal share the King took in its production. Like a mediæval master-painter he may have set the model, sketched the outlines, suggested the character and expression, and left the details to be filled in by his subordinates. Like a modern editor, he may have contented himself with organising and supervising a co-operative undertaking, contributing a preface here and a correction there. Or, like the true student of every period, he may have been attracted by the very toil and drudgery of composition, and have accounted it his highest privilege to be himself an active member of the confraternity of letters, in close sympathy with the living thought and the intellectual endeavour of his time.

In his Boethius, the King pauses in his translation to describe the Mind groping in ignorance as in a dark room, until Wisdom shines upon it like light through the chink of a door. It was towards that heavenly light of wisdom that Alfred was straining, and in throwing open the door for himself he opened it also to his people. He was more than a mere patron of learned men like Charles the Bald, more even than a founder of schools and a pioneer of education like Charles the Great, or Louis the Pious, and it is by no undue stretch of imagination that the direct influence of his steadfast truth-loving spirit has been traced in the books which a venerable and unbroken tradition has associated with his name.

The frequent repetitions in the translation of the Pastoral Care and the double renderings of the same passage may imply that here, at least, the task of transcription was performed by scribes writing to Alfred's own dictation. He names his helpers, indeed, in the preface, Plegmund and Asser,

Grimbald and John, the learned clerks who possibly suggested many of the explanatory additions to the text, as well as the solution of verbal and grammatical difficulties. The fact that Plegmund, who became primate in 890, is called "my archbishop" in the preface, seems to fix the earliest date at which the translation could have been completed. The inclusion of Grimbald, who is thought to have been in Flanders in 892, among the King's advisers, and Asser's omission of any mention of the English version of the Pastoral Care in his Life of Alfred, where he quotes from the original Latin text, may throw it some years later. The King's own words in the preface show that the work was carried on among many distractions and interruptions: "then, amid the various and manifold troubles of this kingdom, I began to turn into English the book that is called in Latin Pastoralis."

The lack of originality in Alfred's literary work in itself marks him out as the child of his age. His books belong to a time when reverence for the written word was strong, and the critical faculty was weak, when a diligent aptitude for collecting and interpreting the thoughts of the past seemed the height of intellectual achievement. Asser compares the King's mental activity to the flight of a bee gathering honey from herbs and flowers, an apt, if somewhat trite, metaphor, for by patient assimilation, selection, and rearrangement of his materials, he transformed them into new creations, subtly compounded of familiar elements. In the Pastoral Care, more than in his other translations, he keeps close to the letter as well as to the spirit of the Latin text, though even here the rendering is free. Words are transposed, two synonymous English words are used to translate one Latin term, and an obvious effort is made to give the meaning of the original, even at the expense of verbal accuracy. The omissions and misinterpretations are few, while the additions are chiefly of the nature of expansions, explaining difficult words and obscure allusions, or simplifying and materialising abstract conceptions, to bring them down to the level of unlearned English readers.

Alfred is less metaphysical and erudite than St. Gregory, less terse and more homely in language. He illustrates the unknown by the known, and in striving to convey the sense of his sixthcentury author, he has incidentally left us a picture of the English life of his own day. Thus Uriah for him is David's "own loyal thegn," KingDavid himself, and the prophets Isaiah,

Jeremiah, and Ezekiel, are "wise men," witegan or witan, Jacob, like Alfred's father Ethelwulf, tithes his inheritance, rulers are "shire-men," servants (ministri) are thegns, slaves (servi) are "theows" (theowas) jugglers (histriones) are "evil gleemen." Purple (purpura) is explained as the kingly robe, because it betokens royal authority, manna is "the sweet food that came down from heaven," adamant is "the hard stone that we call athamans."

The simple piety and humanity of St. Gregory's book, its noble morality and quiet humour, found a ready response in Alfred's nature, and many passages must have appealed to him with special poignancy. The description of the mind lost in worldly cares, rising above them by concentrating itself on study, the comparison of ruler and subjects to the head guiding the feet in the right way, the injunctions to rulers to meditate on high matters, and to subjects to discharge humble duties, the metaphors drawn from war and seamanship, were all alike echoes from his own thought and life. As he translated the comparison of backsliding Christians to the careless folk who, after a victory in the open field, let themselves be taken when fast locked in their burhs, or the exhortation to fortify the burh of the mind against the insidious foe,6 or the reflection that "every army has less strength when it comes, if its coming be known beforehand, because it sees those ready whom it thought7 to find unprepared," his experiences at Chippenham in 878 must have lent point and reality to St. Gregory's Bunyan-like allegory of the city of Mansoul.

In rendering the Latin hostis by the graphic English word stælherigeas, marauders, who "steal" and "harry," a term which the Chronicle applies to the Danes, his fair west country, "all harried and burnt," may have swum once more before his eyes. Or when he wrote of the sluggard who would not plough in winter for spring sowing, of the ceorl at work in his orchard, or "apple-town," of the acres joined one to another and stretching to the boundary of the land, he may have looked out on the English open fields with their acre and half-acre strips narrowing to the horizon, and on hillsides and valleys white with fruit-blossom, and have seen them transfigured with spiritual meaning.

This same love of parable, and perception of the deeper significance of common things, colours also the little original epilogue in alliterative verse which closes the translation of the Pastoral Care. As Alfred sent forth St. Gregory's wisdom, "the waters which the God of Hosts promised as a comfort to us earth-dwellers," his fancy played with concrete familiar images--pure water dispersed, threading marshy fields in shallow murmuring streams, or gathered in a well, deep and still, for the service of man--the leaky pitcher that spills the precious draught, the mended vessel that preserves it--the whole picture painted in simple language, not altogether devoid of poetical beauty, which, like the rudely metrical verses of the prologue, may probably be attributed to the King himself.

The mention in the prologue to the Pastoral Care of the connection of St. Gregory with England, through the mission of St. Augustine, has led to the supposition that the next book to be translated by Alfred and his helpers would be Bede's Ecclesiastical History of the English Nation, in which the course of that mission is described. The stiffness and lack of elasticity in the English rendering of Bede has been also adduced as evidence of the early date of its composition. Mr. Plummer, on the other hand, has maintained the priority of the Orosius on the grounds of its affinity in language and construction with the Alfredian Chronicle, and of the independent nature of the passages in the Chronicle derived from Bede, which appear to have been taken straight from the Latin, and show no traces of the influence of the English translation. The question is further complicated by the doubts which have been thrown upon the authorship of the Bede, but the exact order of the two works is of less importance, if both are assigned to the same phase of literary development, and belong in character and spirit to the more practical and directly educational group of Alfred's writings.

If the translation of the Pastoral Care provided for the instruction of the English clergy, the Orosius and the Bede appealed to a wider public, and the Orosius in particular, remodelled to meet the needs of the English people, became a treasurehouse of curious and useful learning. The Universal History of Orosius was composed in the beginning of the fifth century, as an apology for the Christians, on whom the heathen Romans were inclined to lay the blame for the sack of their city by the Goths in 410 A.D. Orosius himself was the disciple of St. Augustine of Hippo, and his book bore a definite relation to the City of God, which was written with much the same purpose. One-sided and inaccurate as was the work of Orosius, it was the best and most comprehensive historical survey which mediæval scholars possessed, while its distinctively Christian tone won for it the approval of churchmen.

To the topical and polemical character of the original may be attributed the freedom of Alfred's treatment of the text. He was both editor and translator, and he did not hesitate to alter, curtail, and amplify, as he thought best, adapting and shaping the concise Latin constructions to suit the taste and understanding of his Germanic subjects. His English version, if marred by ignorance, haste, and inexperience, is redeemed by freshness, vividness of presentment, and a genuine enthusiasm for knowledge. It has all the characteristic marks of Alfred's style, and its authorship has never been questioned, though the only evidence for it is Ohthere's address, in the geographical section, to "his lord king Alfred," with William of Malmesbury's inclusion of "Orosius" in his twelfth-century list of Alfred's writings.

The oldest extant manuscript of the English Orosius may date from the end of the ninth century, and vies in beauty and interest with the contemporary Worcester manuscript of the Pastoral Care and the later Parker manuscript of the Anglo-Saxon Chronicle. In arrangement and plan it differs widely from the Latin original. Alfred reduces the seven books of Orosius to six, cuts down his two hundred chapters by more than half, and gives laconic chapter-headings which are probably his own. The geographical introduction is expanded and enriched by original additions, the historical portions are expurgated and annotated in accordance with those educational aims which were never far from Alfred's thoughts.

The geographical interpolations, in particular, are of unusual interest and value. They consist, first, of Alfred's description of "Germany," by which he understands all the country from the river Don on the east to the Rhine on the west, and from the Danube on the south to the White Sea on the north, including Scandinavia. The description, though little more than a list of boundaries, was, from the comparative accuracy of its topography, a real contribution to the knowledge of the time, drawn, it may well be, from the reports of travellers visiting the West-Saxon court.

More certainly the two other great additions to the text of Orosius come from this source. These are the travellers' tales of Ohthere or Ottar, the Norwegian, who doubled the North Cape, and of Wulfstan, who sailed in seven days and nights from Haithaby or Schleswig to the eastern shores of the Baltic.

Inserted in the English translation of Orosius, each of these narratives forms a whole in itself, and round each a critical literature has sprung up. Ohthere's story, as an early and independent record of northern adventure, has appealed to Germanic explorers, the heirs of the vikings, in all ages. Hakluyt knew and reproduced it in the sixteenth century, and in these last days it has won the admiring sympathy of the Norwegian sea-captain's countryman and successor Frithiöf Nansen. Ohthere "told his lord king Alfred," of the far north, with its eternal lure for the adventurous spirit of man. He told how he lived northernmost of all Northmen, and how he journeyed from his home to the waste land where the Finns dwelt, who were fishers and fowlers and huntsmen, and the Beormas or Perms, who were an agricultural people, living about the White Sea. He told of whales and walruses, or "horsewhales," whose tusks of fine ivory he brought to the King, and whose hide made good ropes; of seals, too, and of the tame reindeer which were used to decoy their wild fellows. He described how he himself, one of the first men in Halgoland, his "shire," had six hundred reindeer, though only twenty head of cattle, twenty sheep, and twenty swine, while "the little that he ploughed, he ploughed with horses," a striking contrast to the English fashion of using plough-oxen. He told how Norway was "very long, and very narrow," with arable ground lying along the sea, and wild moors inland to eastward, so wide in some parts that it would take two weeks to cross them. He spoke of Sweden, also, of the Cwenas or Cwæns, those north-eastern tribesmen who carried their small light boats overland to the lakes of Norway, when they were at feud with the Norwegians, and of the Danish isles, and the lands in which the Angles dwelt before they came to Britain, lands by which he passed in his five days' sail from Sciringshall in southern Norway to the town of Haithaby or Schleswig.

Wulfstan, whose brief account of his voyage immediately follows Ohthere's more detailed reminiscences, described his visit to eastern Prussia, that marvellous "East-land," full of honey and fish, where every burh had a king, where kings and rich men drank milk, while poor men and slaves quaffed mead, and where strange funeral rites and customs of inheritance were in vogue.

If Alfred's sense of the unity of knowledge, and his practical conception of his own educational function, saved him from any doubt of the propriety of introducing contemporary narratives into a treatise on ancient geography and history, his zeal in the pursuit of information of all kinds made it easy for him to turn from natural science and present realities to the outworn mythology and traditions of antiquity. To his unjaded imagination, indeed, all seemed alike marvellous, Ohthere's walruses and the war-elephants of Pyrrhus, King of Epirus, the fortunes of a Scandinavian trading-ship and the strategy of a campaign in the Persian or Punic wars.

The historical portion of the English Orosius contains less directly original matter than the geographical section, but the independence with which the text is handled is highly characteristic of Alfred's method of editing. He omits and expands, and in the work of selection his own mind and taste stand revealed. He passes by local details of transitory importance, to linger over deeds of heroism, and instances of courage, patriotism, and self-sacrifice. He explains the unfamiliar, a Roman triumph, the temple of Janus, the centaurs, the Amazons, those "poor homeless women," and inserts an occasional fact or anecdote from his private store of knowledge, taken, it may be, from the notes in his Handbook. Thus he adds to the account of Cæsar's invasions of Britain that he fought "in the land which is called Kent-land," or "near the ford which is called Wallingford." Thus, too, he tells how Titus the Emperor thought the day lost on which he had done no good action, a story which appears again in the Anglo-Saxon Chronicle. The picturesque has its charm for Alfred, but he likes to materialise his fancies. In his description of the plagues of Egypt the frogs prevent men from working, and dishes are served up, "as full of reptiles as of meat," while the flies torment men and cattle "with fiery smarting bites." He modernises, also, reading his personal experience into the history of the past. In his version of Orosius, the Persian king deprives an ealdorman of his shire, Tyrtæus, the lame poet-leader of the Spartan army, encourages his men by song and chant in the fashion of an English gleeman, and the poet Homer is transformed into Omarus the scop, the "shaper," "maker," or bard. Philip of Macedon gathers ships, "becomes a viking," and plunders merchant vessels to replenish his empty coffers during his long siege of Byzantium or Constantinople, "a burh on the sea, the highest kingly seat, and head of all the eastern realm."5

The military passages in the text of the Orosius were specially interesting to the soldier-king:-- Pharaoh's "war-waggons" overturned by the God of Hosts, the marches and counter-marches, the sieges and battles, the sea-fights and stratagems of Greek and Persian, Carthaginian and Roman kings and "ealdormen," with their following of "thegns" and "fyrdmen." Alfred, as Mr. Plummer notes, may even have occasionally borrowed a practical suggestion from his historical reading, while his explanations of the text may have been based on his personal experience. The Scythians' fine answer, that it was "dearer" to them "to fight, than to pay tribute," may have roused reluctant thoughts of English treasure yielded to the vikings, and memories of Athelney may have underlain the writing of the passage that told how the king of Egypt with his "folk" was driven out, and pursued, and how all the country was wasted, "save one fenland."

This power of seeing the present in the past lent life and colour to the work of Alfred and his fellow-translators. Their defective scholarship often led them into absurd and childish blunders of fact and language--the subtler shades of meaning nearly always escaped them--they never sounded the depths of the Greek spirit, or understood the full greatness of Imperial Rome. Yet, at least, in their self-imposed task they were neither dry pedants nor mechanical drudges, but teachers seeking diligently after truth, simple lovers of ancient learning, and daring pioneers of a new civilisation. Joint-labourers in that workshop in which the common language was slowly welded into a literary instrument of great force and flexibility, as they experimented in words and turns of speech, they, half unconsciously, fixed a standard for the English of the future.

The recurrent passages in dooms and legal documents, in the Anglo-Saxon Chronicle and the Alfredian translations, the coincidences in expression between the Orosius and the Chronicle, the Bede and the Dialogues of St. Gregory, the Pastoral Care and Alfred's Laws, or, again, between the Boethius and the English rendering of the Soliloquies of St. Augustine, all show the gradual formation of a distinctive English prose style. Some phrases were tried, and found wanting, others stood the test of time, and, ennobled by association, passed into ordinary use. An ingenious fancy may see the hand of Werferth in one place, and the touch of Plegmund in another, or the direct influence of the King throughout, but it matters little how the labour was divided. It is not because Alfred wrote any particular book that he is worthy of a place among the fathers of English literature, but because he was the creator of a scholarly tradition, and the leader of a widespread intellectual movement, a leader capable of inspiring his followers with something of his own idealism, and of sharing with them his hopes and ambitions.

The attribution of the English version of Bede's Ecclesiastical History to King Alfred has been attacked on two grounds,--the stiffness and crudity of the translation itself, and the Mercian characteristics of the dialect in which it is written. The question is still undecided, but the arguments brought against Alfred's authorship are hardly convincing enough to compel the abandonment of that old and pleasant belief. Literal unidiomatic translation would be natural enough if the Bede were one of the King's earlier works, or it might simply result from the fact that the book, concerned with English affairs, needed less alteration and explanation than the Orosius, an "apology" transformed into a text-book, or the more abstruse works of St. Gregory and Boethius. The Mercian character of the dialect has not been established beyond a doubt, and in any case, the oldest extant manuscript, to which alone the argument applies, dates only from the second half of the tenth century, and may quite possibly be a Mercian transcript of a West-Saxon original. Even if it be assumed that the original manuscript was in Mercian dialect, it may merely have been written by a Mercian scribe under the King's direction. The preface to the Pastoral Care shows that Mercia had preserved some traces of its early literary distinction through the desolating Danish wars. When Alfred came to the throne there were still a few Latin scholars "south of Humber," and it was to Mercia that he looked for help in his educational schemes. The most ancient version of the Beowulf epic which has come down to us seems to have been a Mercian recension of the eighth century; the dooms of Offa of Mercia supplied material for Alfred's Code, and the inscription on the famous Alfred Jewel has an Anglian form.

The historical and external evidence for Alfred's connection with the English Bede, again, is too strong, early, and explicit to be lightly disregarded. Not only does William of Malmesbury, in the twelfth century, include Bede's Gesta Anglorum among the books which King Alfred "gave to English ears." The eleventh-century Cambridge manuscript of the English translation of Bede has the Latin distich at the beginning and end:

Historicus quondam fecit me Beda Latinum,

Alfred, rex Saxo, transtulit ille pius.

(Bede the historian made me formerly in Latin,

Alfred, the pious Saxon king, translated me.

It also contains the West-Saxon royal genealogy which precedes the Parker manuscript of the Anglo-Saxon Chronicle, a genealogy which stops at the accession of Alfred, and if, as is probable, both distich and genealogy once formed part of the still older, but now imperfect, Oxford manuscript of the English Bede, of which the Cambridge manuscript is a copy, this evidence will go back to within a century of Alfred's death. To about the same period belongs the very definite statement of the English homilist, Abbot Ælfric, who mentions, in his homily on St. Gregory the Great, "Historia Anglorum, which King Alfred turned from Latin into English." Alfred's claim to be the translator of Bede thus rests on a sound basis of tenth-century tradition, and if, in the absence of direct proof, it must remain unsettled, it seems likely that here, as with the Pastoral Care and the Orosius, the King inspired and directed the work, though much of the actual composition may have been done by others.

The translation itself betrays an unpractised hand. It suggests a learned, if somewhat timid, scholar, testing the possibilities of a novel medium of expression, and interpreting his author so literally "word for word" that he forgets the importance of also giving "sense for sense." There are fewer gross blunders than in the Orosius, but the rendering, though fairly accurate and grammatical, is so overcrowded with Latinisms, transferred wholesale from the text, or from the interlinear explanatory glosses, that at times it is scarcely intelligible.

There are practically no additions to the original, but much is omitted,-- papal and official letters, poems, the account of the Pelagian heresy, the wearisome Paschal controversies of the seventh century, and the borrowed description of the holy places of Palestine, with the chronological summary at the close of the book. The early history, before the coming of St. Augustine, is abridged, and details relating to northern England are left out, though such beautiful episodes as the meeting of St. Gregory and the

English slave-boys at Rome, or the life and death of St. Oswald of Northumbria, are retained in full, and are dwelt upon with evident appreciation and sympathy. In the story of the poet Cædmon, the sweet singer who, "blithe of mood towards all God's men," ended his life in the silence of sleep, the language of the translation is as simple and dignified as its theme.

The English Bede also contains a hymn in West-Saxon dialect which is found in several of the extant Latin versions, and has been very generally accepted as the authentic work of Cædmon, since it occurs in a Northumbrian form, in the earliest existing manuscript of the Historia Anglorum. The absence of any additions to the southern history from the local knowledge of Alfred and his scribes has been variously referred to respect for the text of Bede, and to the possibility that the progress of the Alfredian Chronicle had already rendered such interpolations superfluous.

One of the chief features of historical interest in the original text is the way in which the Latin terminology reflects the Anglo-Saxon social life and institutions of the beginning of the eighth century, more particularly in Northumbria. In spite of local differences between north and south, these institutions were still familiar to the English translators of the ninth century. It was only necessary to strip off the classical trappings of Bede's duces and principes, consules and satrapæ, comites, ministri, and milites, for ealdormen and heretogan, gesiths and king's thegns to reappear. There was no question here, as in the Pastoral Care and the Orosius, of explaining the unknown by the known. The old accustomed manner of life was easy to recognise. The petty king, with his bodyguard of loyal thegns, the assembly of elders and councillors, the witan in their gemot, the fyrd going forth to battle, the royal hall, the small walled town, the populous monastery, as Bede described them, had changed but little in the lapse of a hundred and fifty years, and these at least were common alike to southern and to northern England.

By far the most interesting of Alfred's four great translations, more arresting in its revelations of personality than even the Pastoral Care, is his English version of the De Consolatione Philosophiæ of Boethius, that Consolation of Philosophy which was one of the favourite books of the Middle Ages. This translation was, apparently, the work of Alfred's riper age, completed, perhaps, about 897, some two or three years before his death, when he, like Boethius, was looking towards the calm haven of eternal happiness, after the storms and billows of life.

Anicius Manlius Severinus Boethius, consul and head of the Roman Senate in the early sixth century, under Theodoric, the Ostrogothic King of Italy, was, after years of honour and prosperity, accused of conspiracy against his master, cast into a dungeon, and finally tortured and put to death. A man of vast learning, a philosopher, scientist, and mathematician, versed in music and poetry, and a skilful craftsman, his writings cover practically the whole field of the knowledge of his day. Though he was much more of a Platonist than a Christian, the fact that he was persecuted by the Arian Theodoric won for him the reputation of a Catholic martyr, and he was actually canonised as St. Severinus. The Consolation was written in prison, to soothe his loneliness and sense of injustice. It is in mingled prose and verse, and takes the form of a dialogue between Boethius and divine Philosophy, in which she cheers and exhorts her disciple, and leaves him resigned, resting in the thought of the everlasting righteousness of God.

The almost unrivalled popularity of the De Consolatione was probably due partly to its attractive mixture of poetry with prose, and to its dialogue form--for mediaeval readers were like children in their taste for verses and "conversations"; partly to the abiding interest of its subject-matter, the vanity of earthly greatness, and the stability of heavenly wisdom. Yet that it should be popular is not really surprising, for it is, as Gibbon called it, a "golden volume," breathing high courage and touched with poetic thought. A philosophic treatise which has been translated by King Alfred, Geoffrey Chaucer, and Queen Elizabeth, to which Dante turned for solace after the death of Beatrice, and in which Sir Thomas More found comfort during his own imprisonment1 needs no apology. It must have in it something human and universal, some appeal to fundamental truths and emotions, which even now, when its moralising has grown trite, and its arguments have lost their force, still lingers about its natural cries of sorrow and perplexity, its Joblike wrestlings with the mystery of pain. This one book, moreover, stood for much in mediæval education. It was the authorised manual of moral philosophy, the mirror in which the thinkers of the early Middle Ages saw reflected the mighty shades of Plato and Aristotle.

King Alfred's authorship of the first English prose version of the De Consolatione has never been doubted. It is asserted in the preface to the translation itself: "KingAlfred was the interpreter of this book, and he turned it from book- Latin into English." Ethelwerd says that the King turned many volumes from Latin into the vulgar tongue, among them the "lachrymose book" of Boethius, and William of Malmesbury adds that Asser explained the book of Boethius on the Consolation of Philosophy in plainer words, "a labour necessary in those days, ridiculous in ours," by the King's command, that he might the more easily turn it into the English tongue. The Book of Hyde, on the other hand, makes Werferth translate the Consolation as well as the Dialogues of St. Gregory, but gives no authority for the statement, while an equally unsupported and improbable story lays the scene of the translation at Alfred's hunting-seat of Woodstock near Oxford.

Even independently of external testimony, the internal evidence of the Anglo-Saxon Boethius would be almost enough to decide the question of its authorship. Here, if anywhere, the dead Alfred yet speaks with a living voice, telling of his hopes and fears, his ambitions and difficulties, his ideals and disappointments.

The book has survived in two manuscripts, of which one probably goes back to the tenth century, while the other dates from about the beginning of the twelfth century. This later manuscript gives prose renderings of both the prose and the verse sections, the prosæ and the metra or carmina of the Latin original. The earlier manuscript has a prose version of the prose sections, with a preface, or proem, also in prose, and an alliterative English verse translation of the metra, with a short metrical proem or prelude. As this verse translation is not taken straight from the Latin, but is clearly based on the Anglo-Saxon prose version of the carmina, it is probable that Alfred's original translation was entirely in prose, and it is possible that, as William of Malmesbury says, it was made from Asser's paraphrase.

After the preface, which is perhaps by another hand, Alfred's prose version begins with a short explanatory introduction, giving the history of the wise and book-learned consul or hereloga, "Boetius," who lived in the days when the Goths from Scythia had warred against the Roman Empire, and Theodoric had won all the realm of Italy. Alfred then passes on to the text of the Consolation, which he treats with the utmost freedom, simplifying, explaining, abridging, and expanding, till his translation is almost an original work. This is particularly noticeable in the last chapters, which correspond to the fifth book of the Latin, where, fired by the controversial nature of the questions at issue, he diverges into independent metaphysical speculations on free-will, foreknowledge, and the nature of God, and gives a strongly Christian tinge to the Neo-Platonic philosophy of Boethius. These omissions and additions are in themselves deeply interesting, for they throw light on Alfred's mental and spiritual development, as well as on his taste and judgment. Thus he often forgets altogether that it is Boethius who is speaking, and argues with Wisdom, Reason, or Philosophy, in his own person, or makes the questioner the mind of man.

He enlarges but little on the geographical notices in the book; of these he had perhaps already said enough in the Orosius, but he shows off his classical and mythological knowledge, telling the stories of Orpheus and Eurydice, Ulysses and Circe, at length, and introducing additional notes on Hercules, on Jove and the Titans, and on such famous Romans as Tarquin and Nero, Regulus and Cato, with Homer and Virgil, the best of the Greek and Latin poets, and Cicero, the "Roman heretoga and sage."

It has recently been pointed out1 that many of Alfred's additions to his text are derived from early Latin commentaries on the De Consolatione. If this weakens his claim to originality, it also illustrates his powers of adaptation. His selections from these commentaries show his interest in history, mythology, and natural science, and his love of allegory and symbolism. Thus he adopts and expands the simile of the wheel, its axle God, its nave, spokes, and fellies, men, good and bad, yet all, even the worst and farthest from God, in touch with the divine centre, which itself remains still, though it bears the whole weight of the waggon, and guides its movement. He gives a personal application to the comparison of the "three orders" of men to the tools of a king's trade, identifying himself with the king whose needs he is describing.

"I desired tools and materials to carry on the work I was set to do," he writes, looking back over his struggling reign, and then, in words which come from no commentary, but straight from his own heart, he makes his simple confession of the high aim of his life: "It has ever been my will to live worthily while I lived, and after my death to leave to them that should come after me my memory in good works." Alfred's own, too, in appreciation, if not in conception, is the fine metaphor of the eagle, where Wisdom says: "When I soar up with my servants, we look down on the storms of this world, as the eagle, when he rises in stormy weather above the clouds, where no storm can harm him." Even so, in his last years, Alfred rose above doubt and anxiety into a serene air, whence he could contemplate his varied experience, and frame, from his knowledge of joy and sorrow alike, a philosophy of life and of death.

If, however, King Alfred may be accepted without hesitation as the translator of that English version of the Consolation on which the oldest existing manuscripts are based, his authorship of the Anglo-Saxon verse translation of the Latin metra is more open to doubt. With it, moreover, stands or falls his authorship of the two prefaces, for the prose preface states that when King Alfred had studied the Consolation, and turned it from Latin into English prose, he wrought it up once more into songs, or lays(leothe), "as it is now done," and the metrical prelude begins:"Thus the old tale, Alfred told us, West-Saxons'king. He showed the craft, the skill of song-makers."

That Alfred wrote these lays has been denied on the ground of their inferior poetic quality, and the improbability that the King, after completing the vigorous prose translation, should have turned it into comparatively feeble verse. It has also been urged that, though the lays are based on the English prose version, some of themetra in that version are omitted, where the formula, "Then Wisdom began to sing," which generally introduces the metrical sections, is absent; a piece of carelessness of which the translator of the prose version would hardly have been guilty. Lastly, it is alleged that the writer of the verses betrays ignorance of the classics, as compared with the prose translator. None of these arguments can be taken as conclusive.

That Alfred could write somewhat indifferent verse is seen in his metrical preface to thePastoral Care, and he may have tried to popularise the teaching of Boethius still further by giving it a form which would catch the ear of an unlettered public. The omission of some of the metra is not necessarily incompatible with the King's authorship, and the instances of classical ignorance on the part of the versifier are too few and uncertain to be convincing. Hence the question becomes a matter of opinion, on which critics will probably continue to differ, until decisive evidence is produced on one side or the other. At present, both the supporters and the opponents of Alfred's authorship of the verse translation cast the burden of proof on those who disagree with them, and, as yet, neither side has been able satisfactorily to meet the challenge. The discussion, though interesting from a literary point of view, has little biographical importance, for the Anglo-Saxon metra throw no fresh light on Alfred's character or history.

The King's authorship of the prose preface to the Boethius, which is very generally denied, may also be left undetermined. This "proem" is, in great part, a mere repetition of the preface to the Pastoral Care, but the little prayer with which it ends seems to be original, and recalls a passage in Alfred's translation of the Soliloquies of St. Augustine: "Every one," he there wrote, following out his independent train of thought," rejoiceth, that at least he can understand, according to the measure of his understanding." "Every man," runs the preface to the Boethius, "must speak what he speaketh and do what he doeth according to the measure of his understanding and his leisure." Therefore, King Alfred, with a most winning simplicity "prays, and beseeches in God's name, every man who cares to read this book [the Consolation], to pray for him, and not to blame him if he understand it better than [the translator]." If these are not Alfred's actual words, they at least express the spirit of his work, the cool judgment which could recognise his own limitations, and the brave hopefulness which prevented such recognition from paralysing effort.

There is a remarkable affinity between the prose version of the Boethius and Alfred's last noteworthy translation, his English rendering of the Soliloquies of St. Augustine. This little work consists of a preface, and three books, the first two derived chiefly from the Soliloquies, the third drawn partly from St. Augustine's letter on the Vision of God (De Videndo Deo), partly from the writings of St. Gregory, from the Vulgate, and from other sources. It is often called "Blooms" from the opening and closing phrases of the first and second books: "Here end the blooms of the first book." "Here beginneth the gathering of the blooms (or the anthology) of the second book." The translation, which is only known in a corrupt and mutilated twelfth-century manuscript, has been attributed to Alfred on the strength of the concluding words: "Here end the sayings (cwidas) which

King Alfred collected," and though the King's authorship has been doubted, it is borne out by the evidence of the book itself. The preface, in particular, and the additions to the Latin text, breathe the very spirit of Alfred, as shown in his earlier writings.

Professor Wülker at one time even suggested that the "Blooms" might represent the lost Handbook1 with its collection of "blossoms," or flowers of thought, a theory which seems to be supported by the expression "the sayings" of King Alfred, which tallies with Florence of Worcester's mention of the book called Dicta regis Ælfredi. This theory, however, has now been abandoned, and Professor Wülker is inclined to agree with other critics in treating the Soliloquies as the last of Alfred's completed translations, and the preface as a sort of epilogue to his works.

This is the memorable preface in which Alfred describes his literary labours under the figure of a man gathering wood from a forest for the building of his house. He had collected much, but much remained for those who should come after him. To them he bequeathed his task. "I exhort every one who is able, and has many wains, to wend his way to the same wood." For himself, he turned in thought from the "log-hut" of this transitory life to the "eternal home." It is the same tone which is heard in the Boethius, the voice of a man who has almost done his practical work, and for whom abstract speculation has an increasing attraction.

In form, in treatment, and in subject-matter, the Boethius and the Soliloquies are singularly alike. Both are dialogues between Reason and the soul of man; both are concerned with metaphysical questions, with the definition of good and evil, the nature of God, and the life of the unseen world. The turns of phrase, the similes, metaphors, and illustrations, also correspond so constantly as almost to compel belief in the common source of the two translations.

The first book follows St. Augustine's Latin somewhat closely, though with certain important additions, which strongly favour the theory of Alfred 's authorship. Here he asks what he is, and whether his mind and soul are mortal or immortal. His mind goes "fearing and searching out various and rare things." He compares memory to a good steward, guarding the treasures of knowledge, the soul to a ship, moored to God by the anchors of faith, hope, and love, and God himself to the lord of a household, or to a king, whose subjects flock to his court from every side. He digresses, to describe the natural changes of the seasons, or the blessings of friendship. He dwells on St. Augustine's thought of the student's need of solitude, and expands it, with recollections, it may be, of the many cares which had hindered his own literary work. "Thou wouldst need to have a place retired and empty . . . and a few wise and skilful men who would in no way hinder thee, but help thy ability," he makes Reason declare, and to St. Augustine's answer: "I have none of these," he adds,"neither the leisure, nor the help of other men, nor a place retired enough to suit me for such a task (cræft)."

There are interesting and characteristic touches, too, in the mention of the lord's writ with its seal2, and in the description of the teaching of "the science which we callgeometrica," by means of a ball, an apple, or a painted egg, whereby the motions of the heavenly bodies could be illustrated3.

Echoes of the Pastoral Care and of the Boethius are heard in the phrase, the "craft of crafts," applied to the knowledge of God, in the comparison of men to the "tools" of God, and in the expression of the King's desire for sufficient wealth to enable him to feed and keep the men who depended on him.

The short second book is more independent of the Latin original, especially towards its close. Here Alfred is occupied with the problem of immortality, and he adapts the subject to his English readers by omitting much of St. Augustine's dialectical argument, and relying for his proofs on the witness of Christ, of the Prophets, the Apostles, and the Fathers of the Church, and on the soul's natural craving for eternal life. He uses familiar illustrations, moreover, and reverts to his favourite themes, the love of God, as the highest good and wisdom, God's rule over the kings of this world, and the hollowness of earthly power. He speaks of the Apostles as "Christ's thegns," and reveals his own attitude towards the acquisition of knowledge, when, speaking for St. Augustine, he says that no statement is too incredible for him to accept on his lord's authority, and adds: "Yea, I even have many companions, whom I would believe, if they should say that they saw and heard, just as much as if I myself had seen and heard."

In the third book Alfred tries to complete what St. Augustine had left unfinished. The second book had ended with a question as to the continuance of knowledge and understanding after death. "I do not suppose," writes Alfred, "that the life there will be without reason, any more than it is here with children; in that case there would be too little gladness in that life." St. Augustine referred this question to his own epistle on the Vision of God (de Videndo Deo). Alfred borrows from this, from the City of God, St. Gregory's Dialogues and Morals, and the Vulgate, with St. Jerome's Commentary on St. Luke. He recasts his material in dialogue form, to bring it into harmony with the two former books, and gives the whole the impress of his own personality, as he strives to put into words his thoughts of the life of the soul when it is released from "the prison of the body." The pains of exile and the joy of the banished favourite who returns to his former lord shadow forth for him the happiness of heaven after the sufferings of this world. He pictures hell as the court prison of a king, where the misery of the captives is increased by the sight of the pleasures they have forfeited, and recalls, perhaps, his childish travels, when he shows the difference between belief and knowledge by saying that he does not know who built Rome because he had seen the city, but because it was told him. "Nor even know I of what kin I am," he continues, with his mind still fixed on his boyhood, "or who my father or mother was, save by hearsay.""Therefore," he concludes, in a striking passage, "methinks that man is very foolish and very wretched who will not increase his understanding while here in this world, and also wish and desire to come to the eternal life, where nothing is hid from us."

Since some of the additions to the "Blooms" agree with translated passages in the Anglo-Saxon Boethius, it is almost certain that the English version of the Soliloquies was completed after the Consolation, not long, probably, before Alfred's death. This lends a special interest to William of Malmesbury's statement that the King "began to translate the Psalter, but died when he had hardly finished the first part," for even if this is based on a misunderstanding, it shows the twelfthcentury tradition that Alfred's literary activity only ended with his life. The fact that in an extant eleventh-century Anglo-Saxon version of the Psalter the first fifty psalms are in prose, and the remainder in alliterative verse, suggested to Professor Wülker1 that these fifty psalms might represent Alfred's work.

This Psalter includes the Latin text, and Latin rubrics, and each of the first fifty psalms has a short explanatory and historical introduction in the vernacular. Mr. Plummer, moreover, has pointed out2 that the mediæval psalter was often divided, for liturgical purposes, into three parts, each containing fifty psalms, and that the "first part," of which William of Malmesbury speaks, would thus correspond very well to the fifty prose psalms which precede the alliterative version. The general style of the translation is not unlike that of the Pastoral Care, but the internal evidence is hardly strong enough to outweigh the entire lack of contemporary authority for assigning it to Alfred. Such coincidences as have been traced between the Psalter and his well-authenticated writings may merely be due to the literary fashion of the day, a fashion doubtless set by the King and his collaborators, but persisting after his death.

Alfred's fame as a man of letters early became nebulous, and while his literary ability was exaggerated, and books of many kinds were indiscriminately attributed to him, the true details of his work were forgotten. If the tenth-century homilist Ælfric could write that in his time there were no godly books in the vulgar tongue "save those which King Alfred wisely turned from Latin into English," Ethelwerd declared that the number of the volumes the King translated was unknown, and the Anglo-Saxon Life of St. Neot, which is probably somewhat later in date, vaguely mentions the "many books which King Alfred wrote by the spirit of God." While, then, the authorship of the Anglo-Saxon Psalter must remain uncertain, Alfred's translation of the whole Bible may be dismissed to the realm of legend, in company with his "Domesday Book," his collection of proverbs, his version of Æsop's fables, and his treatise on falconry.

On a different plane is the Anglo-Saxon Martyrology, which, though it has no known direct connection with the King, was probably written in his lifetime, and under the influence of his literary revival. Here many of the characteristics of the Alfredian school reappear, and the short lives of the saints are given with the pithy, straightforward simplicity which distinguishes the English prose of the later ninth century. To have given the impulse to the development of that terse, vigorous, racy native prose, is one of Alfred's chief titles to the gratitude of all Englishspeaking peoples. "Though Saxon were then a naked and scanted Language, destitute both of Phrase and Originals wherewith to express significantly," wrote Sir John Spelman, in his seventeenth-century Life of King Alfred, "yet were his Versions so full, so proper, and with that Lively Expression, that they did infinitely take the Readers." The peculiar character of the Alfredian revival of letters may best be appreciated by a comparison with the corresponding movement on the Continent. The West Frankish court, even in its decadence, was a centre of learning and cultivation, but, except in the poem of the Ludwigslied, and in an occasional public document, Latin was the medium of its literary expression, the language in which treatises and homilies, letters and annals were written. It was, indeed, the very ignorance of the English people which gave birth to English prose literature. It was Alfred's educational zeal rather than his literary taste which led him to turn "book Latin" into the English tongue, and to bequeath to his descendants an unrivalled treasure of vernacular literature. This is the more remarkable, since Alfred had many foreign clerks and Latinists in his court-circle, and was in various ways strongly influenced by Frankish example.

When the Welshman, Asser, set himself to compile the king's Life, he wrote in Latin as a matter of course, and even translated the annals he borrowed from the Anglo-Saxon Chronicle into the common language of educated men. In spite of its classical form, however, Asser's contemporary Life of King Alfred plays much the same part in the ninth-century English revival of letters as Einhard's Life of Charles the Great in the earlier Carolingian Renaissance.

One of the fiercest of modern literary controversies has been waged over the authenticity of Asser's little book. It is worth fighting for, since, were it to be proved a forgery, one of the main sources of Alfredian history would be lost, and the figure of the great King would become even more shadowy than it is at present. The question has been complicated by the destruction of the only manuscript of the De Rebus Gestis Ælfredi in the great Cotton Library fire of 1731. From existing accounts of it, and from the facsimile of a page printed in Wise's edition, it seems to have been written in the eleventh century, probably from a ninth-century original. It was transcribed for Archbishop Parker in the sixteenth century, and two other manuscript copies are also extant, with one seventeenth-century transcript, in addition to the four printed editions, Parker's, published in 1574, Camden's, 1602-3, Wise's, 1722, and Petrie's, 1848.

Though three out of these four editions were issued before the loss of the manuscript, their value is impaired by interpolations, alterations, and inaccuracies. Parker made considerable additions to the text, including the story of Alfred and the cakes, from the Annals of St. Neots, or Annales Asserii, an anonymous post-Conquest compilation, which borrowed freely from the Life of Alfred, and was consequently thought by Parker to represent a fuller text of Asser's work. Camden inserted in Parker's edition the famous passage relating to the University of Oxford, and Wise reproduced the former editions, after a somewhat superficial collation with the still extant Cotton manuscript.

Under these circumstances it is not surprising that Asser's ill-compacted medley of annals and biography should have been regarded with distrust. Thomas Wright, in the middle of the nineteenth century, and Sir Henry Howorth, in more recent times, have even attempted to prove it to be a monkish forgery of the tenth century, or later, connected with the priory of St. Neots. Mr. Stevenson's critical edition, however, has now practically demonstrated the genuineness of at least the nucleus of the book. He has shown that the forgery theory rests to a great extent on misunderstandings of the author's meaning, on inferences drawn from the interpolated sections, or on pure assumption, while there is much positive evidence in favour of the authenticity of the original portions of the text.

Thus the burnt Cotton manuscript, which probably dated from the first half of the eleventh century, was, in all likelihood, a copy of the ninthcentury original.

The language of the biography, again, resembles the Latin written in England and on the Continent in the period before the Norman Conquest, a Latin containing many Frankish and Celtic elements; and the mixture of annalistic and biographical matter, with the abrupt termination, before the King's death, are paralleled in the ninth-century lives of Louis the Pious. The very omissions and confusions of fact and chronology, which would argue great clumsiness in a forger writing some time after the events, are not unnatural in the unfinished work of a contemporary of Alfred. Other signs of an early origin are the writer's mention of St. Gueriir, the Cornish saint, whose popularity was eclipsed in the tenth century by that of St. Neot, and his apparent ignorance of the fame as saint and martyr of the East-Anglian King Edmund.

The Welsh nationality of the author, moreover, seems to be indicated by words and phrases of specially Celtic Latin, by occasional mistranslations of the Anglo-Saxon of the Chronicle, by the mention of the British equivalents for English place-names, and by the accuracy and purity with which the proper names of the Welsh princes are given. The exact knowledge of these obscure names, and of such details as the precise time of the eclipse of 878, or of the reception in Europe of letters from the Patriarch of Jerusalem, with the additions to the accounts in the Chronicle of the battle of Ashdown and the siege of Cynwit, have every appearance of being based on personal information.

Still, Asser's book, even when purged of all interpolated material, can only be used with caution. It is rhetorical and pretentious in style, involved in arrangement, self-contradictory in chronology, and exaggerated in statement. It passes unexpectedly from annals, translated mainly from the Chronicle, to original biography, and back again, with equal abruptness, to annals. The personality of the author is almost as obtrusively present as in the self-conscious writings of a later Welsh ecclesiastic, Giraldus Cambrensis, and the simple, sincere, informal Alfred of the Pastoral Care, the Boethius, and the Soliloquies shows strangely distorted in the glass of flattery and courtly eulogy.

Very little is known of Asser himself, save from the internal evidence of his book. In the preface to the Pastoral Care, Alfred speaks of "Asser my bishop," among those who had helped him in the translation, and there is evidence in ancient episcopal lists that he held the see of Sherborne after Bishop Wulfsige, the date of whose death is unknown. Asser's own death is entered in the Annales Cambriæ, a Welsh Chronicle, under 908, and in the Anglo-Saxon Chronicle under 910, as "Asser bishop . . . who was bishop at Sherborne." He thus survived his royal master some years, and he may possibly be the Bishop of Sherborne to whom Alfred bequeathed a hundred mancuses in his will. His signature as a witness is appended to charters of doubtful authenticity from 900 to 904. His name, otherwise unknown in English documents, occurs in Welsh sources.

According to his own account, Asser was a kinsman of Nobis, Bishop of St. Davids, who died in 873, and was brought up and ordained in western Wales. Summoned by King Alfred to Wessex, which in Welsh fashion he calls Saxonia, he journeyed to the land of the southern or "right-hand" Saxons (Dexteralium Saxonum), another Welsh touch. Here, at the royal vill of Denu, perhaps East Dean or West Dean near the Sussex Seaford, he first met his future master and hero. He refused to accede to Alfred's request to spend at least half of every year at the West-Saxon court, until he had consulted his own people, but he promised to pay the King a second visit in six months' time. As he rode homewards, however, he was attacked with fever in the city of Wintonia, probably Caerwent, on the way to St. Davids, and lay sick for a year and a week.

A correspondence with Alfred followed, and it was arranged that Asser should divide his time equally between Wales and Wessex, spending three months alternately in each. In this way he and his friends at St. Davids hoped to win the support of the West-Saxon King in their struggle with Hemeid, the tyrannical prince of Dyfed, that is Pembrokeshire and part of Carmarthenshire, who had expelled Bishop Nobis1 and Asser from his dominions. In spite of this arrangement, when Asser rejoined King Alfred at the unidentified royal vill of Leonaford, he remained for eight months, reading and studying with the King, and was then only reluctantly allowed to depart. At Christmas he received from Alfred a grant of the two monasteries of Congresbury and Banwell, with a valuable silk pallium and a quantity of incense, accompanied by a hint that further favours were in store.

"In later times, indeed," continues Asser, "he gave me Exeter with all the parish(parochia) which belonged to it in Saxonia (Wessex) and in Cornwall, besides innumerable daily gifts of all kinds of worldly riches." As parochia at this time was used in the sense of "diocese," and as there is no official record of an episcopal see of Exeter till the middle of the eleventh century, this passage has been regarded with suspicion. But it is not improbable that Alfred made Asser Bishop of Devonshire and Cornwall, the Celtic western part of the diocese of Sherborne, before he became diocesan of the whole see. Unfortunately, the exact time when these various events took place cannot be ascertained, owing to Asser's lack of method. The King, however, began to "read and interpret" in 887, the year in which the annalistic portion of Asser's work ends, and he may have come to the West-Saxon court some two or three years earlier. Since in the biographical sections he speaks of Alfred as being "now" in the forty-fifth year of his age, he probably wrote his book in or about 893.

Verbose, prolix, full of wearisome repetitions and tedious moralising, Asser's work has yet achieved something of its avowed object--the recording of what he knew of Alfred's infancy and boyhood, and the description of the life, manners, conversation, and actions of his "lord Alfred, King of the Anglo-Saxons," after his marriage in 868. It is to him that we owe the stories of Eadburh, wife of King Beorhtric, of the revolt of Ethelbald, and his marriage with Judith, of Alfred's mother Osburh and the illuminated manuscript, and the account of the home and court life of his hero, of his frail body and undaunted spirit, his piety and learning, his mechanical skill and artistic tastes, and his wise government of the kingdom. With all its defects, the book remains a most important contemporary authority for the history of the ninth century, and the chief source from which later mediæval annalists drew their knowledge of the life and reign of King Alfred. Florence of Worcester and Simeon of Durham incorporated it in their Chronicles, and their successors borrowed from them in turn. After the appearance of Parker's and Camden's editions, again, the printed text, with its many interpolations, was accepted as the basis of Alfredian biography by more modern writers, and thus the name of Asser came to be as intimately connected with Alfred as Einhard's name with Charles the Great, or Boswell's with Samuel Johnson.

THE SIX YEARS' PEACE, THE THREE YEARS' WAR, AND THE BUILDING OF THE LONG SHIPS, 887-896

THE winning of London was the first step in that reconquest of the Danelaw which Alfred's sons and grandsons were destined to complete. The peace of 886 had left the West-Saxon kingdom shrunken, indeed, but fairly compact and united. Though the lofty pretensions of Alfred's grandfather Egbert had, perforce, been abandoned, they were replaced by a solid, if modest, reality of power.

Kent, with its dependent shires, was now, more truly than ever before, an integral part of Wessex. No Kentish under-king was appointed, as in the days of Ethelwulf, but Plegmund, Alfred's friend and adviser, became Archbishop of Canterbury in 890, and worked in perfect harmony with the King until the close of the reign.

The eastern half of the old Mercian kingdom was in the hands of the Danes, but the western half, with London, was under the government of Alfred's son-in-law, Ethelred, "lord of the Mercians." Ethelred, as his signature to a Mercian charter shows, had held the office of dux or ealdorman in Mercia under Burhred. He married Ethelflæd, the eldest child of Alfred and Ealhswith, probably not earlier than 884, when she would be about fifteen, as she cannot have been born before 869. In 886 Alfred entrusted London to his keeping, and from that year onwards he plays an important part in West-Saxon history as the chief of the Mercian ealdormen, the guardian of London, and the defender of the western frontier against the Welsh. He seems to have occupied a position of almost royal dignity, and even signs one charter subregulus, while Ethelwerd and the Celtic sources call him rex, and Asser states that Anaraut, prince of North Wales, submitted to Alfred on condition that he and his people should stand in the same relation to the West-Saxon King as Ethelred and the Mercians. Ethelflæd might claim to belong to the Mercian royal stock through her maternal grandmother Eadburh, and she, too, is sometimes styled queen (regina).

This was the third marriage alliance between the royal houses of Wessex and Mercia since the accession of Ethelwulf, and each had coincided with a political crisis. In 853 the union of Ethelswith, Alfred's sister, with Burhred, the Mercian King, was, perhaps, connected with the combined West-Saxon and Mercian expedition of that year, against the North Welsh. In 868, according to Asser, Alfred's own marriage with the Mercian Ealhswith took place, in the year when Wessex and Mercia made a joint attack on the Danes at Nottingham. After the cession of western Mercia to Wessex, and the disappearance of the puppet king Ceolwulf, Alfred seems to have chosen the most capable of Burhred's ealdormen as the governor of the new territory, and, by giving him the hand of his daughter, to have bound him closely to the West-Saxon throne. Henceforward, though Mercia preserved a measure of independence, it ceased to be a separate kingdom, and was gradually incorporated in the West-Saxon legal and administrative system.

With the Danish kingdoms of East Anglia and Northumbria, or York, under their Christian kings, Guthrum-Athelstan, and Cnut-Guthred, Healfdene's successor, Alfred was, apparently, on friendly terms. It was Cnut-Guthred who gave the bearers of St. Cuthbert's holy body a restingplace at Chester-le-street, and both he and Guthrum-Athelstan copied Alfred's coins, and to some extent adopted western customs. It has even been suggested1 that the rare Northumbrian penny which bears the name of Alfred on the obverse, and Cnut Rex on the reverse, may point to some recognition of Alfred's suzerainty, but the history of the northern Danish kingdom in these years is very obscure, while of the condition of Danish Mercia and of those midland Danish districts which were afterwards known as the territories of the Five Boroughs, nothing is certainly known.

In Wales, Alfred's supremacy seems to have been widely acknowledged. Asser, writing, it appears, of the time of his own coming to Wessex, before 887, says that at that period and "long before," the "regions of South Britain" had belonged to King Alfred, "and still so belong." He goes on to enumerate the rulers of these lands: Hemeid of Demetica, or Dyfed, and

Helised or Elised ap Teudur, King of Brecknock, who had submitted to Alfred to save themselves from the oppression of the North Welsh princes; Howel ap Rhys, King of Glegwising (Glamorgan and part of Monmouthshire), and the kings of Gwent in Monmouthshire, Brochmail and Fernmail, sons of Mouric, who sought Alfred's protection against their enemies, "compelled by the force and tyranny of ealdorman (comes) Eadred (Ethelred) and of the Mercians."

If 885, the date given for Hemeid's death in the Annales Cambriæ, may be accepted, Alfred must have been suzerain of at least part of South Wales even before the winning of London. The North Welsh came in later, under Anaraut, one of the sons of Rotri, or Roderick Mawr. Roderick himself is said to have been slain by the "Saxons" in 877. Of Anaraut Asser states that,

deserting at last the friendship of the Northumbrians, from which he had gained no good, but rather harm, and diligently seeking the friendship of the King, he came into his presence, and when the King had received him honourably, and had taken him from the bishop's hand as his son in confirmation, and had enriched him with very great gifts, he submitted himself with all his people to the King's lordship, on condition that in all things he should be as obedient to the King's will as Ethelred and the Mercians.

Since the North Welsh helped the English against the Danes in 893, it is probable that this submission was made shortly before Asser recorded it, writing, it may be, in Wales, with access to local information. His assertions are borne out by the later, and somewhat fragmentary, Welsh sources, and the high-sounding dedication of his book to his "venerable and most pious lord, ruler (rector) of all the Christians of the island of Britain, AElig;lfred King of the Anglo-Saxons," may have some justification in fact.

But as the price paid for England's peace had been the suffering of the Continental kingdoms, so the revival of prosperity on the Continent was marked by a fresh attempt to conquer Wessex, and to extend the Danelaw to the English Channel. The Empire had reached its lowest depth of humiliation with the siege of Paris, followed, in 887, by the deposition of Charles the Fat. While Odo, or Eudes, the brave defender of Paris, ruled over the West Franks, the East Franks found a leader of energy and capacity in their new King, Arnulf of Carinthia, who became Emperor in 896. Though the Northmen defeated the Franks in June, 891, on the Geule, a tributary of the Maas, Arnulf led his army in person against the strongly fortified viking position on the Dyle, near Louvain, and, in November of the same year, gained a signal victory. "KingEarnulf," writes the Anglo-Saxon chronicler, "fought against the riding host (ræde here) before the ships came up, and put it to flight." Yet, though the sea-kings Godfred and Sigfred were slain, and the interior of Germany was finally delivered from viking ravages, the "Great Army" was still strong enough to winter at Louvain, and to resume its plunder raids in the following spring.

Not until the autumn of 8921 did the main body of the Northmen, with their wives, their children, and their horses, cross the Channel, leaving a famine-stricken and desolate land behind them. A fleet of two hundred and fifty ships gathered at Boulogne, sailed to the coast of Kent, and penetrated into the heart of the Andredsweald, that "great wood" which was said to be a hundred and twelve miles long and thirty miles wide. They went up the Limene or Lymne, then a navigable stream, now only to be traced from geographical indications and ancient documents. Four miles from the river-mouth they seized an unfinished earthwork, a "half-wrought" geweorc or fæsten, which was only occupied by a few ceorls, possibly the workmen who were building it, in connection with Alfred's scheme of coastal and frontier defence. The vikings proceeded to entrench themselves in winter quarters at Appledore, in southern Kent, now an inland village, but in those days probably situated on the tidal river Lymne.

Meanwhile, a smaller fleet of eighty Danish ships had entered the estuary of the Thames, and had built a fort (geweorc) at Milton, on the Swale, in northern Kent, just opposite the isle of Sheppey. Its leader was Hastein, Hæsten, or Hasting, like Ragnar Lodbrok, Guthrum, or Rollo, a bold and crafty adventurer, in the guise of a typical pirate of romance.

Threatened by this double danger, Alfred's first thought seems to have been to secure the loyalty of the Danelaw. He exacted oaths of fidelity from the Northumbrian and East-Anglian Danes, and took hostages also from the East Anglians, who were now under the rule of Eohric or Eric, Guthrum-Athelstan's successor. The fact that he was able to demand and obtain such pledges suggests that the Anglo-Danish kingdoms had to some extent accepted the superiority of Wessex.

Early in 893 Alfred gathered his fyrd, and stationed himself in Kent, between the two viking armies, in order that he might keep a watch on both. All about him were "the wood fastnesses and the water fastnesses," the forest of the Andredsweald, and the marshes of the Medway. Prevented from seeking the open in force, the Danes resorted to a policy of raids and skirmishes. "They rode along by the forest in marauding bands (hlothum) and troops, skirting the woodland, wherever it was 'fyrdless.' And the [West-Saxons] also sought them almost every day or night, in troops, either from the fyrd, or from the burhs."

It is here that the Anglo-Saxon Chronicle mentions Alfred's division of the fyrd into a field army and a reserve, "besides the men who had to hold the burhs." The order of events is obscured by the confused arrangement of the Chronicle, the one contemporary source, but it was probably at this time that Alfred tried to detach Hæsten from 1 the "Great Army," and win him over by bribes and flattery. The wily viking swore oaths and gave hostages readily enough, and the King, following the precedents of Guthrum, and Anaraut, lavished gifts on him, and stood godfather to one of his sons, while Ethelred of Mercia was the sponsor of another. Hæsten then withdrew from Kent, but only to throw up earthworks and fortify himself at Benfleet in Essex, just across the Thames estuary, in the friendly territory of the East-Anglian Danes, who did not scruple to break their oaths to Alfred.

The "Great Army" now concentrated all its energies on a united effort, broke up the camp at Appledore, and rode northwards, laden with immense booty, to effect a junction with Hæsten at Benfleet, while the ships went round by sea. It was probably to avoid the West-Saxon fyrd that the Danes chose to march by way of Surrey, Hampshire, and Berkshire, but they did not succeed in repeating the manœuvre of 876 and stealing away from Alfred's army, for the mounted fyrd, under the King's son Edward, outrode them, intercepted them at Farnham, near the Hampshire border of Surrey, and drove them in hurried flight over the Thames. They abandoned their spoils, crossed the river without waiting to find a ford, and took refuge in the little island of Thorney, in the Colne, not far from West Drayton. Here the fyrd came up with them, and beset them until the appointed time of service expired, and supplies ran short.

Alfred, with the second division of the fyrd, was on his way to relieve his son, and Edward's troops had already turned homewards, when news arrived of a fresh and daring movement on the part of the enemy. The Northumbrians and East Anglians, acting, it may be, in concert with Hæsten and the "Great Army," made a combined naval attack on the south and west of England. While a fleet of a hundred sail besieged Exeter, forty ships beleaguered an unnamed Devonshire fort or geweorc"on the north sea."

The difficulties and anxieties of this complicated campaign may have inspired a rhetorical but graphic passage in Henry of Huntingdon's description of the ravages of Britain's "fourth plague," the Danes. When, he says, the King of the English marched to fight against them in the east, before they could reach the enemy a messenger would fly up, crying: "Whither goest thou, O King? An immense fleet of heathen men, coming from the south, has seized the coasts of England, depopulating towns and villages, and all is delivered to slaughter and fire." The same day another came running, saying: "Why dost thou fly, O King? A terrible army has landed in eastern England, and unless thou return straightway to meet them, they will think thee a fugitive, and slaughter and flames will pursue thee." On the same day, or on the morrow, came another messenger, who said: "O chiefs, whither are you going? The Danes, landing on the northern shores, are burning your houses, plundering your goods, tossing children on the points of their spears, maltreating and carrying off your wives." The twelfth-century historian pictures King and people weakened and demoralised "in heart and hand" by these alarming rumours. The ninthcentury chronicler, on the contrary, writes that when Alfred heard of the attack on Devonshire, "he turned westwards towards Exeter, with all the fyrd except a very small part," which he left, under Edward, to watch the Danes at Thorney.

The Anglo-Saxon Chronicle now, in trying to tell two stories at once, becomes involved, and difficult to follow, but Ethelwerd supplies some additional details, and, by combining the two accounts, the probable course of the campaign may be traced. It appears that while Alfred went to Devonshire, Edward took over the command of the eastern army. The

Danes had been detained at Thorney by the illness of their king, who had been seri ously wounded at Farnham, but they eventually carried out their original plan, and joined Haesten at Benfleet.

Ethelwerd says that they were first besieged in their island refuge by Edward and Ethelred of Mercia, with the men of London, and that they were compelled to give hostages, and to promise to leave the kingdom. Reinforced both from the west and from London, Edward and Ethelred now advanced into Essex, and while Hæsten was absent on a plunder raid, they fell on the Benfleet entrenchments, scattered the defenders, destroyed the fortifications, and carried off the treasure, with the women and children, to London. Such of the ships as they did not take to London or Rochester they "broke up, or burned." The contemporary chronicler's words were unexpectedly confirmed when, in digging the foundations of South Benfleet station, remains of charred prows of ships were found in the waterway. Hæsten's wife and his two sons, the godchildren of Alfred and Ethelred, were sent to the King. Moved by pious scruples and natural generosity, he restored them to their own people, without conditions.

The shattered remnants of the "Great Army" fell back on Shoebury, and there, with the help of Hæsten's contingent, threw up a new fort or geweorc. The sea has encroached on what was once an island earthwork, but fragments of ditch and bank still witness to the original strength of entrenchments which may with much probability be attributed to this period. In the west, meantime, Alfred had been successful in raising the siege of Exeter, but the viking ships were still lingering about the coast, and the King's forces could not safely leave Devonshire. This was the situation when the Danes at Shoebury, strengthened by reinforcements from East Anglia and Northumbria, struck boldly at the heart of the West-Saxon kingdom, by the waterways of the Thames and Severn.

They may have been co-operating with the western fleet, or the expedition may have been an independent plunder raid. In any case, the event showed the efficiency of Alfred's defensive organisation. If London failed to check the advance of the enemy, it at least saved itself from attack, while, as the vikings marched along the Thames, once the frontier of Alfred's kingdom, now its central avenue of approach, and then "up Severn," they found the country guarded, in spite of the King's absence, by competent local troops, commanded by the ealdormen Ethelred of Mercia, AElig;thelm of Wiltshire, and Ethelnoth of Somerset, with the king's thegns from the burhs "east of Parret, west and east of Selwood, north of Thames, and west of Severn," and--a tribute to Alfred's recent dealings with the Celtic princes-- with "a part also of the North Welsh people." The host thus composed--it is never called a fyrd --closed in on the Danish army at Buttington, "on Severn shore," and blockaded their entrenchments from both sides of the stream. The place indicated is probably Buttington1 in Montgomeryshire, not far from Welshpool, where considerable earthworks may still be seen. So closely was the camp beleaguered that the Danes were forced to eat many of their horses, while others died of starvation.

After several weeks of famine, they sallied out in despair, and gave battle to the besiegers on the east side of the river. The English gained a victory, though with the loss of "Ordeh the king's thegn, and of many another king's thegn also," but the Danes managed to break through the blockading lines, and to retreat to their Shoebury camp. Then, after placing their women and children, their treasure and their ships, in safety, in East Anglia, they gathered together their whole remaining strength, and dashed "at one stretch," riding by day and by night, right across England, from east to west, following, perhaps, the Watling Street, till they came to the old Roman "City of Legions" (Legaceaster), or Chester, in the Wirral, the district between Dee and Mersey. It was still half-ruined, a "waste chester (ceaster),"says the chronicler, but the Danes succeeded in fortifying themselves behind the ancient walls, before the fyrd, riding in hot pursuit, could come up with them.

The English now deliberately starved out the enemy, by harrying the surrounding country, driving off the cattle, burning the corn, and turning their horses loose to graze on the standing crops, while they kept a strict watch on the stronghold, and cut off all stragglers who ventured outside the fortifications. Thus ended the eventful year 893.

Early in 894 the Danes were constrained by famine to evacuate Chester. They raided North Wales for supplies, and then turned towards the Danelaw. Laden with their spoil, they went through the land of the Northumbrians and the East Anglians, "so that the fyrd might not reach them," until they came to the country of the East Saxons, "to an island out in the sea which is called Meresig"--Mersea Island, off the Essex coast, between the mouths of the Stour and the Blackwater. The fleet which had besieged Exeter now also returned home, harrying Sussex, round about Chichester, on the way, only to be beaten off by the "men of the burh;--the town is found in the Burghal Hidage, as the centre of a district of fifteen hundred hides. Once more the new defensive system proved effective. The vikings fled, with a loss of "many hundreds" of men, and of several ships, and the south coast was freed from their ravages. In the late autumn, the Danes in Mersea Island left their camp, sailed up the Thames, and then up the Lea, along the river frontier of the treaty of 886, and took up winter quarters in an earthwork (geweorc) which they raised on the Lea, some twenty miles above London. Here they remained till the following summer, and it is significant of their changed attitude towards the English that there is no record of any attempt on the city, or of any harrying of the neighbouring country. The Londoners were even strong enough to take the offensive. In the summer of 895 they attacked the Danish fort, but were repulsed with the loss of four king's thegns.

Alfred had now returned from the west, and as the harvest season approached, he stationed himself with his troops between the camp on the Lea and London, that the men of the burh, those warlike, yet rustic citizens, might reap their crops in security. Not content with a mere policy of defence, he devised a scheme for ridding the kingdom altogether of the unwelcome intruders.

One day the King rode up the river to reconnoitre where the stream might be blocked, so that the enemy could not bring out their ships. He then ordered two forts (geweorc) to be built, one on either bank of the Lea, probably with some sort of bar or obstruction in the channel between them. The Danes only woke to their danger when the second fort was in course of construction, too late to save the fleet. Leaving the ships to their fate, they established their wives and children in East Anglia, and marched across country to "Quatbridge" on the Severn, not far from Bridgenorth, where they encamped. The fyrd rode after them, while the Londoners triumphantly destroyed some of the deserted ships, and brought all that were still serviceable into harbour "within Londonburh."

After wintering at Quatbridge, the "Great Army," in the summer of 896, at last disbanded. Some went to East Anglia, some to Northumbria, while the more needy and ambitious procured ships, and sailed across the Channel to the Seine, where they renewed their former ravages. "Thanks be to God," writes the Anglo-Saxon chronicler, "the army had not utterly 'broken' the English (Angel cyn). They were, indeed, much more 'broken' in these three years with pestilence among cattle and men, and in these three years many of the worthiest king's thegns departed this life."

The three years' war was over, but peace was not yet. The English Danelaw was restless and disturbed, its old viking spirit revived by the contact with the pirates of the "Great Army." Cnut-Guthred of Northumbria had died in 894. He was succeeded by Sigfred or Siefred, probably the Sigeferth piraticus who is described by Ethelwerd as devastating the English coast at about this time. This seems to be confirmed by Ethelwerd's further statement that Ethelnoth, the Somerset ealdorman, pursued the Danes from York to Stamford, in the country of the Mercians, between the river Welland and "the dense wood of Kesteven." Ethelwerd dates a period of great discord in Northumbria from the death of King Guthfrid in August, 895, the year following this raid. It is not certain that this Guthfrid and Cnut-Guthred are identical, but it is worth noting Simeon of Durham's assertion that King Alfred assumed the right of disposing of the Northumbrian kingdom after Guthred's death. Simeon doubtless exaggerates, but there may possibly have been some attempt on Alfred's part to exercise sovereign power beyond the Humber.

It was, perhaps, in connection with these northern events that, in 896, marauders4 from Northumbria and East Anglia harried the south coast of Wessex, "with the ships which they had built many years before." To meet these old-fashioned vessels Alfred caused his famous "long ships" to be built, "fully twice as long as the others," some with sixty oars, some with more, swifter and steadier than the viking boats, and of a new and original pattern, neither Frisian nor Danish in build, but "as the King himself thought they would be most efficient." As often happens with the first trial of a new type of battle-ship, the immediate results of this invention were disappointing.

At the turn of the year 896 a small fleet of six viking ships devastated the Isle of Wight and the coasts of Dorset and Devonshire. Alfred sent nine of the new ships against them, hoping, it seems, to catch them in Southampton Water. The Danes had beached three of their boats, and the crews had gone ashore. The three remaining vessels gave battle to the English. Two were taken, and their crews were put to death; the third escaped, with only five men left alive on board. The drawbacks of the size and deep draught of the "long ships" now appeared. They went aground, six on one side of the harbour, three on the other side, near the three surviving viking boats. At low tide the Danes crossed the sands on foot, and a fierce battle took place, in which the Danes lost a hundred and twenty men, and the West-Saxons, according to the Chronicle, only sixty-two "Frisians and English," while three Frisians are mentioned by name in the list of worthies who fell in the fight. With the flood-tide the Danes put out to sea, but two of their three vessels were cast ashore in a storm, and the crews were led to the King at Winchester, and were hanged by his orders. The last ship of the little fleet, full of wounded men, made good its retreat to East Anglia.

In this one summer, says the Anglo-Saxon chronicler, no less than twenty ships, with their crews, were lost on the south coast, but he refrains from stating whether he means Danish or English ships, or the total loss on both sides.

There could certainly be no question that the close of the naval campaign of 896 left Wessex stronger and more prosperous than at any time since the strenuous year 871. The contrast between the state of the kingdom at Alfred's accession and at the end of his reign was, indeed, too marked to escape the notice of historians. William of Malmesbury, in writing of Hæsten's invasion, notes that the Danes, reduced in numbers and disheartened by their Continental wars, hung back from attacking the English, while Alfred's men had become accustomed to bearing arms, and were ready both for defence and attack. He is probably right in attributing this happy change to the personal influence of the King, who never knew when he was beaten, and was invincible in his persistent courage and energy.

THE LAST YEARS OF KING ALFRED: PORT AFTER STORMY SEAS.

897-899

KING ALFRED'S restless life is usually supposed to have closed in peace. But this is an assumption from the silence of the Anglo- Saxon Chronicle, and there are indications, both in Ethelwerd's chronicle and in Alfred's own writings, that the Golden Age of his dreams, when "no man had heard of the pirate fleet (sciphere)," remained to the last an unattained ideal.

For four years after the death of King Guthfrid of Northumbria, says Ethelwerd, "foul bands of Northumbrians" caused great discord among the English. As Ethelwerd puts Guthfrid's death in the course of 895, the four troubled years of which he speaks would bring his story up to 899, the year in which he places the death of Alfred. The prose preface to the Boethius, if it may be accepted as contemporary, may also be cited in proof of the disturbed character of the time at which it was written, "among various and manifold worldly cares," and the same may be said of the pathetic passage in the Soliloquies, where Alfred speaks of his vain desire for the leisure and retirement necessary to the fulfilment of his literary ambitions.

The alliance, in the very year of Alfred's death, of his rebellious nephew Æthelwald with the Danes of Northumbria points in the same direction. It was, indeed, the great King's military policy rather than his peaceful activities that his children Edward and Ethelflæd were called on to continue. The invasions of "heathen men" from without were now replaced by risings of the half-Christianised Anglo-Danish settlers within the English kingdoms. The subjection and assimilation of the new Scandinavian element in the English population became, for the next half-century, the main problem of government for the West-Saxon kings.

The Anglo-Saxon Chronicle leaves Alfred in 896 [897], a stern and ruthless conqueror, sending his prisoners of war to the gallows. A more pleasing story of his last years is told by William of Malmesbury, who relates how, noting the grace and beauty of his little grandson Athelstan, the future victor at Brunanburh, he predicted for him a happy reign, and invested him with a scarlet cloak, a jewelled belt, and a "Saxon sword," with a golden scabbard, the insignia, as it seemed to the twelfth-century monk, of knighthood, the outward tokens, it may be, to ninth-century eyes, of the hereditary thegnhood of an ætheling, or prince of the blood royal.

In 897 [898] the Chronicle records the deaths of Heahstan, Bishop of London, and of æthelm, ealdorman of Wiltshire, the King's old friends and trusted councillors. In 898 Alfred, rex Saxonum, is found granting land in Kent to ealdorman "Sigilm," and consulting at Chelsea with Ethelred and Ethelflæd of Mercia about the fortifications of London. But the shades were already closing in, and it was, perhaps, a premonition of impending change which led him to write in the Soliloquies that he would not fear the infirmities of the body, were it not for three things:--heavy sorrow, death, and inability to satisfy the desire for the understanding and knowledge of God.

The annal for 901, in the Parker manuscript of the Chronicle, opens with the entry:

Here departed Ælfred son of Athulf [Ethelwulf] six nights before All Hallows Mass. He was King overall the English people [Angel cyn] except that part which was under the power of the Danes, and he held the kingdom thirty winters all but one and a half [twenty-eight and a half]. And then Edward his son took the kingdom.

A cross in the margin marks the early recognition of the importance of the event, the passing of AElig;lfred Athulfing.

It seems a pity that the dust of controversy should have obscured the dignity of the simple contemporary notice of the great King's death, but unfortunately scarcely anything in Alfred's life has been so keenly disputed as the date of his leaving it. The scribal errors of copyists, and the irregular and arbitrary nature of the systems of chronology used by mediæval writers, make discussion inevitable, and a positive conclusion almost impossible.

The balance of probability, however, is in favour of October 26, 899, as the day of Alfred's death, though October 26, 900, also finds many supporters.

It is, perhaps, indicative of the strictly contemporary character of the original of the Parker Chronicle, that the annal which records Alfred's death makes no mention of his place of burial. According to a twelfth-century tradition, preserved by William of Malmesbury, his body found a temporary resting-place in the cathedral church at Winchester, pending the completion of the New Minster, to which it was removed in 903. The story went that this translation of Alfred's remains was due to the silly fancies of the cathedral canons, who thought, with "English credulity," that the King's ghost walked by night. Be this as it may, Ethelwerd in the tenth century described Alfred as "resting in peace at Winchester," and the Annals of St. Neots, which were probably written in the early twelfth century, state that he was buried at Winchester, the royal city, with due kingly honours, in the church of St. Peter, Prince of the Apostles (the New Minster), and that his tomb was wrought of most precious porphyry.

The fourteenth-century compilation called the "Book of Hyde" (Liber de Hyda) repeats William of Malmesbury's tale of the credulous canons, and gives details of the building of the New Minster, which Alfred himself had planned. Finished in two years, by the pious efforts of King Edward and of Grimbald, its first abbot, it stood in close proximity to the cathedral, on ground which had been bought from the bishop at a mancus of gold the foot. It was dedicated in 903 to the Holy Trinity, the Blessed Virgin, and Saint Peter and St. Paul, but it was commonly called the "New Minster," to distinguish it from the older foundation. In 903, also, took place the solemn reception of a little band of immigrants from Ponthieu, flying from the vikings with the precious relics of the Breton Saint Judoc, who became, with Grimbald, one of the patrons of the house, while in the same year "the most benign king" Edward translated the bones and ashes of his father Alfred to the "most holy place of his own building," with great ceremony and royal dignity. Ealhswith, Alfred's widow, was buried near her husband not many years later, and Edward himself was laid beside his parents before the first quarter of the tenth century was at an end. Grimbald, too, who only lived long enough to see the completion of his abbey, found a grave within its walls, and was reverenced as one of its patron saints. In the twelfth century the bodies were removed in state to Hyde Abbey, the splendid building established by Henry I. just outside the city of Winchester, in place of the New Minster, which had been found to be inconveniently near the cathedral.

At the time of the Dissolution of the Monasteries, Hyde Abbey was so ruthlessly destroyed that Camden, the sixteenth-century antiquary, could write: "At present the bare site remains, deformed with heaps of ruins, daily dug up to burn into lime." In 1788, even these poor remnants were swept away, to make room for a New Gaol or Bridewell. Three stone coffins which were brought to light at this time were recklessly broken up, and their contents were scattered. It can only be guessed that they once held the mortal remains of Alfred, his wife, and his son Edward the Elder. A stone bearing the inscription œlfred rex DCCC LXXXI, and a few fragments of sculpture, alone survive of the stately and beautiful church and monastery. "O, glory of this world! Why do foolish men, with false tongue, call thee glory, when such thou art not?"

Fate, which has obliterated even the memory of the site of Alfred's tomb, has yet, by a curious chance, preserved his last will and testament, his "writing about his inheritance (yrfe-gewrit)." This document, of which the oldest extant copy dates from the early eleventh century, is given in the "Book of Hyde," in three versions, Anglo-Saxon, Latin, and later English.

The time of its composition has been disputed, but it cannot have been earlier than 873, when Werferth, mentioned in it as a Bishop, was consecrated to the see of Worcester, or later than 888, when Archbishop Ethelred of Canterbury, who advised the King about it, died. The name of Plegmund, moreover, does not occur in the list of legatees, whence it has been argued that it is earlier than 884-5, the probable date of his close association with King Alfred. It may also be pointed out that the name of "Ælflæd" occurs in connection with the Wiltshire estate of Damerham. If, as seems likely, this is Ethelflæd, Alfred's daughter, it may be suggested that this will, not the first which the King had made, was drawn up at the time of her marriage to Ethelred of Mercia, probably about 884, or a little later, and that an estate at Damerham formed part of her marriage portion.

Alfred's will is deeply interesting and suggestive, from many points of view. It shows the King in his family relations, as husband, father, kinsman, and lord, disposing of his inherited family lands, of his "bookland," and of his personalty. It shows him, too, consulting with his witan about the interpretation of his father's will, asking their counsel, and obtaining their witness for his own disposition of his property.

When death had swept away many of his kinsmen, and changed his circumstances, he thought it well to cancel his former bequests, and to make a new arrangement for the future. The King "by God's gift," then, with the advice of the Archbishop, and the witness of all the West-Saxon witan, takes thought for his soul, and for the inheritance which God and his forefathers had given him, and declares his will concerning the distribution of his heritage after his death. He recapitulates the events whereby this heritage has been concentrated in his hands, mentions the provisions of his father's will, and then passes to his own bequests.

To his eldest son Edward he leaves lands in the west country, in Cornwall and Somerset, including Wedmore, and "all the bookland which Leofheah held," with other estates in Wiltshire, Hampshire, and Surrey. To the "households" (hiwum) at Cheddar, a royal vill, he commends Edward, as lord, though he admits their right, previously recognised, to choose what lord they will. His bookland in Kent, at Hurstbourne in Hampshire, and at Chisledon in Wiltshire, he gives to Winchester, in accordance with his father's grant, together with the property at Hurstbourne which he himself had formerly entrusted to Ecgulf, perhaps the "horse-thegn" whose death is recorded in 896 [897].

His youngest son receives estates in the south, with the old family property at Meon in Hampshire, and lands in the west, in Wiltshire, Dorset, Somerset, and Devonshire, "all that I have among the Welsh (on Wealcynne) except Triconshire [part of Cornwall]," writes Alfred, with an interesting recognition of the Celtic character of the western counties. His eldest daughter has the Somerset "ham" at Wellow, to the second are bequeathed two Hampshire estates, and to the third, Chippenham, and two other "hams" in Wiltshire. His nephews, Ethelred's sons Æthelm and Æthelwald, are provided for by ample estates in Sussex, Hampshire, and Surrey, and his kinsman Osferth, by lands in Sussex, while his wife Ealhswith has the three "hams" of Lambourn, Wantage, Alfred's birthplace, and Ethandun, the scene of his victory over Guthrum.

The King's personal property he also distributes among his kinsmen and followers: five hundred pounds to each of his sons; one hundred pounds to his wife, and to each of his three daughters; a hundred mancuses (about £12.0.0) apiece to his ealdormen, and the same to his nephews and Osferth; a sword worth a hundred mancuses to ealdorman Ethelred, and "to the men who follow me, to whom I now give gifts at Eastertide," two hundred pounds, duly shared among them. To the Archbishop of Canterbury, a hundred mancuses, and the like sum to each of the Bishops Esne, Werferth, and "him at Sherborne."

Two hundred pounds are further devoted to charity, on behalf of the King and his father, and the friends for whom they were accustomed to intercede: fifty pounds to the priesthood, fifty to "God's poor servants," fifty to poor laymen, fifty to the church in which the King is laid to rest. "I am in nowise certain," he candidly adds, "if there be so much money (feoh), or if there be more; but I think it is so. If it be more, let it be shared among those to whom I have bequeathed money, and I will that my ealdormen and my thenigmenn . . . distribute it thus." Then follow injunctions to carry out his father's will as far as possible, and to pay his own debts, and the long document closes with the famous provisions regulating the succession to his bookland, and securing the liberty to choose a lord which he had granted to certain privileged persons and communities.

In Alfred's Laws he had decreed that bookland should not be alienated from the kindred of the owner, if the original "book" or charter forbade such alienation. Here, in granting bookland, he stipulates that the "men" who receive it shall not leave it away from the royal family, and that in the event of their dying childless it shall revert to his house, in the male line, "on the weapon side," if possible, in accordance with the ancient custom. His own gifts to women, "on the spindle side," are, however, to hold good, and he expressly reserves his right to grant land either to "women's hands" or to "weapon hands," though his kinsmen are enjoined to indemnify any aggrieved male claimants.

The evidence of Alfred's will confirms what Asser says about his family. His two sons, Edward and Ethelwerd, and his three daughters, Ethelflæd, Ethelgifu, and Elfthryth, were worthy descendants of a great father. Ethelflæd and Edward seem to have inherited his practical ability. Both, one as "Lady of the Mercians," the other as his father's successor, left names famous in English history. Ethelwerd, the youngest child, trained in learning and scholarship in the court-school, and Ethelgifu, who took the veil, and became the first abbess of Shaftesbury, were the heirs of Alfred's intellectual and literary tastes. Elfthryth, the wife of Baldwin II. of Flanders, renewed and carried on an old alliance. With her sons, Arnulf and Adelolf, who was probably named after King Ethelwulf, she is found in 918 granting lands in Kent to the Abbey of St. Peter at Ghent. Asser also mentions other children who died in infancy.

It is one of the little intimate touches which strengthen belief in the genuineness of Asser's book, that he describes the different methods of education adopted with the elder children and with the youngest, Ethelwerd, and yet, apparently, knows little of their later history. Though Ethelflæd was already married when he wrote, Elfthryth was still a girl in her father's house, and Ethelgifu was a nun, indeed, but not yet an abbess. William of Malmesbury, in relating Edward the Elder's mythical love-story, makes him meet his future bride at the house of his old nurse, the wife of a villicus or reeve: an incident which suggests that the royal children may have been brought up on the King's country farms, in wholesome rustic fashion. In later days, Edward himself seems to have entrusted the education of his son Athelstan to Ethelflæd and Ethelred of Mercia.

At the opening of the tenth century, then, the figure of King Alfred appears, for a brief space, clear and distinct, before the distorting mists of legend and tradition gather about it. If now, sweeping aside all these later accretions, we try to see the King as his contemporaries saw him, and as he has revealed himself in his writings, the conventional perfection of "the First Founder of the English Monarchy" gives place to something warmer and more human, a living personality, a character of native simplicity and honesty, disciplined by experience into a rare nobility and purity.

Of Alfred's personal appearance there is no record except Asser's stereotyped phrases1 describing his childish beauty. The busts on his coins, even if they could be taken as attempts at portraiture, are too rude to be much help, though it may, perhaps, be inferred from them that the King was beardless, with rather long hair, framing a regular-featured face. His delicate, painwracked body probably looked frail enough, yet he was able to hunt, and fight, and to bear hardships which might have discouraged stronger men. His early fear of blindness, with the frequent recurrence in his writings of references to the value of clear vision, may imply both that his own eyesight was imperfect, and that the pleasures of sight specially appealed to him. The difficulty in reconstructing Alfred's physical characteristics is, however, less to be regretted, since he himself desired chiefly to be remembered by his good works. This was the wish of an active lover of his kind, the ambition of a man who, for all his idealism, was determined to leave some material traces of his passage through the world.

His mind seems to have been constructive rather than creative. The scientific spirit, the intense desire for knowledge and love of truth, combined with the instinct for applying knowledge to practical ends, were stronger in him than even his feeling for beauty, or his religious mysticism. Yet he had the mediæval fondness for parable and simile. All to him was symbolical--the sea and the shipping, the starry sky, the common incidents of rural life, the routine of the court, or the labour of the workshop. His imagination was quick and vivid, but his intellectual powers were, probably, richer and fuller than his emotional capacity. He speaks much of friendship, but little of earthly love. He touches high passion only when he faces the mysteries of the spiritual world, when he asks himself, with fear and searchings of heart, what he is, and whether his mind and soul are "mortal and perishable, or ever-living and eternal."

What would I care for life [he writes] if I knew nothing? What is the highest wisdom, other than the highest good? Or what is the highest good, except that every man in this world love God as much as he loveth wisdom? . . . So much as he loveth wisdom, so much doth he love God.

Here, surely, in this burning love of truth, lies the clue to Alfred's character, and much of the secret of his enduring charm. By his sincerity of purpose and clearness of spiritual vision he penetrated below the changing surface to the eternal heart of the things that never grow old. He touched the hidden springs of life and death, of wonder and fear, of joy and sorrow, and, by virtue of his sympathy and humanity, he won the love of his people, and has been remembered for a thousand years with a familiar affection and a straightforward unromantic esteem which are a fitting tribute to the "wise king," "Alfred the truth-teller" (Ælfredus veridicus), "England's darling."

King Alfred has been classed with Canute, William the Conqueror, Henry

II., and Edward I., as one of the "conscious creators of England's greatness." If this be so, his closest affinity is with Henry II. Like him, he was an adapter rather than an originator. Like him, too, he modified foreign ideas, even while accepting them, and gave them an English dress which practically transformed them. If he saved England for the English by repelling the flood of Danish invasion, and setting bounds to it in the Danelaw, he saved it again by preserving the ancient laws and customs, and giving them a permanent literary shape, in the vernacular tongue.

Yet again, though he borrowed from other civilisations, he did not slavishly follow either Frankish or Scandinavian models. He selected and combined, and gave his subjects what he thought needful for them, in a language which they could understand. Building on the foundations which Ine of Wessex had laid, he established a tradition of government which was carried on by his descendants:--a policy of centralisation, wherein, nevertheless, the king and witan worked through the local communities of the land, and the monarchy, balanced by a powerful aristocracy, rested on a broad basis of popular support.

Elaborated by Edward the Elder and Athelstan, by Edmund and Edgar and Ethelred II., the system was strong enough to withstand the double shock of the Danish and Norman conquests of the eleventh century. If Alfred had fallen at Ethandun, it can hardly be doubted that England would have become Scandinavian, and her lot would have been cast with the northern European nations, while, if Alfred's legal "Code" had never been compiled, the Latin element would, almost inevitably, have predominated in English law. But for Alfred, too, English might never have become a literary language. He rescued, restored, and transmitted the scattered fragments of past achievement, historical, intellectual, and political.

The Anglo-Saxon Chronicle, the Laws, and the four great translations are his abiding monuments. His very timidity, and fear of rash innovation, worked for the good of his kingdom, and secured continuity of social development, where a bolder reformer would have completely broken with the old order. For these services alone the Englishspeaking and English-governed races owe him lasting gratitude, but even deeper is their debt to the English King who first lent the weight of a great name and a stainless reputation to the fine theory that public office is a sacred trust, and that the privileges of high place are only justified by unswerving devotion to its attendant duties.

Thy true Nobility of Mind and Blood,

O Warlike Alfred, gave thee to be good.

Goodness Industrious made thee; Industry

Got thee a name to all Posterity.

NOTE ON THE DATE OF KING ALFRED'S DEATH

(Eng. Hist. Rev., vol. xiii., p. 71; Two Saxon Chron., ii., p. 112; British Numismatic Journal, series 1, vol. iv., p. 241 ff., vol. v., p. 381 ff.; Athenæum, 1898, Nos. 3672-5, 3688, 3690, 3693; 1900, Nos. 3804, 3810-11, 3814, 3817; 1901, Nos. 3819-20, 3870. F. M. Stenton, Æthelwerd's Account of the Last Years of King Alfred's Reign. Eng. Hist. Rev. vol. xxiv. p. 79.)

The era from which the Anglo-Saxons computed the beginning of the year in the ninth century is uncertain, though there is some evidence for a calendar year beginning either at "midwinter," or Christmas Day, December 25th, or on "the harvest equinox," September 24th, which seems to have been the date recognised by Bede.

Another possible New Year's Day was the Annunciation, or Lady Day, March 25th, preceding the Christmas of the Julian year. Thus the year 901 might begin, according to modern reckoning, with March, 900, with September, 900, or with December, 900.

When it is remembered that the annalistic and ecclesiastical years might have different beginnings, and that the regnal years did not correspond to either, while the regnal year itself might date from the king's accession, or from his coronation, some idea may be formed of the complexity of the chronological problem.

Alfred's death has been assigned to three different days in October, the 25th, the 26th, and the 28th, and to three separate years, 899, 900, and 901.

For the day of the month, the evidence is strongly in favour of October 26th, "six nights before All Hallows Mass" (November 1st). This is the date given by the Parker Chronicle (A) and by the two Abingdon Chronicles (B and C). It is repeated, in the Roman form, the 7th of the Kalends of November, by the Worcester and Peterborough Chronicles (D and E), by the bilingual Canterbury Chronicle (F), and by the Annals of St. Neots. The King's obit is also entered under the same date in a tenth-century calendar, in the "Psalter of King Æthelstan," and in two metrical calendars of the eleventh century1, while in four manuscripts of the Chronicle the death of King Athelstan, on October 27th (6 Kal. Nov.), 940 is said to have occurred "forty years all but a day" after Alfred's death.

Against this full and early evidence for October 26th, Florence of Worcester's date, October 28th (5 Kal. Nov.) cannot stand, while Ethelwerd's statement that Alfred died on the seventh day before All Saints, October 25th, is unsupported by contemporary authority.

The ancient metrical calendars, then, may be held worthy of credence when, under October 26th (7 Kal. Nov.) they inscribe the line:

Ælfred rex obiit septenis et quoque amandus. (Alfred the King, who died on the seventh, is still to be loved.) The question of the year of Alfred's death is less easy of solution. The Parker Chronicle gives 901, and is followed by all the other manuscripts, by Florence of Worcester, and by the Book of Hyde Abbey (Liber de Hyda), the place of the King's burial. On the other hand, the passage in the Chronicle which places Athelstan's death in 940, forty years after the death of his grandfather, implies that Alfred died in 900, and this is the date in the Annals of St. Neots, in the Annales Cambriæ, and in two Winchester charters issued in 900, "in the year when King Alfred died"; "when the King died, and King Edward his son took the kingdom."

Since the chronology of the Chronicle at this period is untrustworthy, and the insertion of a second annal for 891, for the purpose of describing the comet of that year, appears to have pushed the events of 892 into 893, it has been conjectured that the annals continue for some time to be a year in advance of the true date, and that 901 may therefore be read 900.

This, however, is far from certain, and in any case the sequence of the chronology is broken here, as the entry for 901 immediately follows the annal for 898. Perhaps the strongest objection to the 900 theory is the fact that the Parker Chronicle says that Alfred reigned for twenty-eight and a half years, and as he undoubtedly came to the throne "after Easter" in 871, this would make 899 the year of his death.

Mr. Stevenson has argued with great force and probability in support of this year. It is the date assigned to Alfred's death by Simeon of Durham, by the Lindisfarne Annals, and by Ethelwerd, all of them, apparently, resting on an earlier northern source, a significant fact, when the special association of Alfred with St. Cuthbert is recalled. This date is strikingly confirmed by a rule (computus) for calculating the year of the Incarnation, which occurs in a tenth-century manuscript. Illustrating from the "present year, which is the thirteenth year of Edward, King of the Saxons," it shows this year to be 912, which throws back his accession and his father's death to 899.

Ethelwerd, moreover, says that Edward the Elder was crowned on Whitsunday (June 8), 900, a date which cannot be reconciled with Alfred's supposed death in the following October. Nor does the date 899 necessarily conflict with the passage in the Chronicle on Athelstan's death, or with the two charters which make 900 the year of Edward's accession, for his regnal year would run from October, 899, to October, 900, and the fortieth year of his reign would be 939-940. Here, then, the controversy may be left, undetermined, but with Mr. Stevenson's theory in the ascendant, that October 26, 899, was the date of King Alfred's death. If, however, it could be satisfactorily proved that the Anglo-Saxons in the ninth century began their year either with the 25th of March preceding the Christmas of the Julian calendar, or with September 24th, many of the chronological difficulties would disappear, and it might be shown that Alfred died on October 25th-26th, in 899, according to modern reckoning, but in 900 according to the contemporary system of computation.

This would still leave unexplained the date 901 in the Chronicle, but it would harmonise almost all the other discrepancies in the early accounts of the death of Alfred, and the accession and coronation of Edward the Elder.

THE MYTH OF KING ALFRED

THE King Alfred of English legend shows pale and lifeless beside the heroic Charlemagne of the French chansons de gestes, or the mysterious Arthur of Celtic romance. The elements of pity and terror are lacking in his story, as his people told it after his death. He is no unconquered warrior, who can be compared to Odin the thundergod, no high-souled victim of a lost cause and a tragic love. His life of quiet virtue and unobtrusive success was not brilliant or passionate enough to attract the court poets and chroniclers. The influences which went to the creation of his myth were chiefly popular, ecclesiastical, or academic, and the victor of Ashdown and Ethandun was forgotten in the fame of the scholar-king, the friend of the poor, and the favourite of the saints.

The tradition of Alfred's wisdom, which eventually made of him an English Solomon, may be traced in the century immediately following his death, in the appeal to his judgment as to a standard, in the reference to his laws as "the doombook," a recognised authority, in the name of "the wise king," given to him in one of the charters of Ethelred II., and in the eulogy pronounced upon him by Ethelwerd, himself a member of the royal house: "The magnanimous King Alfred, the immovable pillar of the West-Saxons, a man full of justice, keen in arms, learned in speech, imbued above all with the divine writings."

The popular tradition was also, in all likelihood, growing up during the tenth century; the people, it can hardly be doubted, were already beginning to tell fireside tales of good King Alfred, and to point out the scenes of his sufferings and victories, though there is no record of such legends till after the Norman Conquest. The renewal of Danish invasion in the last quarter of the tenth century seems to have dimmed the memory of the earlier struggle with the vikings, while Edgar's reign of peace and good government came to be regarded as England's Golden Age.

It was not until the opening of the twelfth century that interest in early English history revived, as part of the general literary activity of the time. Florence of Worcester, who died in 1118, compiled his work mainly from the Anglo-Saxon Chronicle and from Asser. How fully he appreciated the greatness of Alfred is seen in the fine tribute which he pays to the "King of the Anglo-Saxons, the son of the most pious King Ethelwulf": famous, warlike, victorious; the diligent provider for widows and children, for orphans and the poor; the most skilful of Saxon poets, most dear to his people, affable to all, and most generous; endowed with prudence, fortitude, justice, and temperance; most patient in the infirmity from which he constantly suffered; a most discreet investigator in the execution of justice; most watchful and devout in the service of God.

Henry of Huntingdon, too, writing in the first half of the twelfth century, thinks Alfred's laborious reign worthy to be sung in verse, 1 and dismisses him in his summary of the lives of the early kings as one of whom nothing could be said briefly, because he did so many admirable deeds. In the twelfth century, also, that period of monastic revival, the name of Alfred was indissolubly associated with the English saints Neot and Cuthbert; his works were copied and read; his reputation as a writer and lawgiver grew apace, and the obscure remembrance of his history still lingering in local gossip took literary form in folk-tales inserted in chronicles, in saints' lives, and in homilies.

The most famous of these tales, the story of "Alfred and the cakes," is first found in the Annals of St. Neots, and in three lives of St. Neot, two in Latin, and the third, a homily intended to be read an St. Neot's day, in Anglo-Saxon. All three lives, in their present shape, appear to belong to the twelfth century, but they probably embody older material, and they may go back to tenth-century originals, which incorporated still earlier oral traditions. 1

The fact that the English homily gives what seems to be a folk-tale, of a fox which stole St. Neot's shoe, somewhat strengthens the probability that the story of the cakes is also derived from a popular source. That old familiar story is worth retelling, in what is, apparently, its earliest English form. Its broad humour, its crude contrasts of good and evil fortune, the sudden transition from the squalour of the peasant's hut to the glory of the heavenly vision, are like a scene in a medi- æval Morality, and have appealed to the English imagination for at least nine hundred years.

In the English homily, then, Alfred visits St. Neot in his Cornish retreat, "for his soul's need." The saint foretells his future trials, and urges him to turn from his sins, and to make offerings to Romeburh, and to Pope Martin (Marinus), who rules the English school at Rome. Alfred receives Neot's blessing, and obeys his behests. The saint dies, and Guthrum the heathen King arrives in "the eastern part of the Saxon land (Sexlandes)" with his bloodthirsty host.

When King Alfred . . . learnt that the army (here) was so strong, and so near to England, he straightway for fear took to flight, and forsook all his warriors and his captains (heretogen), and all his people, treasure, and treasure-chests. . . . He went skulking by hedge and lane, by wood and field, till by God's guidance he came safely to Athelney, and took refuge in a swineherd's house, and obeyed him and his evil wife very willingly. It chanced on a day that the swineherd's wife heated her oven, and the King sat by it, warming himself at the fire, for they knew not that he was the King. Then the evil wife waxed wroth of a sudden, and said to the King, in angry mood: "Turn the loaf, so that it does not burn; I see every day what a lusty eater thou art." He straightway obeyed the evil wife as needs he must.

The "good king" then pleads to God for mercy, and his prayer is heard. All falls out as St. Neot foretold. The saint appears in a dream, shining brightly, and comforts the King, saying: "I go before thee, follow thou after me, together with thy people." Alfred now defeats Guthrum, who is baptised, and returns to "his own country." Alfred's kingdom increases, and his fame spreads far and wide, for in knowledge of the divine writings "he surpassed bishops and mass-priests and archdeacons (high deacons), and Christianity flourished well in those good times." The King, moreover, wrote many books, concludes the homilist, and within the space of two and twenty years he forsook this earthly life for the life eternal: "so God granted it to him for his righteousness."

The Annals of St. Neots and the Latin lives tell the same tale with elaborations. In the Annals, which refer to the "life of the holy father Neot," the swineherd becomes a neatherd (vaccarius), and Alfred, as he sits by the fire, busies himself with his bow and arrows, "and other instruments of war," and forgets the loaves. The "unhappy housewife" runs up and turns them, and rates the "most unconquered king" in Latin hexameters:

Heus homo

Urere, quos cernis, panes gyrate moraris,

Cum nimium gaudes hos manducare calentes?

(Canst set and see the Bread burn thus thou sot

And canst not turn what thou so well lov'st hot?)

An account of Alfred's youthful tyranny and lack of sympathy with his people follows, and St. Neot, his "kinsman," duly rebukes his sins, and prophesies impending misfortunes. He subsequently appears to the King in his time of need, and consoles him, and finally, the night before the battle of Ethandun, he promises to lead the English to victory on the morrow.

The earlier of the two Latin lives is interspersed throughout with fragments of verse, and exhibits, as the sixteenth-century antiquary Leland said of it, an "affectation of eloquence rather than the honest fidelity of history." St. Neot, who is himself of royal East-Anglian blood, here threatens his kinsman Hœluredus, King of the English, with the pains of hell, if he persists in his immoderate tyranny, and bids him send to Rome to ask Pope Marinus to free the English school. Alfred, deeply moved, obeys, and receives a piece of the true cross from the Pope. St. Neot dies. The heathen tyrant Gytrum invades England. He hears from fugitives of Alfred's wealth, and learns where he intends to winter. The Athelney incident is then introduced; the name Æthelinga-ig is explained to mean the "Isle of Princes," Clitonum Insula;the King seeks hospitality from a swineherd (subulcus) and stays with him for some days; he is scolded by the swineherd's wife in the same hexameters as in the Annals of St. Neots, but he turns the bread himself, and watches it till it is ready. He then goes forth, and builds the fort at Athelney. St. Neot appears, and encourages him. Alfred gathers his men by the sound of trumpets; Guthrum also prepares for battle, and exhorts his troops. St. Neot again appears as a venerable old man, with shining face and vesture, and arms in his hand. Alfred addresses his men before the fight, and St. Neot in person leads the English army at Ethandun. The siege of Chippenham and Guthrum's baptism are described, and Guthrum's submission is compared to the conversion of St. Paul.

The second Latin life is wholly in prose, and adds a few details to the story. St. Neot becomes the son of Edulfus or Ethelwulf, King of one of the four English kingdoms. He visits Pope Marinus in Rome, and Alfred by his advice endows the English school. The swineherd's wife reproves the King's idleness with bitter reproaches. Alfred, "like another job," bears it patiently, and attends to the cakes. St. Neot, before Ethandun, exhorts the King and his followers to fight "as beseems the athletes of Christ," a phrase often used in the eleventh and twelfth centuries, to describe the Crusaders. During the battle Alfred sees "Neot, the glorious servant of Christ," leading the army as the royal standard-bearer. He calls the attention of his fellow-warriors to the presence of " Neot, Christ's most unconquered knight," and assures them of victory. Guthrum, who is compared to Goliath, is defeated, and baptised. Saul becomes Paul; the wolf is turned into a lamb. Alfred also renounces his evil ways, and follows justice for the rest of his life, "ruling piously under the most pious King."

The militant Christianity of these lives, their profusion of scriptural quotation and comparison, their stirring battle scenes, and edifying speeches, were well suited to the taste of the Crusading epoch, and in later days Archbishop Parker's inclusion of the story of "Alfred and the cakes" in the first printed edition of Asser's Life of the King won it credence as part of the original text. The omission of the miraculous element from the account of St. Neot's relations with Alfred, moreover, probably made it more popular with Protestant readers than the unexpurgated legend which connected the Athelney adventure with St. Cuthbert.

The twelfth-century records of the history and miracles of that great northern bishop and saint 1 relate how Cuthbert appeared to King Alfred at Athelney, and cheered him with hopes of better times; how, after hiding for "three years" in the Glastonbury marshes, the King gathered together his followers, and defeated the Danes, and how on his deathbed Alfred commended the church and monastery of St. Cuthbert to his son Edward, and bade him offer two bracelets (armillas) and a golden censer (thuribulum) at the shrine of the saint. 1

In these records Cuthbert comes as a pilgrim to Alfred and his wife, who are left with a single attendant, while their followers go out to fish. Alfred gives the wanderer his only remaining bread and wine; the attendant remonstrates, the saint vanishes, and the King's men return with a marvellous draught of three shiploads of fish. That night Cuthbert reveals himself in a vision, and gives Alfred assurance of victory. Next morning the King winds three blasts on his horn, his troops assemble, and he defeats the Danes.

Another version of the story makes Alfred give half his bread and wine to the saint, and find the remainder miraculously undiminished. St. Cuthbert, "Christ's knight," appears in a flood of light which illuminates the King's small sleeping-chamber, and says: "Be faithful to me and to my people, because all Albion is given to thee and to thy sons. . . . Be just, because thou art chosen King of all Britain."

William of Malmesbury, that delightful medi- æval story-teller, gives yet another form of the St. Cuthbert legend. The misfortunes of Alfred are treated as the penalty of England's national sins, while the saint in a vision brings the King hopes of pardon, and, as a sign of the truth of his words, works a miracle. The attendants who are out in search of food take a great draught of fish in spite of frost and ice. Alfred's mother, who shares his exile, is also visited by St. Cuthbert, as she snatches a little troubled sleep on her hard bed.

To William of Malmesbury is further due the preservation of the picturesque tale of Alfred venturing into the Danish camp disguised as a minstrel or gleeman. He uses the knowledge thus obtained to win the victory of Ethandun over the indolent and careless enemy. "Gudrun, whom we call Gurmund," is baptised, and all ends happily. A similar story is told of the Northman Anlaf, who penetrated into the English camp before the tenthcentury battle of Brunanburh.

Another "floating folk-tale" of like nature may be traced in William of Malmesbury's mention of the golden bracelets which Alfred ordered to be hung up at the cross-roads, unguarded treasures which none durst steal, so great was the peace and security of the kingdom. That William of Malmesbury also attributes to Alfred the institution of hundreds and tithings, as a police measure, shows that even before the middle of the twelfth century he was beginning to be regarded as the type of the just king, and this association of his name with judicial and administrative reforms is peculiarly interesting from its appearance at a time when Anglo-Norman lawyers and statesmen were trying to bring order and coherence into the tangle of Anglo-Saxon customs and "dooms."

Even when, in the middle of the twelfth century, Geoffrey of Monmouth was charming the western world with the fantastic adventures of Merlin and King Arthur, the more prosaic Alfred was not forgotten. If Arthurian romance took court and camp and hall by storm, the didactic piety, legal fables, and moral tales of the Alfredian legend were cherished in the monastery and the council chamber, in the peasant's hut and the village ale-house. Layamon, the English paraphraser of Wace's metrical adaptation of Geoffrey of Monmouth's History of the Britons, introduces Alfred into his rhymed chronicle, if only as a lawgiver, the translator into English of the British law of Queen Marcie, a personification of Mercia,:

Seotthen [subsequently] ther after

Mani hundred winter

Com Alfret the king

Engelondes deorling2

And worhte [wrought] the lawe an Englis [in English]

The thirteenth century, which saw the growth of English national feeling and the long fight for freedom in the reigns of John and Henry III., saw also the development of the English element in literature. As in the previous period the vulgar tales of the countryside had found a place in Latin prose, so now the tradition of Alfred's justice and wisdom, his piety and love of his people, found voice in English verse. Already in the twelfth century the chronicler Ailred or Ethelred of Rievaulx wrote of Alfred's "parables" (parabolæ), which tended to edification, delight, and mirth, and a Winchester chronicler described him as so "brilliant in proverbs," that he had never been surpassed. It seems likely, then, that he was quoted as a source of popular wisdom before the thirteenth century, when, in the poem of the "Owl and the Nightingale," "Alured king," "Alured that was wise," is credited with the proverbial sayings which are introduced into the dialogue between the two birds.

A much more elaborate collection of rhymed sayings of the same kind has been preserved in two thirteenth-century manuscripts, under the name of "Precepts" or "Saws" of King Alfred (Documenta Regis Aluredi). This poem opens with a meeting of the witan-thegns and bishops, book-learned men, earls and knights-at Seaford, in Sussex, under King Alfred:

Englene herde,England's (shep)herd,

Englene derling,   England's darling,

In Engelonde he was king.   In England he was king.

The prologue ends with further praise of the King who taught his people how to lead good lives:

Alfred he was in Englelonde a king,

(Alfred was in England king,)

Wel swithe strong and lufsum thing;

(A very strong and lovesome thing;)

He was king and cler,

(He was king and clerk,)

Ful wel he lovede Godis werc;

(Full well he loved God's work;)

He was wis on his word,

(He was wise in his word,)

And war on his werke;

(And wary in his work;)

He was the wisiste mon

(He was the wisest man)

That was in Englelonde on.

(That was in England.)1

Alfred, "the comforter of the English (Englene frowere), then harangues his subjects on the duties of Christians in general, and of Christian kings and nobles in particular, in verses which read like an expansion on feudal lines of the passage in the Boethius on the three orders of men. King, earl and ætheling, clerk and knight, are to judge rightly, and to rule by law, while the knight is specially bidden to guard the land, and give peace to the rich, and quiet to the ceorl, to enable him "his seed to sow, his meads to mow, his ploughs to drive." The "saws of King Alfred" follow, maxims on the uncertainty of life and of earthly wealth, each preceded by the words "thus quoth Alfred."

The second part of the poem begins with an exhortation to Alfred's "dear friends" to listen, and to learn "wit and wisdom." The proverbs in which this wisdom is enshrined echo the popular philosophy of the time, the pithy familiar sayings of the English peasantry: "Wise child is father's bliss"; "Better is child unborn than unbeaten"; "Fool's bolt is soon shot"; "Whoso letteth his wife become his master, shall never be lord of his word." The somewhat cynical common-sense of the warnings against trusting in wife, or friend, or wealth, and the injunctions to reticence and prudence, are relieved by passages which, if only Alfred's in name, are full of his spirit of gallant endurance:

If thou hast sorrow, tell it not thy foe; Sit thy saddle-bow, and ride thee singing; or: Whithersoever thou wendst, say thou at the end Let be what may be, God's will be done;

a thought which agrees well with Alfred's own words: "I say, then, as say all Christian men, that the divine purpose rules, and not fate."

The third and concluding part of the "Proverbs" contains advice to the King's son. Here each section begins: "Thus quoth Alfred: 'My son so dear.'" The son, presumably Edward the Elder, is enjoined to be a father and lord to his people, a father to the child and a friend to the widow, to comfort and defend the poor and weak, to rule himself by law, and to remember his God. It is the old ideal of the king below the law, as Alfred had known it in the ninth century, recurring after more than three hundred years, mixed up oddly enough with traditional folk-lore and homely counsel, yet still, as the Barons' War was soon to show, powerful for inspiration and guidance, a rallying-cry in the struggle for liberty.

Matthew Paris, the thirteenth-century monk of St. Albans, whose chronicle gathered up the work of his predecessors, and became the standard mediæval history of later ages, pieces together the story of Alfred from many sources, and makes of it a consecutive and interesting narrative. Alfred burns the cakes, fortifies himself in the isle of Athelney with "towers and ramparts," goes to Cornwall to visit St. Neot, returns to the island and sees St. Cuthbert in a vision, vows to build a monastery at Athelney, wins the battle of Ethandun, enfeoffs Gytro or Guthrum with East Anglia, raises Denewulf, whom he had first met as a swineherd at Athelney, to the see of Winchester, divides England into hundreds and tithings, hangs up golden bracelets at the cross-roads, and dies as monarch of all England except Northumbria and East Anglia.

In the beautiful contemporary manuscript of his Chronica Majora which Matthew Paris presented to St. Albans, is a portrait of Alfredus rex, as the monastic draftsman pictured him: a bearded, regular-featured prince, wearing a crown of thir teenth-centuryfashion, and holding a scroll inscribed: Primus in anglia regnavi solus, scilicet monarcha.

The image of Alfred, "the first monarch of the English," thus impressed itself on the minds of patriotic Englishmen, to the exclusion of the more imposing figure of the conqueror of the vikings. The memory of those old fights with the "heathen men" was gradually merged in the dazzling fictions of crusading romance, while Guthrum and Hæsten and Rollo developed legends of their own, and the fame of Alvrekr or Alrekr, King of the English, lingered but faintly in the northern sagas During the fourteenth century the Alfredian myth developed chiefly on ecclesiastical and academic lines. The Mirror of Justices (Miroir des Justices), which may date from the end of the thirteenth century, reflects an Alfred who hangs fortyfour unjust judges in one day, and in whose reign trial by jury was already an old English institution. A new element is introduced by the later Liber de Hyda, which places the foundation of the University of Oxford in 886, "in the presence of the most glorious and invincible King Alfred, whose memory will dwell like honey in the mouths of all," and before the assembled clergy and people of the realm. A regular staff of "regents," professors, and readers is appointed. St. Neot teaches theology, St. Grimbald divinity, Asser, grammar and rhetoric, John, the monk of St. Davids, logic, music, and arithmetic, another John, apparently the Old-Saxon, geometry and astronomy. This passage was, doubtless, inserted to do honour to Grimbald, the first abbot of Hyde, who, with King Alfred, is described as addressing the national assembly on their ignorance and need of instruction.

Ralph Higden, in his Polychronicon, goes a step further, and makes Alfred, by the advice of St. Neot, establish "public schools for the various arts" at Oxford. Another tradition, which became current about this time, that Alfred was the founder of University College, Oxford, was turned to practical use when in 1379 the Master and Scholars of " Mickle University Hall in Oxenford" successfully petitioned Richard II., as the royal foundation of his noble progenitor King Alfred, to evoke a lawsuit in which they were involved, from the court of King's Bench to the Privy Council. From the Book of Hyde comes, also, Alfred's appropriation of a definite portion of his revenues to the maintenance of the Oxford schools, his division of the kingdom into counties as well as hundreds, and the wild tale of his youthful journey to Ireland, to be cured of his incurable malady by the Irish Saint Modwenna, who afterwards founded two nunneries in England, at Streneshale and at Pollisvytham, where Ethelwulf's sister, "the holy Edith," was professed.

The fourteenth-century legends reach their highest point of pure imagination in the fairytale of Nestingus, the beautiful child, robed in purple, with gold bracelets on its arms, which was found in an eagle's nest at the top of a tree when Alfred was hunting in the forest, and educated at the King's expense.

The lively fancy of the romantic historians of the fifteenth century added fresh details to the Alfredian legend, without substantially altering it. The "noble King Alfred" now, after the fashion of the period, founds three halls at Oxford, "in the name of the Holy Trinity," for the study of grammar, logic or philosophy, and theology, and sends his own son Ethelwerd to the University, of which Grimbald becomes the first Chancellor. The King himself is "a perfect clerk," and translates into English:

The lawes of Troye and Brute, Lawes Moluntynes and Marcians congregate,
With Danyshe lawes that were well constitute, And Grekysche also well
made and appropate.

So high, indeed, was Alfred's historic and legendary fame at this period that
in 1441 Henry VI. applied to Pope Eugenius IV. for the canonisation of
"the first monarch of the famous realm of England," and though the
request was refused, he may surely be counted a saint, "though not in the
Pope's, yet in the People's Calendar."

With the revival of learning in the sixteenth century, the myth of King
Alfred entered on a new phase. Though the early history of England was at
first somewhat neglected, in the absorbing interest of classical studies, those
studies led in time to a more scientific and critical appreciation of the
treasures of antiquity. While the great poets and dramatists of the
Elizabethan era drew inspiration from Celtic rather than from Anglo- Saxon
sources, scholars and antiquaries turned with growing enthusiasm to the
records of England's past.

In 1574 appeared Archbishop Parker's edition of Asser's life of Alfred,
Ælfredi Regis Res Gestæ, an epoch-making book, in spite of its many
shortcomings. It was printed in Anglo-Saxon letters, "out of veneration for
the antiquity of the archetype," and had a fancy portrait of King Alfred on
the title-page. Camden's edition followed in 1602-3, with the interpolated
passage on the University of Oxford, which had been printed in 1600, in an
edition of the great antiquary's Britannia, nominally from "an excellent
manuscript copy of Asser, who was at that time professor." Oxford is here
represented as already an ancient seat of learning in the ninth century, when
Grimbald arrives in the character of a reformer, and gives great offence to
the "old scholars" (scholastici) whom he finds there, by his innovations in
the methods of teaching. Alfred comes to Oxford to settle the dispute,
hears the arguments on both sides, and receives proof from the chronicles
that the routine of the schools had been established by such pious and
learned men as "St. Gildas, Melkinus, Nennius, Kentigern, and others," and
approved by St. Germanus when he visited Britain. The King then exhorts
the disputants to maintain unity and concord, but Grimbald retires in
dudgeon to the new monastery which Alfred had founded at Winchester,
and removes thither the tomb which he had prepared for his burial in the

crypt of the stone church of St. Peter, which he had built in Oxford.

There can be little doubt that this wonderful piece of fiction was a deliberate forgery, intended to support the claim of Oxford to be an older university than Cambridge. A fierce controversy on this subject had resulted from a speech of the Cambridge orator in 1564, on the occasion of Queen Elizabeth's visit to the University. The Cambridge champion began by asserting that whereas Oxford University could claim no higher antiquity than the reign of Alfred, his own foundation went back to Cantaber, an exiled Spanish prince, who took refuge with the British King Gurguntius, or, if this origin were rejected as fabulous, it had a historical founder, of much earlier date than Alfred, in Sigebert, the seventhcentury King of East Anglia, who established schools of learning in his kingdom. Later on, the line of attack was changed, and the validity of Alfred's claims was denied, on the ground that no life of the West-Saxon King mentioned the Oxford schools. Camden's interpolation, then, came in opportunely, for it not only gave contemporary historical evidence for Alfred's restoration of the University, but relegated its foundation to the days before the Germanic invasions of Britain.

From the first, however, the paragraph was viewed with distrust, and Camden was suspected of having concocted it with the help of his fellowantiquary, Sir Henry Savile. The discrepancies between dates and facts' were noted, and Sir John Spelman, who firmly believed that Alfred founded the University, writes of the attempt to make him merely a restorer: "As new Pieces never suit handsomely in an old Garment, so that Insertion not squaring well with other Circumstances, discovers itself to have been a Patch of a late hand." Still, the legend persisted, and Alfred continued to be regarded as the founder, or the restorer, of the University.

Sir John Spelman describes a "fair window" in St. Mary's Church, in Oxford, "where both the Story and the Glory of the Universitie's Foundation by Alfred was beautifully set forth both in Picture and Verses," and on St. Martin's Eve prayers were accustomed to be offered in the Oxford schools for all benefactors, and for the souls of those departed, "more especially for the soul of King Alfred, the first founder of this University."

The publication of Parker's edition of Asser, moreover, with the learned disputations which followed the appearance of Camden's edition, thirty years later, did much to revive the failing popular interest in King Alfred. The story of the cakes assumed a new form in a rude ballad, which can be traced back to 1578, four years after the publication of Parker's Asser. Alfred goes forth, dressed as a beggar, in quest of sport:

Thus coasting thorowe [through] Somersetshire Neere Newton-Court he met A shepheard swaine of lusty limbes That up and downe did jet.

They fight, after deciding that the victor shall have the food in the shepherd's scrip as a prize:

So soundly thus they both fall to't, And giving bang for bang At ev'ry blow the shepheard gave, King Alfred's sword cride [cried] twang.

Alfred now demands a truce. The shepherd engages him as his man, gives him a "penny round" as earnest-money, and brings him to his cottage and his churlish wife, "old Gillian." Then comes the cake incident:

But as he sate with smiling cheere The event of all to see, His dame brought forth a piece of dowe [dough] Which in the fire throws she;

Where lying on the harth to bake

By chance the cake did burne:

"What! canst thou not, thou lout," quoth she,

"Take pains the same to turne?

"Thou art more quick to rake it out

And eat it up half dowe [dough],

Than thus to stay till't be enough,

And so thy manners show.

"But serve me such another tricke,

I'll thwack thee on the snout:"

Which made the patient king, good man,

Of her to stand in doubt.

The next morning, Alfred blows his horn; his "Lords and Knights" assemble, the shepherd and his wife expect to be hanged, but the King is gracious to them, gives them sheep and pastureland, and changes their cottage into a stately hall. In return, the shepherd is to offer the King a milkwhite lamb each year, and Gillian is to bring wool for coats at New Year's tide. The grateful shepherd says:

"And in your prayse, my bag-pipe shall

Sound sweetly once a yeere,

How Alfred our renownèd king

Most kindly hath beene here."

The ballad of " King Olfry and the Old Abbot" probably also refers to Alfred in its earlier form, where the abbot saves his life by getting his brother, a shepherd, to personate him, and answer the three questions set by the King.

Even the political troubles of the seventeenth century did not altogether break the Alfredian tradition. In the reign of James I. a new departure was made by the appearance of a Latin tragi-comedy, written by William Drury, a Roman Catholic, on the subject of Alvredus or Alfredus. Some years later, in 1634, Robert Powell published his singular little book, The Life of Alfred, or Alvred, The first Institutor of subordinate government in this kingdome, and Refounder of the University of Oxford. Together with a Parallel of our Soveraigne Lord K. Charles untill the yeare, 1634. In this medley of legendary absurdities and fulsome adulation, Neote, the first Oxford divinity reader, becomes the second son of Ethelwulf, by Judith, and Alfred refounds that "renowned Seminary," the "Garden of Art and Learning," Oxford University, which had been "laid waste and even with the dust," in the Danish wars, while all the old fables are served up again, in their most exaggerated form. Stress is laid on Alfred's "Princely piety" in enforcing the payment of tithes, "the just alimony of the painefull ministry," and the book concludes with a minute and laboured comparison of that "paire of Peerlesse Princes," Alfred and Charles I.

A far more creditable and scholarly production is Sir John Spelman's Life of Elfred the Great, which seems to have been written while its royalist author was at Oxford with Charles I., after the outbreak of the Civil War. Here, in the summer of 1643, he died of the camp disease, leaving his book in manuscript. It was published in a Latin translation in 1678, with comments by Obadiah Walker, Master of University College, Oxford, and a dedication to Charles II., comparing him to Alfred. Walker's notes were regarded as "Popish," and in 1686 the stone statue of King Alfred which had been set over the gate of University College in 1683 was ignominiously "plucked downe" by ardent Oxford Protestants.

Spelman is the first to give Alfred the formal title of The Great, which he derived from Baronius, the sixteenth-century Italian Cardinal and church historian, who, under the year 878, speaks of him as "deservedly called the Great" (Magnus, merito nuncupatus).

Credulous and uncritical as this first attempt at a complete English life of Alfred seems, when tested by modern standards, Spelman had read widely, and treated his subject with learning and eloquence. If he saw the institution of trial by jury in Alfred's provision for "the Purgation of the King's Thaines by twelve of their Peers," and "in the Purging of Borsholders by the oath of twelve Borsholders," a confused attribution to Alfred's days of the police system of frankpledge, yet he knew that there was no trustworthy documentary evidence for Alfred's division of England into shires and tithings, and fell back on the convenient supposition that some of the West-Saxon laws had been lost, while in the matter of the University of Oxford, he made an honest effort to weigh the arguments, and to arrive at a fair conclusion.

The Civil War turned the thoughts of Englishmen to sterner themes and more vital problems than the leisurely pursuit of antiquarian studies. Yet if Waller's Roundhead soldiers scattered the ashes of Anglo-Saxon kings to the winds, the Puritan poet Milton2 could admire Alfred's "noble mind, which rendered him the Mirror of Princes," and plan a tragedy, or "a heroical poem," on his adventures in the isle of Athelney.

At the opening of the eighteenth century, a strong impulse was given to the scientific study of archæology by the publication of Hickes' celebrated Thesaurus, which contains excellent engravings of the recently discovered "Alfred Jewel." In 1722 Francis Wise published his interesting edition of Asser, with a long "Apology" for Camden's interpolation in the text. Wise, also, in his "letter to Dr. Mead," printed in 1738, discusses the site of the battle of Ashdown, and the meaning of the White Horse on the hill, which he took to be a memorial of the victory, and a representation of the "standard," or "arms," of the Saxons. With much that is ridiculous, Wise combined great good sense and discrimination, and he wrote with real eloquence of King Alfred, "the most perfect monarch that ever adorned the English throne." He certainly did not deserve the savage attack made on him by Philalethes Rusticus, in "The Impertinence and Imposture of Modern Antiquarianism Display'd", where it is maintained that Alfred's "arms" were not a horse, but a cross, between five martlets, as shown on Kempsford Tower, in Gloucestershire. The writer clinches his argument by a reference to "that most Authentick Record the Oxford-Almanack for 1735: Where we have K. Alfred in all his Glory, seated upon his Royal Throne, under his own Ensign, which is exhibited as the very same upon the Tower aforesaid, bating one Martlet only." Wise rejoined, supporting his original position by amazing arguments, drawn from Hengest and Horsa, and the White Horse of Hanover, but explaining that he believed the cross to have been adopted as the royal arms in the reign of Alfred.

While learned antiquaries were thus transferring the Scholasticism, Chivalry, and Heraldry of the later mediæval period to the age of Alfred, the story of Alfred himself, the model prince of the Germanic races, found favour with the minor poets and dramatists of Hanoverian England.

In 1740, Thomson, who in his Seasons calls Alfred the "best of kings," produced, in conjunction with David Mallet, the masque of Alfred, in which the song of "Rule Britannia" first appeared. Blackmore's heavy epic, in twelve books, on the same subject, was dedicated, with unconscious irony, to Frederick, Prince of Wales, the dissipated son of George II., as suited for the "forming of a young Prince for Empire and the right Government of a people." Though Dr. Johnson's contemplated "Life of Alfred" was never written, no fewer than six dramas or poems on Alfredian history and legend followed in quick succession between 1750 and 1850, including a five-act play by Home, the author of Douglas. The titles of these ephemeral publications sufficiently indicate the conditions under which they were composed. The Patriot King, The Battle of Eddington, or British Liberty, Alfred, or the Magic Banner, suggest the influence of the French Revolution, and the dawn of the Romantic movement in literature.

In the early nineteenth century, the same tendencies are visible. If Shelley, in his "Ode to Liberty", devotes only a line or two to "Saxon Alfred", Wordsworth has commemorated the "Lord of the harp and liberating spear", the "Mirror of Princes", and "Darling of England", in two fine sonnets on Alfred and his descendants.

In 1849 the millenary of the great King's birth was celebrated at Wantage with feasting and merry-making; a medal was struck, and a Jubilee edition of Alfred's works, in an English translation, was issued, with illustrative essays on the history of the ninth century. About this time, too, in the year of revolutions, 1848, the German patriot, Reinhold Pauli, soothed his exile in England by writing the life of Alfred, the constitutional King of a free country.

Meantime, not serious literature alone, but fiction, burlesque, and farce were busy with Alfred's name. He figured in sentimental romance and in tales of adventure, in Christmas pantomime and in musical comedy, in the satire of Thackeray, and in the pages of Punch. The stories of the cakes and the minstrel harp were told in every nursery and village school in England, and the "old White Horse" and his annual "scouring" became familiar to all readers of the vigorous prose of Tom Hughes. In 1872 a dinner was actually given in University College, Oxford, to celebrate the supposed millenary of its foundation, and though King Alfred's name no longer heads the list of pious founders and benefactors whom the University yearly commemorates, the Oxford University Calendar still records that "the Great Hall of the University, commonly called University College in Oxford . . . is said to have been founded in the year 878 by Alfred the Great."

Finally, in 1901, the commemoration of the millenary of Alfred's death called general attention once more to his life and works. His statue, by Hamo Thornycroft, was set up at Winchester, with pageantry and oratory, thanksgiving and song. Again a medal was struck in Alfred's honour, and a battle-ship, the King Alfred, was launched, in remembrance of the reputed founder of the English navy, while books were written and lectures delivered on every aspect of Alfredian history and literature.

In all these celebrations, nothing was more striking than the way in which they emphasised the continuity of the ancient legends, and the consensus of European opinion on the fame of the great English King, and on his perfection of character: "the practical character, fired half unconsciously with imagination," in which Lord Rosebery has seen the secret of true greatness.

Thus every age has had its own vision of King Alfred, dim, fantastic, distorted, even grotesque it may be, yet always a reflection, however faint, of "the light that rose out of darkness," in the middle of the ninth century. Much regretful sentiment has been lavished on the ruthless destruction of old romance by the modern scientific historian. In reality, the genuine popular traditions are indestructible, for they are rooted deep in the national life. The myths of the past make the history of the future, and it is not so much by truth itself as by what men believe to be true that they are inspired to action. The legendary tales which have gathered about the name of King Alfred may be shadows from the actual events of his life, or merely the dreams of later ages concerning him. In either case they show, by their very simplicity, that his appeal has been to humble folk, that the poor have seen in him their helper, and that his memory still dwells in good works in the country for which he fought and suffered, the England which might say, in the words of the golden legend encircling the Alfred Jewel:

ÆLFRED MEC HEHT GEWYRCAN.

(Alfred bade me be wrought.)

Made in the USA
Monee, IL
30 August 2023

41884197R00149